MARRIAGE AND RELATIONSHIP EDUCATION

Marriage and Relationship Education

WHAT WORKS AND HOW TO PROVIDE IT

W. Kim Halford

THE GUILFORD PRESS
New York   London

© 2011 The Guilford Press
A Division of Guilford Publications, Inc.
72 Spring Street, New York, NY 10012
www.guilford.com

Printed in the United States of America

This book is printed on acid-free paper.

Last digit is print number: 9   8   7   6   5   4   3   2   1

The author has checked with sources believed to be reliable in his efforts to provide information
that is complete and generally in accord with the standards of practice that are accepted at the
time of publication. However, in view of the possibility of human error or changes in behavioral, mental health, or medical sciences, neither the author, nor the editor and publisher, nor
any other party who has been involved in the preparation or publication of this work warrants
that the information contained herein is in every respect accurate or complete, and they are not
responsible for any errors or omissions or the results obtained from the use of such information.
Readers are encouraged to confirm the information contained in this book with other sources.

Library of Congress Cataloging-in-Publication Data

Halford, W. Kim.
   Marriage and relationship education : what works and how to provide it / W.
Kim Halford.
      p. cm.
   Includes bibliographical references and index.
   ISBN 978-1-60918-155-0 (hardcover : acid-free paper)
   1. Man–woman relationships.   2. Intimacy (Psychology).   3. Interpersonal
communication.   4. Interpersonal conflict.   5. Interpersonal
relations.   6. Marriage.   I. Title.
   HQ801.H3135 2011
   646.7'80715—dc22

                                                           2010032231

The practice of couple relationship education blends the deeply personal with professional practice. My research, my professional practice, my conversations with family and friends, and my experience being married to Barbara—all convince me that sharing the journey with someone special is central to a healthy life. I dedicate this book to my son, Chris Halford, and daughter-in-law, Ai Ito, who married during the time I worked on this book; and to a great couple educator, a pioneer of the field, and a wonderful friend, Howard Markman. It is my fondest hope that Chris and Ai will continue to cherish each other all their days, and be enriched by a long, loving, and healthy marriage. Howie inspired me to think beyond therapy for distressed couples, to seek to enrich and strengthen love right from the outset. I have learned much from him, and we have shared many wonderful discussions and fun experiences in exotic parts of the world. Thanks for everything so far, Howie, and I look forward to our future adventures together.

About the Author

W. Kim Halford, PhD, is Professor of Clinical Psychology at the University of Queensland in Brisbane, Australia. He was previously Professor of Clinical Psychology at Griffith University (1995–2008) and Director of Psychology at the Royal Brisbane Hospital (1991–1995). Dr. Halford has published four books and over 130 articles on couple therapy and couple relationship education. He works with couples adjusting to major life stresses and changes, including developing committed relationships, cancer diagnosis in a partner, becoming a parent, and forming a stepfamily. Dr. Halford leads the international team that developed the Couple CARE relationship education programs, is active in work with couples, and has provided training in work with couples to approximately 20,000 professionals in more than a dozen countries.

Preface

In this book I present an evidence-based approach to marriage and couple relationship education (CRE).[1] CRE is intended to assist couples who currently view their relationships as happy to sustain and strengthen those relationships. CRE is of use to couples at a variety of life stages in a relationship, including couples in the early years of commitment (marrying, planning to marry, or living together), couples having a child together, couples repartnering to form stepfamilies, couples facing major life changes, and couples confronting crises.

CRE is distinctive from couple therapy. CRE is focused on relationship enhancement, relationship commitment, and prevention of relationship distress. CRE uses the positive feelings of the partners as a resource to build momentum for positive change. In contrast, couple therapy is focused on the treatment of existing relationship distress. Couple therapy necessarily deals with resolving long-standing grievances, negative thoughts, and negative feelings about the relationship. CRE is an attempt to steer couples away from the cliff of relationship distress, whereas couple therapy is the ambulance at the bottom of the cliff available to treat those couples who have fallen. We need couple therapy to treat the hurt, and we also need relationship education to promote healthy couple relationships and prevent injuries.

CRE is most commonly provided to groups of couples in face-to-face sessions. This book focuses on how to provide CRE for groups of couples. It also is possible to make CRE available in a range of other formats. For exam-

---

[1] While most research on committed couple relationships has been with heterosexual married couples, I believe most of what is described in this book can enhance a variety of forms of committed relationships (e.g., married, cohabiting) of couples, be they heterosexual or homosexual. I use the generic term *couple relationship education* to reflect this broad applicability.

ple, many educators work face to face with one couple at a time. Recently there have been successful CRE programs built around self-directed learning materials that couples complete at home, usually with telephone- or Internet-based support from a relationship educator. This book describes all of these possible formats, and how they can be used to provide CRE to couples.

This book has 10 chapters. The first two chapters analyze the most relevant research evidence on what influences couples' relationship outcomes, and what approaches to CRE are most effective. Chapter 3 describes an evidence-based approach to CRE. The remaining chapters describe a flexible curriculum for those providing CRE to use. Chapter 4 covers the importance of assessing couple relationships for CRE, and how assessment and feedback can be a brief form of CRE.

Chapters 5 through 10 describe the Couple CARE program. There are suggestions of content areas to be covered, and specific exercises are described. I also describe how the needs of couples vary according to the strengths and challenges each partner brings to the relationship, the social context in which the couple live, and the life stage of the couple. The book includes suggestions about how the content and process of CRE can be tailored to meet unique couple needs. I hope that my writing captures the blend of applied science and humane practice that I think characterizes good CRE.

Acknowledgments

In the last 25 years I have been very fortunate to develop collaborations and friendships with a number of excellent couple researchers, marriage educators, and couple therapists.

In the last 10 years I have collaborated closely with Keithia Wilson. Her wisdom about adult learning processes has informed my thinking, her influences are reflected in my approach in this book, and she is a coauthor of the Couple CARE program. Liz Moore is a former student who became a colleague, and Charles Farrugia and Carmel Dyer are colleagues; all three were central to the development of the original Couple CARE program. Their enthusiasm and combination of skills brought the program together. I am very fortunate to have worked with them.

Jemima Petch and I began collaborating when she was my student, and she is now a valued colleague working with me on the continuing development of the Couple Care for Parents (CCP) program. Debra Creedy has been working with Jemima and me on the CCP program for a number of years. Debra's professional background is as a psychologist and a nurse. Her knowledge and skills about the transition to parenthood, combined with her professional dedication and good humor, make her a terrific colleague. Jeffry Larson, Dean Busby, and Tom Holman of Brigham Young University have been wonderful collaborators for more than 5 years. Their pioneering work developing the RELATE couple assessment system inspired me, their generosity in sharing their expertise and the RELATE resource have enriched my work, and we continue to work together to develop RELATE's applications.

I have been very privileged to work closely with my good friend Matthew Sanders for more than 25 years. Matt's incredible energy and enthusiasm for early intervention to help families, and his extraordinary accomplishments in disseminating evidence-based parenting programs, have inspired and guided my own efforts. Don Baucom, Andy Christensen, Rick Heyman, Kurt Hahl-weg, Doug Snyder, Bob Weiss, Tammy Sher, and Amy Slep all have been valued colleagues and friends for many years. Each of them taught me many valuable lessons on how to work with couples (and how to enjoy conferences), and each of these people is a great friend and professional colleague. My work also has been greatly influenced by a circle of professional colleagues whose willingness to share their ideas and dedication to understanding couple rela-tionships have enriched my thinking. I offer a special thank you to Suzanne Chambers, Nina Heinrichs, Amy Holtzworth-Munroe, Hy Hops, the late Neil Jacobson, Jan Nicholson, Pat Noller, Stef Occhipinti, Dan O'Leary, Galena Rhodes, and Scott Stanley. I am grateful for the exciting discussion and debates each of these people shared with me at various times, and in vari-ous exotic locations, over the last 25 years.

I have worked with many very gifted and dedicated students. The ideas developed in the pages of this book owe much to their creativity. I particularly want to acknowledge the contributions of Lisa Babon, Brett Behrens, Ruth Bouma, Marjolein Broers, Alison Carey-Newman, Jill Charker, Adrian Kelly, Zoe Pearce, Sue Osgarby, Trish O'Rourke, Maddy Phillips, Suzie Sweeper, and Bronwyn Watson. Each of these people taught me valued lessons.

I also thank audiovisual producer, camera operator, sound guy, and cre-ative technical whiz Kevin Judge, who provided the technical expertise and creativity in the making of the Couple CARE and Couple CARE for Par-ents DVDs. Without him, the flexible delivery program development could not have happened. A special thank-you to Stephen May and all the team at Australian Academic Press for their support and expertise in producing and distributing the Couple CARE program materials.

Over 8,000 couples have entrusted my clinical research team with the challenge of helping them to enhance their relationships. Some couples came as volunteers in research projects, others sought out access to our education programs. Their openness to consider the possibilities of change, willingness to fill in so many forms, and preparedness to have the intimacies of their lives recorded and analyzed inspired and informed the work in this book.

I wrote most of this book while on sabbatical leave at the Chinese Uni-versity of Hong Kong. I am most grateful to the Psychology Department there for hosting me and beginning my education in cross-cultural psychol-ogy. I am particularly thankful to my hosts Patrick Leung, Michael Bond, and Fanny Cheung. I thank Michael's applied social psychology gang for let-ting me hang out with them and discuss ideas, and for sharing their energy and enthusiasm to reinspire me when writing slowed. Final editing was accomplished on beautiful Stradbroke Island at my long-time friends Sue and Brian's beach house. Thanks, dear friends, for once again letting me retreat there to write. Thanks also to Philippa Neary, who did a great job assisting me with final manuscript preparation. Throughout the writing I received great help from the team at The Guilford Press in shaping my ideas into a book, and I owe particular thanks to Jim Nageotte, Senior Editor at Guilford, who has been exceptionally helpful. Working with the Guilford team has been a pleasure.

Finally, and most important, I thank my wife, Barbara, who gave me space and time to do this. I look forward to some extra time to spend with her, now that this is done.

W. KIM HALFORD

Contents

MARRIAGE AND RELATIONSHIP EDUCATION

CHAPTER 1

What Is Couple Relationship Education? Why Is It Needed?

Tears welled up in the corners of Rachel's eyes as she held out the plush-covered album page for me to see. The single large color photo showed her and David holding hands facing each other; another couple stood beside them also holding hands, also facing each other. The marriage celebrant stood between and slightly behind the two couples. The backs of the heads of gathered family and friends were in the foreground, with their smart clothes, and various eccentric, feathered hats perched on some of the women. In the photograph Rachel and David looked a little younger than they looked on that day in my office, perhaps 4 or 5 years younger. In the photo they looked radiant, smiling, eyes locked on each other. In my office they had strained expressions, slight downward turns at the corners of their mouths, with their taut eyes fixed on me.

David's voice quavered as he spoke. "Deb told us last week that she and Jeff are divorcing. Rach and I are gutted . . . our best friends . . . we shared our wedding day with them."

Like almost all couples who marry, David and Rachel, Debra and Jeff, had made commitments to each other that their respective relationships would be lifelong and loving. David and Rachel were still deeply in love, they spoke about each other warmly, and they often held hands in the sessions they had with me. They had fun together, sharing an eclectic set of passionate interests: martial arts, football, hiking, and classical music. They supported each other in their times of stress, each gently describing having jointly coped with the struggle as Rachel's mother became ill and died of breast cancer. They communicated often and closely, regularly sitting to talk about things that mattered to them, particularly their plans for the future—children, a new house that was closer to their families. I never met Debra and Jeff, but I heard about how their arguments had become frequent, and more unpleasant, over time. Fun,

1

communication, and sex seemed to have all but disappeared from their lives; the sense of a shared future, of the commitment to be together, had eroded. Toward the end of our first session Rachel sighed heavily. "With Deb and Jeff splitting, it makes us . . . I don't know. . . . "

I interjected, "Unsure, anxious maybe?"

Rachel replied, "Yes, like they were once in love like we are now. . . . So what does this mean for us?"

The divergent pathways of these two couple relationships reflect the diversity of what happens to couples in all developed countries of the world: almost all couples start out highly satisfied with their relationship, a lot of couples sustain that satisfaction and make their relationship work, but a lot of couples do not. In our work together, Rachel and David essentially posed two questions of me. "How does this happen, that two people so in love can lose their way?" and "What can we do to strengthen what we have and not finish up like Jeff and Debra?" This book is my attempt to address those questions in a way that is useful to professionals who work with couples.

A key assumption that is the foundation of this book is that there are crucial skills, attitudes, and knowledge that give partners a better chance of developing and sustaining a healthy, mutually satisfying couple relationship. Some people acquire these attitudes, skills, and knowledge through life experiences, but many people do not. Couple relationship education[1] (CRE) is the provision of structured learning experiences to help couples develop their relationship knowledge, attitude, and skills. CRE typically is targeted at couples who identify themselves as currently satisfied with their relationship, and builds on the strengths in the relationship to enhance commitment and healthy interaction. The key goals of CRE are to help couples sustain a healthy committed relationship, to prevent the erosion of relationship satisfaction that many couples experience, and to reduce the considerable personal and social costs of relationship distress and separation.

This book is a detailed guide on how to conduct evidence-based CRE. Evidence-based CRE draws upon the substantial research on what influences couple relationship satisfaction and stability, and uses an approach to CRE

---

[1] I use the term *couple relationship education* to describe education for marryied couples or for couples who are in other forms of a committed relationship. In most cultures the majority of heterosexual couples who remain in a long-term committed relationship choose to marry, and there is some evidence that marrying has advantages for those couples. However, in many Western countries the majority of heterosexual couples choose cohabiting either as a prelude or an alternative to marriage. I believe most of what is described in this book can enhance the relationships of couples in any form of committed relationship. However, most research on committed couple relationships has been with heterosexual married couples. When a research finding is based just on married couples I use the term *marriage*, otherwise I use *couple relationships*.

that has been evaluated in well-designed research trials. Evidence-based CRE is brief, ranging in length from a single session (involving an assessment of the relationship with discussion of current strengths and challenges) to 12–14 hours of a skill training curriculum. (See Chapter 2 for a detailed review of the evidence on effective CRE.)

CRE is distinct from couple therapy. CRE works with couples who are currently satisfied in their relationship, and who are committed to that relationship. CRE builds upon the high level of positive emotion typical of currently satisfied couples, and has a strong emphasis on building the positive foundations for a great life together. In contrast, couple therapy is for people who are distressed in their relationship. Couple therapy often has to manage the high levels of negative affect in the relationship, and address the ambivalence many distressed couples feel about whether they wish the relationship to continue (Halford, 2001). Couple therapy is often extensive in duration, with evidence-based approaches often involving 15, 20, or more sessions of therapy (Snyder, Castellani, & Whisman, 2006).

The intended audience for the current book is anyone who works as a couple relationship educator. By the term *couple relationship educator* I mean anyone who works with couples on their relationship, particularly those professionals who seek to strengthen couple relationships and prevent future problems. Many priests, ministers, rabbis, imams, and other religious leaders provide education and counsel to couples about their relationships. Psychologists, psychiatrists, social workers, marriage and family therapists, and other mental health professionals also work extensively with couples. Often these mental health professionals work predominantly, or even exclusively, with distressed couples. I hope this book will encourage these professionals to expand their practices to include CRE as a form of early intervention with couples. Some community and religious organizations support a tradition of relationship mentors. Relationship mentors can be individuals, but most often are couples who support other couples in their relationship. This book is intended to assist all these people to work as effective couple relationship educators.

WHY PROVIDE COUPLE RELATIONSHIP EDUCATION?

Sustaining a healthy, mutually satisfying relationship across a lifetime is a substantial challenge. Almost all marriages and other committed couple relationships begin with high relationship satisfaction (Bradbury, 1998). The partners usually hope (and expect) that the relationship will be lifelong. Unfortunately, for many couples, their initially positive feelings decline with time. Between one-third and one-half of marriages in developed countries deteriorate to the point where distance or conflict become predominant, at least one of the partners gives up on the relationship, and the couple separates. The rates of relationship deterioration and separation are even higher in cohabiting couples. However, the erosion of relationship satisfaction that many couples experience is not inevitable. Couples who develop core relationship knowledge, skills, and attitudes greatly enhance their chance of sustaining a healthy, mutually satisfying relationship.

Figure 1.1 summarizes 12 key reasons for professionals to provide, and couples to attend, CRE. This figure is a useful handout to provide to couples. The next two sections of this chapter review the evidence to support the statements included in the figure.

The Significance of Couple Relationships for Adults

Sharing a lifelong committed relationship with a partner is an almost universal aspiration. For most people, that means getting married. More than 90% of people marry by age 50 across almost all countries, cultures, and religions (United Nations Economic and Social Affairs Population Division, 2003). Even among those who choose not to marry in Western countries, the vast majority of people enter "marriage-like" cohabiting couple relationships (Australian Bureau of Statistics, 2008; Statistics Canada, 2003; U.S. Census Bureau, 2003). The desire to be in a committed partner relationship is so pervasive that some psychologists have argued that it reflects an evolutionary imperative (Buss, 2003).

When people achieve their aspiration for a strong, mutually satisfying marriage, this is a very powerful predictor of positive health and well-being in the partners. In an extensive review of research evidence, Diener, Suh, Lucas, and Smith (1999) concluded that being in a satisfying marriage was one of the strongest determinants of life satisfaction for adults, and that this was true across a diverse range of cultures. In addition, a mutually satisfying marriage is associated with resilience to the negative effects of life stresses (Coie et al., 1993), high self-ratings of health and well-being (Waite & Gallagher, 2000), low rates of diagnosed psychological disorder (Halford, Bouma, Kelly, & Young, 1999), greater life expectancy (Hu & Goldman, 1990; Waite & Gallagher, 2000), fewer diagnosed health problems (Schmaling & Sher, 2000), and better coping with major illness (Schmaling & Sher, 2000).

Being happily married is also associated with financial well-being. Relative to single or unhappily married individuals, happily married individuals have greater career achievement and earn higher incomes (Daniel, 1995; Forthofer, Markman, Cox, Stanley, & Kessler, 1996; Schoeni, 1995; Waite & Gallagher, 2000). While some of this "marriage premium" is likely due to selection effects, there is evidence that marriage is associated with higher pro-

1. A loving, lifelong couple relationship promotes a long and healthy life.

2. A loving, lifelong couple relationship helps your career and finances.

3. A loving lifelong couple relationship protects you and your partner against stress.

4. Being raised by parents in a loving, lifelong couple relationship is really good for children.

5. A loving lifelong couple relationship is usually valued by extended family and friends and assists you to feel part of a broader community.

6. Strong, loving couple relationships can be strengthened with couple relationship education.

7. Despite usually starting with love and commitment, about one in three marriages and one in two cohabiting relationships end within 10 years.

8. There is key relationship between knowledge and skills, which can be learned, that help people sustain a loving lifelong couple relationship.

9. Most adults have learned some, but not all, of the important relationship knowledge and skills.

10. Across a lifetime there are inevitable stresses that can strain a couple relationship, but having the right relationship knowledge and skills helps manage the strain on your relationship.

11. Many separated people report that they wish they had worked harder on their relationship, but they did not know what to do.

12. Should problems develop in your relationship, knowing what to do and going for help early gives you a much better chance of solving those problems.

FIGURE 1.1. Twelve good reasons to attend couple relationship (marriage) education. For most—though not all—people, a loving, lifelong couple relationship involves being married. There is evidence that, on average, married people are more likely to be happy and to stay together than people who live together. Some readers might prefer to describe what they offer as marriage education, and to explain the benefits of a loving, lifelong marriage.

ductivity and achievement even when controlling for selection effects (Waite & Gallagher, 2000). Furthermore, married people have fewer days of work absenteeism (Rodriguez & Borgen, 1998), and are much less likely to need social security support (Blank, 1997; Thomas & Sawhill, 2005). In contrast, divorce is a major predictor of financial difficulties and the need to seek social security (Funder, Harrison, & Weston, 1993; Thomas & Sawhill, 2005).

The Significance of Couple Relationships for Children

Children benefit from a strong, happy relationship between their parents. Children who grow up in a stable home with both parents in a satisfying marriage have better mental, physical, educational, and peer-related adjustment than other children (McLanahan & Sandefur, 1996; Sanders, Nicholson, & Floyd, 1997). In contrast, parental conflict and divorce are risk factors for child depression, conduct disorder, poor social competence, health problems, and academic underachievement (Amato, 2001). Moreover, these negative effects of parental discord influence offspring adjustment into adulthood. People whose parents or grandparents divorce are at increased risk for divorce themselves (Amato, 2000; Amato & Cheadle, 2005), and parental marital distress when children are growing up predicts distress in the marriages of the offspring in adulthood (Amato & Booth, 2001).

I do not highlight the negative effects of parental divorce to suggest that couples should remain together in high-conflict or violent marriages. The research evidence indicates that children benefit from living in homes with parents in low-conflict, mutually satisfying marriages. Moreover, countless single mothers and fathers are doing their very best to provide a safe and stable home for their children, and single parenthood can be the best option available to some parents. However, where it is feasible, growing up in a home based on a loving marriage seems to convey many advantages to children. For example, relative to other children, the children of happy stable marriages are much less likely to grow up experiencing poverty (Funder et al., 1993; Smock, Manning, & Gupta, 1999), or abuse (Waite & Gallagher, 2000).

The strong links between marital functioning and a wide range of adult and child outcomes has led to a growing recognition among researchers and policymakers that this entity that most people desire in their lives—happy marriage—has important public health consequences (see, e.g., Hahlweg, Baucom, Bastine, & Markman, 1998; Halford, Markman, & Stanley, 2008). As a result, policymakers across many nations strive to implement programs that can help couples achieve their aspirations for a mutually satisfying relationship and family stability (for examples of trends and issues, see Halford, Markman, & Stanley, 2008; Seefeldt & Smock, 2004). An important element of these new family policies is encouragement and funding of CRE, which is strongly supported in countries as diverse as Australia, Germany, Norway, Hong Kong, Malaysia, Singapore, the United Kingdom, and the United States (Hahlweg, Baucom, et al., 1998; Halford & Simons, 2005; Huang, 2005; Thuen & Lærum, 2005).

Couple Relationship Education and Couple Therapy

Marriage and family therapists, psychologists, and other mental health professionals traditionally have addressed the problem of couple relationship distress almost exclusively through providing therapy to distressed couples. Several approaches to couple therapy (e.g., cognitive-behavioral and emotion-focused therapies) can improve relationship satisfaction for the majority of couples who present for therapy when treatment is delivered by highly trained therapists (Snyder et al., 2006). However, it is clear that couple therapy is often challenging to deliver effectively. By the time many couples present for therapy they have developed ingrained maladaptive communication and conflict management patterns, and high levels of negative thoughts and feelings about the relationship. Positivity toward each other is significantly eroded. These patterns are resistant to change, making successful therapeutic outcomes (namely, achieving sustained reestablishment of relationship satisfaction) difficult to achieve (for discussion of the management of these couple therapy challenges, see Christenen, Doss, & Atkins, 2005; Epstein & Baucom, 2002; Halford, 2001; Snyder & Whisman, 2003).

Couple therapy as applied in routine practice achieves small effect size gains in couple relationship satisfaction, effect sizes substantially lower than the large effect sizes reported in research studies evaluating the efficacy of couple therapy (Hahlweg & Klan, 1997). Furthermore, in clinical practice the rates of dropout from couple therapy are often high (Hahlweg & Klan, 1997), and consumer satisfaction with couple therapy is low relative to satisfaction with other forms of psychotherapy (Seligman, 1995).

CRE has the advantage of working with couples when they are most positive and enthusiastic about their relationship, and seeks to harness that commitment and energy to promote positive relationship functioning. In contrast to couple therapy, dropout from CRE typically is rare (Halford & Simons, 2005). Moreover, couples completing CRE overwhelmingly report that the experience was positive, and that they learned important relationship-enhancing ideas and skills (Halford, Markman, & Stanley, 2008).

Another advantage of CRE is that it seems relatively easy to deliver effectively. There is considerable evidence that people other than mental health professionals, such as clergy, lay leaders (Markman, Williams, Einhorn, & Stanley, 2007), or midwives (Halford, Markman, & Stanley, 2008), can deliver CRE effectively after relatively brief (10–15 hours) training in CRE delivery.

In contrasting couple therapy and CRE I am not arguing that couple therapy is ineffective or should not be offered. However, I am suggesting that CRE has an important contribution to make in helping more couples realize their ambition of sustaining a healthy, mutually satisfying relationship. The need for CRE becomes clear when the challenges of sustaining a healthy couple relationship are analyzed.

THE CHALLENGE OF SUSTAINING A HEALTHY RELATIONSHIP

The Changing Context of Marriage

Across most nations of the world with reliable data, marriage rates have declined and divorce rates have increased since the 1970s (United Nations Economic and Social Affairs Population Division, 2003). Table 1.1 presents the ratio of marriages to divorces in selected countries from Western Europe, Australasia, North America, and Asia. The extent of the changes varies greatly from country to country, with marked differences between developing and developed countries. Across almost all countries people are delaying marriage and getting married at older ages, but this trend is much more marked in developed than developing countries (United Nations Economic and Social Affairs Population Division, 2003). Divorce rates increased in most countries between the 1950s and 1990s, and are substantially higher in developed than developing countries. The median divorce rate in developing countries increased from 13 to about 25 per 1,000 population between the early 1970s

TABLE 1.1. Changes in the Ratio of Marriages to Divorce in Selected Countries

	Marriage-to-divorce ratio	
	1980	2005
Australia	3.1	2.1
Canada	3.0	2.2
Germany	3.5	2.0
Italy	28.5	6.4
India	—	63.9
Japan	5.0	2.5
South Korea	12.5	2.1
United Kingdom	2.6	2.0
United States	2.0	2.7

and 2000, and in developing countries from six to 14 per 1,000 (United Nations Economic and Social Affairs Population Division, 2003).

The decline in marriage rates and increase in divorce rates reflect, in part, the side effects of some positive socioeconomic changes. In the last half-century declining marriage rates and increasing divorce rates correlate with women gaining more access to education, greater control over their fertility (i.e., more access to reliable contraception), and greater participation in the paid workforce (United Nations Economic and Social Affairs Population Division, 2003). In the 1950s almost all women in developed countries needed to get married to attain economic security. Women found it very difficult to leave a marriage—no matter how dysfunctional the marriage might have been—because they typically had many dependent children and lacked the economic means to support themselves and their children (Coontz, 2005).

Socioeconomic change around the world is moving marriage toward being a voluntary union between partners, rather than a social arrangement shaped by circumstances. This trend is well illustrated in the world's most populous country: China. Economic development in China has occurred at the extraordinary growth rate of more than 10% of gross domestic product (GDP) every year from the early 1990s to 2008, but this development has disproportionately benefited the large urban areas (Chinese National Bureau of Statistics, 2003). In the poor rural areas of China where education is rare, and female wages are low or nonexistent, marriage rates are high, and divorce rates remain stable and very low; in the industrialized boom areas surrounding the cities of Beijing and Shanghai, divorce rates in 2002 were more than triple those in the rest of the country and growing rapidly (Chinese National Bureau of Statistics, 2003). Similarly, in the developed countries of North America, Western Europe, and Australasia, increasing divorce rates correlate across time with increasing education and participation of women in the workforce (United Nations Economic and Social Affairs Population Division, 2003). Even in the wealthiest country in the world, the United States, there is a longitudinal correlation over time between women's labor force participation and divorce rates (South, 1985).

Coontz (2005) documented the changing nature of marriage in the United Kingdom, noting that marriages arranged by family members were the normal process for arranging marriage for much of recorded history. Such arranged marriages were seen by the families and the partners as economic arrangements based on mutual benefit. Concepts of social good, duty, economic security, capacity to raise a family, and benefit to the extended family were strong in the rhetoric surrounding marriage. Only in the last few hundred years have notions of marriage as a romantic arrangement based on mutual attraction between the partners become more common. Arranged marriages still are common in many developing countries, such as India and rural China, and the reported satisfaction of partners in such arranged marriages is at least as high as in romantic marriages, and the divorce rates are much lower (Huang, 2005). Interestingly, a number of social commentators in Western countries have recently criticized a perceived overemphasis on individual partner satisfaction in marriage, arguing that more attention needs to be paid to the social good resulting from continuing strong marriages (e.g., Australian National Marriage Coalition, 2004; Bradford et al., 2005).

Changing laws about divorce also have shaped the nature of marriage and divorce. In developed countries divorce laws typically date from the 19th or early 20th centuries[2] (Gonzalez & Viitanen, 2006). When first introduced, most divorce laws required establishing that a partner had done a blameworthy act, such as perpetrating violence or adultery (Gonzalez & Viitanen, 2006). Since the 1960s most Western countries have made legislative changes to introduce "no-fault" divorce law. Under no-fault divorce law, the only required grounds for divorce are that the couple has separated, and in most legislatures the process of divorce has been made less expensive than under earlier legislation (Gonzalez & Viitanen, 2006). Thus, in Western countries marriage has rapidly evolved from a union often enforced by economic imperatives and difficult divorce processes to a voluntary union that can be dissolved by unilateral action by either partner.

Increased Life Expectancy

Increased human life expectancy has substantially lengthened the duration of a lifetime marriage, which some commentators argue make it more likely that partners will change, grow apart, and ultimately divorce (Pinsof, 2002). In now-developed countries like the United Kingdom and the United States, it has been estimated that during the preindustrial era marriages lasted on average 15 years (Pinsof, 2002). The majority of marriages in that era ended through death of a partner, attributable to the combination of the high maternal death rates and the effects of infectious disease producing a low mean life expectancy. The current estimated mean duration of marriages in the United States is about 16 years (U.S. Census Bureau, 2003), which is similar to the mean duration 150 years ago. However, now marriages of the mean duration of 16 years most often end in divorce, whereas 150 years ago the death of a partner was the most common cause of marriages ending at the average duration of 15 years.

---

[2]It is noteworthy that divorce was banned in some developed countries until relatively recently; Italy only permitted divorce from 1970, Spain from 1981, and Ireland from 1996.

The Rise of Cohabitation

In most Western countries cohabitating heterosexual couples are a substantial and increasing minority of all couple households. For example, cohabiting couples now make up 8% of all U.S. couple households (U.S. Census Bureau, 2003). The rates of cohabitation have increased in the last 30 years in most Western countries. For example, cohabiting couples as a percentage of all couple households has increased from 2% in 1970 to 16% in 2006 in Australia (Australian Bureau of Statistics, 2008), and from 6% in 1980 to 16% in 2001 in Canada (Statistics Canada, 2003).

The trend for more couples to cohabit has been a significant source of concern to some prominent religious leaders, social scientists, and social policy analysts, who have made public pronouncements about the importance of marriage (e.g., Australian National Marriage Coalition, 2004; Bradford et al., 2005; Wilson, 2002). A key issue for many of these commentators is that marriage is an accepted social institution involving a firm commitment to the partner, that commitment is often based on strongly held social and religious values, and that there are broad social supports for marriage from extended family and community. In contrast, cohabitation lacks the social and religious underpinnings of marriage, the level of long-term commitment to the relationship is often unclear, and often extended family and the broader community are less supportive of the relationship than of a marriage. Commentators have expressed concern that cohabitation is (wrongly) seen as equivalent or even superior to marriage (e.g., Australian National Marriage Coalition, 2004).

There is substantial social science research showing that cohabitation is different from marriage. While marriage is universally accepted as a commitment intended to be lifelong (even if that intention is not always realized), cohabiting couples vary substantially in their long-term commitment to the relationship. In Australia about half of couples who have recently begun cohabiting report they think they are likely to marry their partner, one-quarter state they are not sure, and one-quarter think they probably will not marry their partner (Qu, 2003). Most often cohabitation is a transitional arrangement for couples that either leads to marriage or to separation. Across a range of Western countries, more than 80% of cohabiting couples either marry or separate within 5 years (Qu & Weston, 2001). Cohabitation is now the most common means for couples in Western countries to begin a committed relationship. The vast majority of couples in these countries who married in this century cohabited before marrying, with recent research showing that 85% of marrying couples in Australia cohabited premaritally, 84% in Canada, and 74% in the United States (Australian Bureau of Statistics, 2008; Statistics Canada, 2003; U.S. Census Bureau, 2005).

One often-expressed concern is that premarital cohabitation undermines the chance of successful marriage. Research up to and including the 1990s found a robust association across Western countries between premarital cohabitation and an elevated risk of divorce (DeMaris & Rao, 1992; de Vaus, Qu, & Weston, 2003b; Hall & Zhao, 1995; Kieran, 2002). However, this correlation does not show that premarital cohabitation causes increased risk of divorce. Individuals who choose to cohabit have an overrepresentation of certain personal characteristics that make them more likely to have relationship problems (Clarksburg, Stolzenberg, & Wake, 1995). Cohabitation is most common among people who are young (under age 25), have been previously married, have children from a past relationship, are poor or socially disadvantaged, or who have some level of psychological disorder, all of which predict increased risk of divorce (de Vaus et al., 2003b). Many of these characteristics compromise long-term relationship commitment. For example, in the United States, studies show that many parents forming a stepfamily express concern about whether their children will get on with a new partner, and whether the new partner will parent their children in a manner acceptable to them (Hetherington & Clingempeel, 1992; White & Booth, 1985). When one statistically controls for the differences between people who choose to cohabit or not cohabit, then the claimed negative effects of premarital cohabitation on marrying couples' risk for divorce are close to zero (Hewitt & de Vaus, 2009).

Cohabitation is much more widely accepted in most Western countries now than it was a generation ago (de Vaus, Qu, & Weston, 2003a). As the extent of social deviance associated with cohabitation has declined, the magnitude of any effect of premarital cohabitation on divorce rates has declined. After controling for the effects of the individual characteristics of partners who choose to cohabit, there is no negative effect of premarital cohabitation on separation in cohorts of couples married after the early 1990s (Hewitt & de Vaus, 2009), at least in countries where premarital cohabitation is widely practiced (Liefbroer & Dourleijn, 2006).

In the United States there have been repeated claims (e.g., Why Marriage Matters, 2007) that premarital cohabitation is associated with increased risk for divorce in the United States. However, U.S. couples who expect to marry their partner when they start living together have similar relationships, and no higher risk of divorce, than couples who only begin living together after they get married (Stanley, Whitton, & Markman, 2004). Thus, in the United States low long-term commitment to the relationship when cohabiting, rather than cohabiting per se, is associated with poor relationship outcomes.

In summary, in contemporary Western cultures cohabitation is of two general forms: committed couples, who probably are planning to marry; and less committed couples, who often are young, forming stepfamilies, or socially disadvantaged. These less committed couples sometimes decide to marry, but often separate. Cohabiting couples who do marry seem to suffer no ill effects from premarital cohabitation. Whatever the moral stance one might take, social science evidence suggests that cohabitation is probably unrelated to relationship outcomes when cohabitation occurs within a relationship of strong commitment. However, marriage remains the most common way that strong relationship commitment is expressed in most contemporary Western cultures (Qu, 2003).

Declining Thresholds for Initiating Separation and Divorce

Social change has modified the determinants of divorce. As noted earlier, prior to the move to no-fault divorces, legal dissolution of a marriage required establishment of specific negative behaviors by one spouse, the most common of which were adultery or violence. The majority of marriages that ended in divorce in that era had severe problems, though some divorces are known to have been obtained by one or both spouses falsely claiming the required conditions (e.g., adultery) existed to allow divorce (van Poppel & de Beer, 1993).

The high threshold to initiate divorce in earlier eras reflected social attitudes that now have changed. In the 1960s the majority of adults in the United States and Australia endorsed the view that divorce should only occur when the marriage had severe problems (Australian Institute of Family Studies, 1997; Thornton & Young-DeMarco, 2001). However, by the late 1990s the majority of adults in the United States (Thornton & Young-DeMarco, 2001), most countries of Western Europe (de Graaf & Kalmijn, 2006), and Australia (Australian Institute of Family Studies, 1997), endorsed the view that divorce is acceptable if the partners no longer wish to remain together. Relative to the 1960s, in the early 2000s more people describe psychological motives ("I felt we had grown apart," "We were not communicating") as the reasons for their divorce (de Graaf & Kalmijn, 2006), rather than severe conflict, violence, or adultery. Both cross-sectional (Kalmijn & Poortman, 2006) and longitudinal studies (Amato & Rogers, 1997) show that severe marital problems like violence or adultery now predict the occurrence of only a minority of divorces. Separation is often the outcome for relationships that initially have only mild problems (Amato & Rogers, 1997), and relationships that were once highly satisfying (Johnson & Booth, 1998). In other words, the threshold for marital dissolution has declined.

Women are more likely to initiate divorce than men (Kincaid & Caldwell, 1995). Women report more marital dissatisfaction, and exhibit more severe psychological adjustment problems, than men prior to the separation (Bloom

& Caldwell, 1981; Diedrick, 1991; Riessman & Gerstel, 1985). Moreover, women's relationship dissatisfaction is a stronger predictor of divorce than men's dissatisfaction (Amato & Rogers, 1997). The decline in the threshold for initiating divorce is particularly noticeable for women.

Separation does not have the benefits expected by many people contemplating leaving an unhappy relationship. It is true that people leaving marriages with severe problems benefit. For example, Aseltine and Kessler (1993) showed that among respondents who were experiencing severe marital conflict or violence, separation was associated with a decrease in depression. However, as noted earlier, most people who separate are not leaving a violent or high-conflict relationship. Almost all people who separate from a committed relationship report substantial distress, and significant difficulties in adjustment, at least initially (Sweeper & Halford, 2006). It is noteworthy that the level of adjustment difficulties seems similar in people recently separated from marrying and cohabiting relationships. While for most people these adjustment difficulties abate with time, problems sharing parenting responsibilities with a former partner are very common and often chronic sources of stress (Sweeper & Halford, 2006).

Many people who leave a marriage and form a new relationship do report a better relationship the second time around (Johnson & Booth, 1998). However, at least some of the negative behaviors partners exhibit in a first distressed marriage, they carry over into their second marriage (Johnson & Booth, 1998; Prado & Markman, 1998). If there are children from the first marriage, then the challenges of the next relationship are substantial. Stepfamilies have particularly high rates of couple relationship distress and separation (Hetherington & Stanley-Hagen, 2000).

In contrast to the option of leaving a distressed relationship, many couples find they can enhance a troubled marriage. High proportions of couples who report marital dissatisfaction at one time, but persist with their relationship, report that their relationship subsequently improves (Waite & Gallagher, 2000). This is not to say that people should be forced to stay in relationships they find unsatisfactory. However, CRE can usefully highlight that separation often does not produce the desired benefits, at least in the case of people leaving relationships without severe problems. In other words, working on a distressed relationship often can be a useful option.

In summary, couple relationships historically were social and economic marriages arranged by extended families. In Western cultures couple relationships have evolved to be love-based arrangements between partners, which most often begin with cohabitation that sometimes leads to marriage. In the past marriages were almost universally lifelong, and divorce was rare and only available if serious problems were evident. Now in Western countries breakup of couple relationships is more common and determined to a large extent by the degree to which the relationship is mutually satisfying to the partners. Given the centrality of relationship satisfaction to the fate of couple relationships, it is important to understand the influences on couple relationship satisfaction.

AN ECOLOGICAL MODEL OF THE INFLUENCES ON COUPLE RELATIONSHIPS

Relationship satisfaction in couples is almost universally high at the time of marriage (Bradbury & Karney, 2004; Glenn, 1998). Couples also have generally positive expectations of their relationship, and despite the well-known statistics about high divorce rates, see themselves as highly likely to be married to their partner for life (Fowers, Lyons, & Montel, 1996). However, the average relationship satisfaction decreases markedly across the early years of marriage (Bradbury & Karney, 2004; Glenn, 1998); about 3–4% of couples separate each year in the first 10 years of marriage (Glenn, 1998). There is now a large research base investigating the variables that predict couples' future relationship outcomes (i.e., relationship satisfaction and separation; Bradbury & Karney, 2004; Holman, 2001).

The variables that predict couple relationship outcomes fall into four broad categories (Halford, 2001), which can be integrated into the ecological model depicted in Figure 1.2.

1. At the outermost level of influence are sociocultural variables, which provide the context in which relationships occur. The previous section of this chapter outlined a range of socioeconomic, legal, and cultural developments that have changed the nature of marriage. There also are contextual variables that operate at a local level that differentially influence couples within a given culture. For example, positive support of the couple relationship by family and friends predicts sustained high relationship satisfaction (Larson & Holman, 1994).

2. Life events include major life events (e.g., birth of a child, a change of job) and daily uplifts and hassles (e.g., being praised by the boss, getting caught in traffic, an argument with a coworker). Stressful life events and daily hassles each predict deteriorating relationship satisfaction (Story & Bradbury, 2004). As depicted in the diagram, some life events are shared by the couple; other life events are experienced specifically by one partner.

3. Individual characteristics are relatively stable individual differences that partners bring to the relationship, such as negative family-of-origin experiences, low partner education, psychological disorder, and certain person-

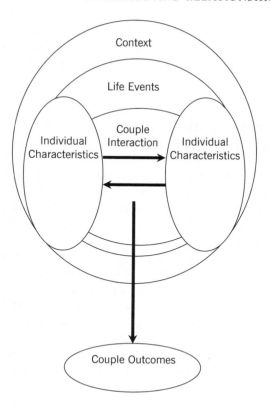

FIGURE 1.2. An ecological model of influences on couple relationships.

ality variables, each of which predict deteriorating relationship satisfaction (Bradbury & Karney, 2004; Holman, 2001).

4. Finally, couple interaction includes the partners' behaviors, thoughts, and feelings during interaction. For example, positive couple communication and shared realistic relationship expectations predict sustained relationship satisfaction and stability (Bradbury & Karney, 2004; Holman, 2001).

Context

Couple relationships occur within a cultural context that defines how couple relationships are supposed to be. The earlier sections of this chapter highlighted some general assumptions about relationships shared across Western cultures. There also are important variations both within and between those cultures. For example, German couples without relationship problems engage in similar levels of verbal negativity as Australian distressed couples (Halford, Hahlweg, & Dunne, 1990), suggesting that greater levels of negativity are more acceptable in the German cultural context than in Australia. Partners who differ in their ethnic, racial, or cultural background often differ in their expectations and beliefs about relationships (Jones & Chao, 1997). This diversity in partner assumptions and beliefs can be a source of great strength for a relationship when the partners are able to draw on the wisdom and strengths of different cultural traditions. At the same time, substantial differences in expectations can be a significant source of conflict between the partners (Jones & Chao, 1997). Marriages in which partners have very different cultural backgrounds break down at somewhat higher rates than other marriages (Bitrchnell & Kennard, 1984; Kurdek, 1993).

A related issue is the relationship between religiosity and marital satisfaction. Research suggests that when both partners attend religious services regularly they have a somewhat lower risk for marital dissolution and report higher marital satisfaction (Call & Heaton, 1997; Heaton & Pratt, 1990; Mahoney, Pargament, Tarakeshwar, & Swank, 2001). Taken with the research presented above on the effects of cultural similarity, it seems that the association between shared religiosity and couple relationship satisfaction can be partly attributed to the partners sharing core values and beliefs. In addition, since almost all religions emphasize and support the value of marriage, it is likely that religious couples both endorse such values and receive support from their community for their marriage (Mahoney et al., 2001).

In Western countries, poverty and social disadvantage are associated with a low probability of getting married (Haskins & Sawhill, 2003; McLaughlin & Lichter, 1997). Many young, unemployed, poor people see marriage as requiring being financially stable and view such financial stability and marriage as personally unattainable (Edin & Kefelas, 2005; McLaughlin & Lichter, 1997). Yet, ironically, getting married is associated with increased likelihood of escaping poverty (Haskins & Sawhill, 2003). Some social policy analysts recommend CRE as a poverty reduction strategy by developing in the disadvantaged skills and knowledge that enable marriage (Haskins & Sawhill, 2003). However, chronic social disadvantage is associated with high risk for divorce in married couples (Orbuch, Veroff, Hassan, & Horrocks, 2002), and in particular, economic strain from unemployment predicts deteriorating relationship satisfaction (Vinokur, Price, & Caplan, 1996). It seems likely that there is a reciprocal influence between social disadvantage and the probability of staying happily married.

Work provides the resources that allow people to perceive marriage as a reasonable aspiration (Haskins & Sawhill, 2003), and often provides extra stimulation and ideas to enrich the relationship (Thompson, 1997). However, stressful jobs can impact negatively on couple relationships. In particular, stress experienced at work is associated with increased negative affect in marital interactions (Krokoff, Gottman, & Roy, 1988). Chronic stress, such as social disadvantage, often exacerbates negative responses to work stress, which in turn can have a negative impact upon marital interaction and satisfaction (Karney, Story, & Bradbury, 2005).

There are consistent findings that approval of one's spouse and relationship by friends and extended family predicts high couple relationship satisfaction and stability (Booth & Johnson, 1988; Kurdek, 1991a, 1991b). At the same time, excessive intrusion by family on selection of dating partners and subsequent mate selection predicts relationship problems (Benson, Larson, Wilson, & Demo, 1993). In summary, young adults are wise to heed concerns about a new partner expressed by close family or friends, and family are wise to express real concerns to their loved one but to watch that they are not being intrusive in the couple's relationship,

Life Events

"Life events" refer to developmental transitions and acute circumstances that impinge upon a couple or individual partners. Relationship problems have been argued to be more likely to develop during periods of high rates of change and stress (Karney et al., 2005), and high rates of stressful life events predict deteriorating couple relationship satisfaction (Neff & Karney, 2004; Story & Bradbury, 2004). For example, declines in couple relationship satisfaction are often associated with the transition to parenthood (Cowan & Cowan, 1992; Doss, Rhoades, Stanley, & Markman, 2009; Feeney, Hohaus, Noller, & Alexander, 2001; Shapiro, Gottman, & Carrere, 2000), loss of work (Gore, 1978), and increased stress at work (O'Driscoll, Brough, & Kalliath, 2006).

There are a variety of mechanisms by which life events impact upon couple relationships. Some life events modify the time available for positive couple activities. For example, becoming parents adds about 40 hours of work per week to a household, and modifies the social activities couples can engage in, which typically is associated with decreases in quality time shared just with the partner (Cowan & Cowan, 1992; Feeney et al., 2001). Similarly, a work promotion often increases work responsibilities and can reduce couple time (O'Driscoll et al., 2006). Life events can also influence partners' moods, and this can spill over into couple interactions. For example, fatigue from coping with the demands of infant care or high stress at work are both associated with more negative affect in marital interactions (Gottman & Notarius, 2000; Halford, Gravestock, Lowe, & Scheldt, 1992).

Stressful life events do not have a uniform effect on couples. For example, while most couples report some deterioration in relationship satisfaction at the transition to parenthood, some couples report that the transition to parenthood enhances relationship satisfaction (Belsky & Rovine, 1990; Shapiro et al., 2000). Couples with more positive couple communication and effective mutual support and problem solving are believed to be more resilient to the negative effects of stressful life events (Markman, Halford, & Cordova, 1997; Pasch & Bradbury, 1998). When couples use these skills effectively, then they develop a shared way of understanding and responding to stressful events, which Bodenmann and colleagues describe as "dyadic coping" (Bodenmann & Cina, 2006). If partners use dyadic coping through stressful events, this predicts sustained or even enhanced relationship satisfaction (Bodenmann & Cina, 2006; Shapiro et al., 2000). For example, mutual support and dyadic coping through severe illness in one partner is reported by many couples to bring them closer together (Halford, Scott, & Smythe, 2000).

Individual Characteristics

"Individual characteristics" refer to stable historical, personal, and experiential factors that each partner brings to a relationship. Many normal personality variations do not predict relationship satisfaction (Gottman, 1994; Karney & Bradbury, 1995; Markman, Stanley, & Blumberg, 2001). However, neuroticism is one personality trait that consistently predicts relationship satisfaction (Karney & Bradbury, 1997). *Neuroticism* is the extent to which an individual experiences and has difficulty managing negative feelings like depression and anxiety (Costa & McCrae, 1980).

A second personality trait that is associated with low couple relationship satisfaction is an insecure attachment style (Collins & Read, 1990; Davila & Bradbury, 2001; Feeney, 1994; Kobak & Hazan, 1991). *Insecure adult attachment* is the extent to which an individual feels anxious about, or tends to avoid, emotional closeness in intimate relationships (Hazan & Shaver, 1987). Insecure attachment is alleged to develop primarily in childhood through early experiences of caregiving by parents (Bowlby, 1973). Sensitive and responsive parenting leads a child to develop secure attachment, which reflects positive expectations about the behavior of others in close relationships (Ainsworth, Blehar, Waters, & Wall, 1978). Inconsistent, harsh, or unresponsive parenting leads to insecure attachment, which involves either high anxiety that others will abandon you, and/or discomfort with emotional closeness (Ainsworth et al., 1978). In essence, Bowlby (1973) argued that attachment style serves as a foundation for the interpretation of adult relationship experiences, which shape the individual's cognitive, emotional, and behavioral responses to others (Collins & Read, 1994).

While attachment style is seen as being developed in childhood, it also can be modified by adult relationship experiences (Bowlby, 1973). Experiencing a mutually satisfying relationship predicts increasing attachment security in the partners, particularly a reduction in anxiety over abandonment (Davila, Burge, & Hammen, 1997; Davila, Karney, & Bradbury, 1999). However, significant childhood trauma can establish relatively stable insecure attachment that can impact on couple relationships. For example, children who are maltreated or sexually abused by family members show sustained attachment insecurity (Wekerle & Wolfe, 1998), and insecure attachment predicts increased risk of relationship distress, violence, and divorce in adulthood (Dutton, Saunders, Starzomski, & Bartholomew, 1994; Holtzworth-Munroe & Meehan, 2004; Kesner & McKenry, 1998; Pistole & Tarrant, 1993).

Aside from normal personality variations, a major risk for relationship distress is if one or both partners suffer from psychological disorder. High rates of relationship problems consistently have been reported in populations with severe psychological disorder (Halford, 1995). The most prevalent psychological disorders associated with relationship problems are depression, alcohol abuse, and some anxiety disorders, especially panic disorder and general anxiety disorder (Emmelkamp, De Haan, & Hoogduin, 1990; Halford et al., 1999; Halford & Osgarty, 1993; Whisman & Uebelacker, 2003). Relationship problems and individual psychological disorder seem to exacerbate each other (Halford et al., 1999; Whisman & Uebelacker, 2003). For example, alcohol abuse at the time of marriage predicts deteriorating marital satisfaction (Leonard & Roberts, 1998), while the onset of alcohol abuse is predicted by low marital satisfaction (Whisman, Uebelacker, & Bruce, 2006). Similarly, depressive symptoms and marital distress reciprocally predict each other (Davila, Karney, Hall, & Bradbury, 2003). In addition, certain personal vulnerabilities may dispose people to both psychological disorders and relationship problems. For example, deficits in interpersonal communication and negative affect regulation are risk factors that predict the onset of both alcohol abuse (Block, Block, & Keyes, 1988) and relationship problems (Arellano & Markman, 1995; Clements, Cordova, Markman, & Laurenceau, 1997; Lindahl & Markman, 1990; Markman & Hahlweg, 1993).

Negative experiences in the family of origin predict low relationship satisfaction. In the family of origin, having parents who divorced (de Graaf, 1991; Glenn & Kramer, 1987; Glenn & Shelton, 1983; Pope & Mueller, 1976), or who were violent toward each other (e.g., Burgess, Hartman, & McCormack, 1987; Mihalic & Elliot, 1997; Widom, 1989) predicts low couple relationship satisfaction and increased risk of separation. In contrast, a positive lifelong marriage between one's parents is associated with more positive expectations of marriage (Black & Sprenkle, 1991; Gibardi & Rosen, 1991), and with more positive communication and conflict management in couples prior to marriage (Halford, Sanders, & Behrens, 2000; Sanders, Halford, & Behrens,

1999). Positive expectations and communication are likely learned from parents' relationships and subsequently mediate positive adult relationships of the offspring. Consistent with this interpretation, Story, Karney, Lawrence, and Bradbury (2004) found that negative communication mediated an association between parental conflict and divorce with the couple's own relationship distress and divorce.

Each partner's and the couple's relationship history are associated with relationship outcomes. Individuals who have had a cohabiting relationship with someone other than their current spouse, or who have had large numbers of sexual partners prior to marriage, are at higher risk for deteriorating relationship satisfaction than people without those histories (Holman, 2001; Teachman, 2003). The reason for this effect is not entirely clear, but might be related to having a low threshold of commitment to enter cohabiting relationships, and being more willing to end those low-commitment relationships if difficulties arise. Couples who know each other for at least 12 months before marriage are more likely to sustain high relationship satisfaction than couples who marry quickly (Birchnell & Kennard, 1984; Grover, Russell, Schumm, & Paff-Bergen, 1985; Kurdek, 1991b, 1993). This effect of time is likely attributable to the extended dating period allowing partners to select effectively for compatibility, and for them to develop shared and realistic relationship expectations.

Couple Interaction

"Couple interaction" refers to how couples think, feel, and act when they are together. Almost all couples planning marriage report relationship satisfaction consistent with relationship happiness, but couples reporting premarital relationship satisfaction toward the lower end of the happy range are more likely to experience later relationship distress and divorce (Clements, Stanley, & Markman, 2004; Holman, 2001; Huston, Caughlin, Houts, Smith, & George, 2001). Couples who commence marriage only moderately happy seem to struggle to adapt in the early years of marriage. Once some relationship dissatisfaction is established early in the marriage, it tends to persist (Johnson & Booth, 1998). Couples with modest initial relationship satisfaction are at high risk to separate in the first few years of marriage (Holman, 2001; Huston et al., 2001).

Holding realistic and shared relationship expectations is important to couple relationship outcomes. In particular, realistic and shared expectations about the importance of communication, appropriate methods of conflict resolution, the balance of couple versus individual time, and gender roles is cross-sectionally correlated with (Baucom, Epstein, Rankin, & Burnett, 1996; Eidelson & Epstein, 1982) and predicts future relationship satisfaction

(Holman, 2001; Larsen & Olson, 1989; Olson & Fowers, 1986; Williams & Jurich, 1995). In contrast, unrealistically positive expectations (e.g., "We will never disagree") predict deteriorating relationship satisfaction (Larsen & Olson, 1989; Olson & Fowers, 1986). In addition, premarital reports of disagreements about core relationship expectations and values predict elevated risk for divorce (Clements et al., 2004; Holman, 2001).

Shared and realistic relationship expectations are not just relevant to couples early in marriage: relationship expectations impact on the couple when they experience major life transitions. Couples becoming parents who disagree about how they should manage household and parenting responsibilities are at high risk for relationship distress after they become parents (Feeney et al., 2001; O'Brien & Peyton, 2002). For example, if a woman expects her partner to share these responsibilities equally, and the man does not meet these expectations, this predicts deteriorating relationship satisfaction (Feeney et al., 2001). Similarly, shared and realistic expectations about roles and activities after retirement predict marital satisfaction in older couples retiring from paid employment (Higginbottom, Barling, & Kelloway, 1993).

Another key attribute of couple interaction is the extent to which partners work to sustain and strengthen their relationship, which my colleagues and I refer to as "relationship self-regulation." The notion of self-regulation has a long history in psychology, and there have been several comprehensive formulations of the role of self-generated events in the regulation of behavior (e.g., Bandura, 2001; Karoly, 1993). Across these conceptualizations, there is a central assumption that individuals can regulate their own behavior. That is, people do things at one time, with the intent that this influences their later behavior. For example, if you check the weather forecast and learn that it is likely to rain today, you might put your umbrella by the front door to remind you to take it when you leave the house.

Applying self-regulation theory to couple relationships, Halford, Sanders, and Behrens (1994) proposed that couple relationship self-regulation (RSR) consisted of appraisal, goal setting, and change implementation. *Appraisal* involves being able to describe one's own current relationship behaviors and the major influences on those behaviors in a manner that facilitates relationship enhancement. *Goal setting* involves defining specific and actionable goals for change in one's own behavior, based on one's appraisal of relationship functioning. *Change implementation* involves taking active steps to achieve relationship goals. The RSR process is iterative and cycles back to appraisal of the extent to which desired behavior changes were achieved, and whether this produced the desired relationship changes. For example, consider a couple relocating for work. High RSR would involve appraising current behavior and the likely impact of the relocation on the relationship (e.g., "We will both be busy in new jobs, and missing family and friends. Under pressure I have tended to focus on work and neglect my partner and after the move she might be feeling isolated"); goal setting (e.g., "I want to give this move the best chance of working for both of us. I need to be supportive and focused on us as well as the new job"); and implementing self-change to help sustain the relationship satisfaction of both partners (e.g., "I will take one night every week and every second weekend for couple time, and we will talk each week about how the move is working for each of us").

In addition to these RSR competencies, conceptualizations of self-regulation often refer to persistence in self-change efforts. For example, Bandura (2001), in a comprehensive review of self-regulation, documents the substantial variation in individuals' persistence in the use of self-control strategies in the face of initial adversity. In the context of couple relationships, such persistence might be important. Thus, in our example of the relocating couple, adaptation to a new city is likely to require continuing, persistent attention to the couple relationship.

RSR is associated with relationship satisfaction in recently married and long-married couples (Wilson, Charker, Lizzio, Kimlin, & Halford, 2005), and predicts later relationship satisfaction (Halford, Lizzio, Wilson, & Occhipinti, 2007). In particular, the extent to which each partner individually reflects upon the relationship, and takes personal responsibility to enhance the relationship, predicts sustained relationship satisfaction (Halford et al., 2007). In contrast, partners who attribute any relationship difficulties to stable characteristics of the spouse are unlikely to take responsibility for the relationship or make an effort to enhance the relationship (Halford et al., 2007). A negative pattern of attributing relationship difficulties to the behavior of the partner predicts deteriorating relationship satisfaction (Fincham, Bradbury, Arias, Byrne, & Karney, 1997; Fincham, Harold, & Gano-Phillips, 2000).

Another aspect of the couple relationship is the way the partners think about their relationship. Gottman and colleagues assess what they call "couple bond" by asking couples to conjointly describe their relationship history (Carrere, Buehlman, Gottman, Coan, & Ruckstuhl, 2000; Shapiro et al., 2000). Couple bond is seen as reflecting whether the partners have strong relationship commitment, and see their lives as a shared experience with their spouse. A strong couple bond is associated with the partners describing their relationship history with a shared view of events as a common experience (labeled as a sense of "we-ness"), positive expressions of affection and valuing of the spouse, and descriptions of jointly working to overcome adversity (labeled as "glorifying the struggle"). A strong couple bond predicts sustained relationship satisfaction in newlywed couples (Carrere et al., 2000) and in couples expecting their first baby (Shapiro et al., 2000).

The concept of dyadic coping is a similar idea to the couple bond. As described previously, dyadic coping predicts sustained high relationship satisfaction when couples are confronted by a major life stress, such as one of them having a serious or potentially life-threatening illness. Furthermore, couples who describe such threats as a shared experience requiring dyadic coping discuss their emotional responses to the threat together, and who provide mutual support, show substantially better individual adjustment to the stress (Bodenmann, 2005; Coyne & Smith, 1991, 1994; Lichtman, Taylor, & Wood, 1988; Scott, Halford, & Ward, 2004). Thus, a common theme in the couple bond and dyadic coping concepts is that couples who see themselves as a team and their lives as a shared journey tend to sustain high relationship satisfaction.

Couple Communication

Couple communication has been the most extensively studied aspect of couple interaction, with the majority of research focusing on how couples communicate when discussing topics that are a source of disagreement between the partners. As couple communication is often the major focus of most evidence-based relationship education programs (Halford, Markman, Kline, & Stanley, 2003), the research on couple communication as an influence on couple relationships is examined carefully in the section that follows.

Positive communication when discussing conflict topics is associated with relationship satisfaction (Karney & Bradbury, 1995; Markman & Hahlweg, 1993). Specifically, high relationship satisfaction is associated with partners listening respectfully to each other; asking questions to clarify meaning; speaking clearly, positively, and succinctly about problems; and showing positive feelings. On the other hand, high rates of criticism, disagreement, interrupting each other, sarcasm, and negative feelings predict deteriorating relationship satisfaction, and this deterioration is often evident across the early years of marriage (Clements et al., 1997; Gottman, Coan, Carrere, & Swanson, 1998; Markman, 1981; Markman & Hahlweg, 1993; Pasch & Bradbury, 1998).

A somewhat different approach to examining the association of couple communication with couple relationship satisfaction is to focus on patterns of couple communication. Demand–withdraw is the most widely researched communication pattern. *Demanding* involves one partner seeking to discuss an issue in the relationship, often by stating unhappiness or criticism of the partner. *Withdrawal* from conversation of that topic usually involves changing the topic, not responding to the partner, or physically leaving the discussion. The occurrence of demand–withdraw is reliably associated with low and deteriorating relationship satisfaction (Caughlin & Houston, 2002; Christensen & Heavey, 1993; Christensen & Shenk, 1991; Gottman & Krokoff, 1989; Heavey, Christensen, & Malamuth, 1995; Kurdek, 1995). Overall it is more common for women to demand and men to withdraw, than vice versa (Christensen & Heavey, 1993; Christensen & Shenk, 1991). However, if men are seeking change from their female partners, then men become more demanding and women tend to withdraw more (Christensen & Heavey, 1990; Heavey, Layne, & Christensen, 1993).

There are important limitations to the research on couple communication and relationship satisfaction. While most studies find an association of relationship satisfaction with communication, the specific associations vary between studies, with satisfaction being correlated with different specific aspects of couple communication (Heyman, 2001). For example, deteriorating newlywed relationship satisfaction is predicted by low rates of positive verbal communication during conflict discussions in some studies (Johnson et al., 2005), but not others (Kiecolt-Glaser, Bane, Glaser, & Malarkey, 2003; Markman, 1981). High rates of negative verbal communication during conflict predict deteriorating relationship satisfaction (e.g., Kiecolt-Glaser et al., 2003; Markman, 1981), though the effects of negative communication might not be evident when there is coexisting positive affect (Johnson et al., 2005). High negative affect is a reliable predictor of deteriorating relationship satisfaction, though it is variously suggested that it is the occurrence of specific affects (e.g., contempt, disgust) or the ratio of the rates of positive and negative affect that is crucial (Gottman, 1994; Gottman et al., 1998). Even with the relatively robust finding that demand–withdraw predicts deteriorating relationship satisfaction, this effect is only evident for women's but not men's relationship satisfaction in some studies (e.g., Heavey et al., 1995), and not evident at all if the partners also express high levels of positive affect (Caughlin & Huston, 2002).

The inconsistent observed association of relationship satisfaction with specific communication behaviors and patterns is likely due, at least partially, to the methodological limitations of studies. Most studies have modest sample sizes, assess numerous indices of communication, and typically only a few of these indices predicted satisfaction; this raises significant concerns about the power of studies to detect modest magnitude associations and the reliability of any detected associations (Heyman, 2001). Furthermore, differences in the systems used to code couple communication, and variations in methods of consolidating individual codes into summary codes, make it difficult to determine the consistency of findings (Heyman, 2001). Finally, except for a small number of recent studies, most longitudinal research predicting marital satisfaction from couple communication assessed satisfaction at only two time points (Bradbury, Cohan, & Karney, 1998). This approach does not allow modeling of the trajectory of change, which can generate unreliability in findings (Bradbury et al., 1998). Despite the many studies assessing couple communication and satisfaction, the only clear, well-replicated findings are that overall negativity and withdrawal each predicts deteriorating relationship satisfaction (Heyman, 2001).

Aside from methodological issues, inconsistent findings on the communication–satisfaction association probably reflect the fact that the specific communication behaviors that help sustain relationship satisfaction vary between couples. For example, the exact communication behaviors associated with relationship satisfaction vary by culture (Halford et al., 1990), and by which partner nominated the topic being discussed (Johnson et al., 2005). Furthermore, deficits in couple communication of social support predict deteriorating relationship satisfaction only in couples that experience high rates of stressful life events (Pasch & Bradbury, 1998). Thus, a range of variables moderates the association of particular aspects of communication with relationship satisfaction.

It is noteworthy that in at least some studies the communication observed in engaged couples does not correlate with their reported relationship satisfaction at the time (Markman & Hahlweg, 1993; Sanders et al., 1999). It seems that communication difficulties often do not stop couples from falling in love or forming committed relationships, but sustaining relationship satisfaction is more likely when there is good communication (Markman, 1981; Pasch & Bradbury, 1998). For couples who have been married for some time, these same communication assets predict sustained relationship satisfaction and decreased risk of relationship breakup (Clements et al., 1997; Gottman, 1993, 1994; Notarius & Markman, 1993).

Emotion

The expression of negative emotion is central to distressed couple interaction. Specifically, the expression of anger, contempt, or disgust by one partner toward the other predicts low and deteriorating relationship satisfaction (Gottman et al., 1998). Greenberg and Goldman (2008) propose that these negative emotions are secondary emotions that result from often unexpressed primary emotions, such as anxiety over possible abandonment, a sense of inadequacy, shame, or fear. For example, Greenberg and Goldman propose that someone who worries that his or her partner might leave him or her is often demanding of the other person during arguments, expressing anger and dissatisfaction about the relationship. They also propose that withdrawal is often associated with lack of emotional expression, or disregard for the other demanding partner, and that these secondary emotions are underpinned by primary emotions of a sense of inadequacy or resentment.

In the context of couple therapy, Greenberg and Goldman (2008) seek to facilitate access to the unexpressed primary emotions, arguing that this helps resolve relationship distress. In a similar vein in CRE, Markman and colleagues (2007) suggest that assisting couples to recognize that there are often deeper unexpressed feelings that can lead to destructive conflict is useful in helping couples sustain high relationship satisfaction.

Violence

National representative surveys across many countries in the world show that interpersonal violence between partners in couple relationships is common (Mouzos & Makkai, 2004). For example, in the United States about 15–20% of married and cohabiting couples report at least one act of physical violence in the past year (e.g., Schafer, Caetano, & Clark, 1998; Straus & Gelles, 1990). Furthermore, numerous United States–based studies suggest that aggression and violence are particularly common for young, recently married couples (Leonard & Senchak, 1996; O'Leary et al., 1989). Verbal aggression early in marriage predicts later occurrence of physical violence (Murphy & O'Leary, 1989; Schumacher & Leonard, 2005). Once it occurs in early marriage, physical violence is often a persistent problem recurring over a number of years (O'Leary et al., 1989), particularly if the initial level of violence is frequent or severe (Quigley & Leonard, 1996). Both verbal aggression and physical violence predict deteriorating relationship satisfaction, and physical aggression predicts risk for marital separation across the early years of marriage (Lawrence & Bradbury, 2001; Rogge & Bradbury, 1999; Schumacher & Leonard, 2005).

There are widely differing levels of violence in couple relationships, and there is increasing evidence that at least two distinctive types of violence exist that can be classified on the basis of the severity of male violence (Holtzworth-Munroe & Meehan, 2004). Severe violence is characterized by frequent, high-severity, male-to-female violence such as beating up of the partner; is associated with injury, psychological domination, and intimidation of the female partner; and male perpetrators of this severe abuse show distinctive characteristics such as frequent substance abuse and other antisocial behaviors (Holtzworth-Munroe, Meehan, Herron, Rehman, & Stuart, 2000; Johnson, 1995). Less severe violence is characterized by infrequent, low-level violence (most commonly, pushing, slapping, and shoving); most often involves both male-to-female and female-to-male violence; and males in this category do not show the same psychological characteristics seen in severely violent men (Holtzworth-Munroe et al., 2000). Longitudinal research suggests that less severe couple violence is unlikely to escalate to severe violence (Holtzworth-Munroe, Meehan, Herron, Rehman, & Stuart, 2003). Although less severe couple violence is not associated with the same level of risk of injury for women as severe violence, less severe violence is much more prevalent (Holtzworth-Munroe & Meehan, 2004).

Interaction of Factors in the Ecological Model

The different components of the ecological model interact to influence couple relationship outcomes. For example, consider the following two couples who attended couple relationship education.

> Terri and Dirk are both successful professionals in their early 30s. They were introduced to each other by mutual friends through their local church, have been dating for 18 months, and recently decided to get married. Each of them has had previous long-term dating relationships, but they state that their relationship feels like "this is the one." Terri and Dirk moved in together 3 months ago, and are busy making plans for their wedding. Both Dirk and Terri's parents are delighted the two of them have decided to make a life together.

> Mia is a 34-year-old divorced woman who met Tony, who is 36 years of age, at the bank where they both worked. They started dating 7 months ago and have been living together for 4 months. Tony has never been married, and lived with his divorced mother before moving into Mia's house. Mia's son, Ben, is 9 and does not get on that well with Tony. Mia and Tony report they love each other very much, but disagree on how to parent Ben, and what to expect of Tony and Ben's relationship. They also disagree about whether to get married. Mia was let go from the bank following an economic downturn a month ago and her savings are being rapidly depleted. Tony wants to marry Mia, stating she is his "soulmate." Mia is wary about marrying again, reporting that her first marriage was violent and unhappy. Mia also is struggling with her mother's disapproval of the relationship with Tony. Mia's mother is Chinese and had an unhappy marriage that ended in divorce from Mia's father, who was German. Mia's mother feels Mia should only marry someone from her own Chinese culture.

A shared characteristic of the relationships of Dirk with Terri and Mia with Tony is that they are in the early stages of a committed relationship. The early stages of a committed relationship are good times for CRE. Couples typically have high relationship satisfaction as both these couples report, and are highly motivated to strengthen their relationship. At the same time couples face significant challenges in these early years. Most couples find that initial overwhelming attraction to their partner moderates, new relationship roles and routines need to be developed, and means of negotiating conflict need to evolve (Huston, McHale, & Crouter, 1986; Veroff, Douvan, & Hatchett, 1995). Both these couples have these challenges before them.

The two case examples also illustrate how couples have diverse strengths and challenges in their relationship. Dirk and Terri have considerable financial resources they bring to the relationship, strong support from extended family for their relationship, and come from families of origin in which the parents have sustained mutually satisfying marriages. In contrast, both Tony and Mia have experienced parental divorce and Mia has herself been divorced. They collectively have had little exposure to successful marriages. Mia is currently unemployed, and their finances are stretched. The couple knew each other for a relatively brief period before beginning to cohabit, and they are unresolved about whether to get married. Mia and Tony have the challenge of developing their relationship together while Mia must also attend to the responsibilities of caring for her son, Ben. Like many partners in stepfamilies, they struggle with how the stepparent should be involved with child care. They also have different cultures of origin and a lack of family support for their relationship.

Given this complex of differences between couples, how best does one focus couple relationship education? The research evidence is clear that the strongest predictors of couple relationship satisfaction from within the ecological model are at the level of couple interaction (Bradbury & Karney, 2004; Halford, 2001; Holman, 2001). Furthermore, the predictors of couple relationship satisfaction at other levels operate through couple interaction. For example, it is likely that being raised by happily married parents exposed both Terri and Dirk to effective models of communication and conflict management. The commitment in Dirk's and Terri's parents' respective marriages might well also be reflected in the effort each of the fathers and mothers put into their marriage. Often parents will model the importance of relationship self-regulation by reflecting on the relationship and doing small but important behaviors like a spouse supporting the other in times of stress, active planning to have quality time together, and speaking warmly to and about each other. In contrast, Mia and Tony each were raised by their mothers, and did not get exposure to models of effective couple communication or relationship self-regulation skills. Thus, while a range of factors at different levels of the ecological model influences sustaining a mutually satisfying and stable relationship, often the patterns of couple interaction seem the strongest influences. And the good news is that healthy patterns of couple interaction can be learned relatively easily when couples are in currently satisfying relationships.

IMPLICATIONS OF RESEARCH ON COUPLE RELATIONSHIPS FOR EDUCATION

There are a number of important implications of the research evidence summarized within the ecological model of couple relationships for the practice of CRE. First, CRE has a crucial role to play in helping couples to sustain a mutually satisfying and stable relationship. Couple interaction is the most powerful predictor of couple relationship outcomes, and CRE can assist couples to develop crucial knowledge, attitudes, and skills that promote positive couple interaction. (The evidence showing the effects of CRE is reviewed in Chapter 2.)

Assessing Couples to Ensure Relationship Education Is Appropriate

At least some couples forming relationships have significant personal problems that can impact upon their relationship. For example, hazardous drinking, other substance abuse, depression, and major psychiatric disorder are all substantial risk factors for future relationship distress and instability (Whisman & Uebelacker, 2003). Given the frequency of these problems, it is advisable to do some assessment of couples to identify whether psychological disorder presents a risk for the couple. Chapter 3 describes how to do such an assessment, and to how to use such an assessment to decide if CRE is appropriate to address a particular couple's needs.

To illustrate the need for assessment for suitability of CRE, consider the case of Hian and Zac, who have been cohabiting for 12 months and are planning to get married. Zac has a history of bipolar disorder. Psychoeducation for the couple could improve each partner's understanding of the nature of bipolar disorder, the role of medication and psychological treatments in managing the disorder, and how they can work together to manage the disorder (Birchwood, 1998). Such education has been shown to reduce stress in the partner of someone with bipolar disorder, reduce rates of relapse in the patient, and enhance patient functioning (Miklowitz, George, Richards, Simoneau, & Suddath, 2003; Rea et al., 2003). However, provision of such education might be beyond the scope of competence of many people who provide CRE. This is not to say that CRE would be irrelevant to couples like Hian and Zac, but that other forms of help might be needed.

Focusing Limited Education Resources on Couples Most Likely to Benefit

A third implication of the ecological model is that some couples have relatively low risk for developing couple relationship problems. In most Western countries 50% or more of couples who marry remain together for the rest of their lives (United Nations Economic and Social Affairs Population Division, 2003); the vast majority of these couples report being satisfied in their relationship at least most of the time, and most have not received CRE (Halford & Simons, 2005). Thus, it is clear that considerable numbers of couples sustain mutually satisfying relationships without CRE.

CRE provided to low-risk couples may make little difference to relationship satisfaction or stability, as many of these couples would have stable, mutually satisfying relationships without any education. From a social policy perspective, expanding the availability of publicly funded, potentially expensive CRE to all couples might be unwise. In response to concern about divorce rates, many governments are committing substantial funding to marriage education. For example, the U.S. Senate approved an appropriation bill on February 1, 2006, committing an extra U.S. $500 million on CRE. Ensuring that large and increasing sums of money expended on marriage education are deployed cost-effectively is a major social policy challenge.

One approach to making CRE cost-effective is to have an integrated system of education that include steps of increasing intensity of education, with more expensive and intensive education being offered selectively to couples at high risk of future relationship problems (Halford, 2004). This has the advantage for low-risk couples of only giving them as much education as they really need, and only suggesting more time-consuming education when it is likely to be helpful. I elaborate more on this stepped approach in Chapter 3.

Given that CRE is likely to be of particular benefit to high-risk couples, attracting high-risk couples to relationship education is important (Halford, O'Donnell, Lizzio, & Wilson, 2006; Sullivan & Bradbury, 1997). Yet, CRE typically is offered to all couples entering committed relationships, irrespective of risk level. This might not matter if high-risk couples self-select to attend relationship education. Unfortunately, there is some evidence that shows high-risk couples are less likely to attend education than low-risk couples (Halford, O'Donnell, et al., 2006; Sullivan & Bradbury, 1997). Specifically, couples who are repartnering, bringing children from prior relationships, and who are less religious are less likely to attend CRE than other couples (Halford, O'Donnell, et al., 2006). These are couples who are at high risk of future relationship problems. Therefore, enhancing the accessibility of CRE to high-risk couples is important. I offer specific suggestions on how to increase accessibility of relationship education, particularly for high-risk couples, in Chapters 2 and 3.

Providing Education at Relevant Times in the Couple's Life

The ecological model makes clear that times of change and stress are associated with risk for relationship deterioration. The vast majority of research on, and implementation of, CRE has focused on providing education when couples are entering marriage (Hunt, Hof, & DeMaria, 1998). Entry to marriage is a good time for relationship education because couples often face significant challenges early in marriage. As noted earlier, almost all partners entering committed couple relationships report high initial relationship satisfaction. However, in Australia and the United States, average relationship satisfaction declines across the first 10 years of marriage, between 10 and 15% of couples separate within the first 3–4 years of marriage (Glenn, 1998;

McDonald, 1995), and 33% of couples divorce within 10 years of marriage (Australian Bureau of Statistics, 2008). Thus, helping marrying couples to establish effective relationship roles and communication is likely to be beneficial.

CRE also needs to be extended beyond married or marrying couples. As noted previously, in most Western countries a majority of couples choose cohabitation as either a prelude or an alternative to marriage. For these couples the transition to marriage might never happen, or might happen after many years of cohabitation when patterns of couple interaction might be well established. If we consider the example of Tony and Mia, this couple is at high risk for relationship problems, and the welfare of Mia's son, Ben, is dependent upon how their relationship develops. Assisting them as cohabiting couples could help them to decide whether to commit to each other, and to enact their choice as effectively as they can.

In addition to when couples are getting married or first living together, there are a number of other life events that might be associated with receptiveness to CRE. For example, the transition to parenthood, relocation in place of living, and major illness are all associated with increased risk of relationship problems (Gagnon, Hersen, Kabacoff, & van Hasselt, 1999; Shapiro et al., 2000), and couples often are receptive to couple-focused education at these times (Halford, 2004).

The transition to parenthood is an example of a major life change that warrants particular attention as a time for CRE (Cowan & Cowan, 1995). Approximately 85% of first-married couples have children (McDonald, 1995) and becoming parents is uniformly reported to bring a wide range of changes in the partners' relationship with each other (Cowan & Cowan, 1999). In Western countries the vast majority of couples having their first child attend antenatal education; these couples report that they want education about how to work as a couple and manage the relationship changes they expect to come from parenthood (Nolan, 1997). Unfortunately, most existing antenatal education largely ignores the couple relationship (Gagnon & Sandall, 2007).

In many couples, both married and cohabiting, relationship satisfaction progressively deteriorates and leads to contemplation of dissolution of the relationship (Gottman, 1993). In couples with long-standing, severe relationship distress, motivation to change the relationship can be low. Thus, long-term success rates for couple therapy are modest (Halford, 2001; Snyder et al., 2006). Low levels of presenting relationship satisfaction (Whisman & Jacobson, 1990), greater length of time of experience of distress (Johnson & Talitman, 1997; Whisman & Jacobson, 1990), and severe problems in managing conflict (Snyder, Mangrum, & Wills, 1993) are associated with poor response to couple therapy. Thus, presentation for assistance early in the process of satisfaction erosion is likely to enhance prognosis.

Couples with early warning signs of relationship difficulty might be willing to present for brief CRE, even if they would not seek out couple therapy (Larson & Brimhall, 2005). In one quasi-experimental study (Cordova, Warren, & Gee, 2002) and a randomized controlled trial (Cordova et al., 2005), Cordova and colleagues evaluated a "relationship checkup" in which they recruited couples who believed they might be beginning to have difficulty in their relationship. The "checkup" involved systematic assessment of the relationship and motivational interviewing to promote self-directed relationship enhancement. Significant gains in relationship satisfaction after the checkup were maintained for at least 12 months (Cordova et al., 2002, 2005). Thus, brief CRE for mildly distressed couples also holds out some promise.

Focusing the Content of Relationship Education Appropriately

The large number of predictors of couple relationship outcomes usefully can be classified into two categories of static indicators and dynamic factors. Static indicators cannot be changed through intervention. For example, mature age at marriage and positive family-of-origin experiences are static indicators that predict marital stability and sustained relationship satisfaction (Sabitelli & Bartle-Haring, 2003). In contrast, dynamic factors are changeable. For example, realistic relationship expectations and effective couple communication predict sustained relationship satisfaction, and these can be developed in relationship education (Halford et al., 2003).

Many static indicators can be measured relatively easily. For example, parental divorce, age, previous marriages, length of time the partners have known each other, cohabitation history, and the presence of stepchildren can be assessed by simple questions. Assessment of these indicators can help determine a couple's risk level for future relationship problems. Moreover, these static indicators often are associated with dynamic factors that are changeable. For example, interparental physical aggression in the family of origin is associated with negative communication and aggression in adult committed relationships (Skuja & Halford, 2004).

Dynamic factors, such as couple communication and relationship expectations, often are more time-consuming to assess than are static risk indicators. For example, observed communication is a reliable predictor of relationship satisfaction, but it requires sophisticated recording equipment and highly trained observers to conduct the assessment. However, some dynamic factors are reliably associated with certain static indicators. For example, parental relationship stability in the family of origin is associated with positive communication in engaged couples (Sanders et al., 1999). Thus, it is possible to evaluate couples on easily assessed indicators like parental stability, and these protective indicators are markers of likely positive communication. In couples without these protective indicators, promotion of positive communication can be targeted in relationship education. When communication improves in couples who are low in protective indicators (i.e., couples at high risk of relationship problems), this helps couples sustain relationship satisfaction (Halford, Sanders, & Behrens, 2001). Thus, the content of CRE should focus on dynamic factors established through research as predictors of couple outcomes.

Tailoring the Content of Education to Address Couple Challenges

Another implication of research on the ecological model of couple relationships for CRE is that each couple has a somewhat different profile of relationship strengths and vulnerabilities. These varying relationship profiles imply that different couples will need to learn different knowledge or skills to enhance their relationship. However, much existing CRE fails to attend to the heterogeneity of couples' relationship profiles. Almost all existing relationship skill training programs have a relatively fixed curriculum (Halford, 2004). Although all programs have multiple components, they all place substantial emphasis on enhancing couple communication and preventing destructive conflict. For example, these elements are suggested to be the most important aspect of PREP and central to its claimed benefits (Markman, Renick, Floyd, Stanley, & Clements, 1993). This focus on enhancing communication is based on the research showing that negative communication in newlyweds predicts poor couple outcomes (Heyman, 2001). However, research also shows that differences between newlywed couples' communication predicts differences in future relationship satisfaction and divorce. This prediction can only occur if at least some marrying couples have low levels of negative communication that predict them being able to sustain high relationship satisfaction. As noted previously, there are diverse factors that put couple relationships at risk such as unrealistic expectations, poor communication, destructive conflict, poor individual stress management, hazardous drinking, aggression, and lack of support from family and friends (Bradbury & Karney, 2004; Halford et al., 2003). CRE needs to tailor its content to address individual couples' relationship risks.

Recognizing the Limitations of Relationship Education

The ecological model also suggests that CRE has limitations in what it can achieve in strengthening couple relationships. CRE aims to promote the couple's knowledge and skills to enhance their chance of sustaining a mutually satisfying relationship. In other words, CRE primarily targets change at the level of couple interaction, and to a lesser extent changes in individual characteristics. However, as illustrated in the contrasting relationships of Dirk with Terri and Mia with Tony, the broader context within which the couple relationship exists influences relationship outcomes. Changing these contexts is often beyond the scope of CRE.

Social and economic changes, rather than CRE, might be needed to address important contextual factors. For example, many couple relationships might benefit from the implementation of social policies to ameliorate the negative effects of economic change that produce high unemployment. Looking back to the case of Tony and Mia, Mia might need assistance to get further education and training to enhance her employment prospects. CRE is not a substitute for these services, but CRE might well be a useful part of the overall process of assisting couples like Tony and Mia.

The recognition of the importance of contextual factors, and the limitations of what CRE alone can achieve, has led some people to form "marriage movements." For example, in the United States such marriage movements have sought to strengthen marriage by addressing relevant laws, social policies, and cultural factors that influence couple relationship satisfaction and stability (Birch, Weed, & Olsen, 2004).

CONCLUSIONS

There is strong evidence that mutually satisfying marriage conveys considerable benefits to the adult partners and any offspring they have. Sustaining a committed, mutually satisfying relationship is a challenge for many couples, partly as a function of changing social circumstances, and partly as a function of the high expectations many people have of their marriage. A large body of research evidence, which can be summarized into an ecological model, gives us guidance on the influences on couple relationship outcomes. It shows that couple relationship satisfaction and stability is, to a substantial extent, predictable. Our current knowledge does not allow us to predict for any given couple their relationship future, but it does allow us to identify risk factors for future relationship problems. CRE needs to address the dynamic risk factors that predict relationship satisfaction. CRE needs to attract couples at high risk of relationship problems, to offer education at times of change in couples' lives, and to tailor the content of education to address the profile of relationship strengths and vulnerabilities of particular couples.

CHAPTER 2

Approaches to Couple Relationship Education and Their Effectiveness

This chapter reviews the most widely used approaches to CRE and the research evidence on the effectiveness of those approaches Psychotherapy research draws an important distinction between efficacy and effectiveness *Efficacy* refers to the empirical status of psychological interventions as they are evaluated in research, most commonly within controlled trials *Effectiveness* refers to the impact of psychological interventions with people who present to routine services This chapter presents an analysis of the evidence on both the efficacy of CRE in controlled trials, and the effectiveness of CRE in its routine provision to couples

APPROACHES TO COUPLE RELATIONSHIP EDUCATION

The Scope of Current Relationship Education

Structured CRE began with the work of religious organizations and evolved from the brief counsel often offered by religious marriage celebrants, such as priests, rabbis, and ministers, to marrying couples (Hunt et al, 1998) Across many Western countries CRE continues to be offered primarily by religious organizations, and predominantly targets committed, married, premarital, or remarrying couples (Markman & Halford, 2005) In the United States and Australia more than one-third of marrying couples attend some form of premarriage education (Halford, O'Donnell, et al, 2006; Simons, Harris,

& Willis, 1994; Stanley, Amato, Johnson, & Markman, 2006; Sullivan & Bradbury, 1997) Rates of attendance at premarriage education have increased dramatically since the first half of the 20th century Stanley and colleagues (2006) reported in a representative survey of adults in four midwestern US states that of people married in the 1930s only 7% attended premarriage education, which increased to 22% of individuals married in the 1960s, 32% in the 1980s, and 44% in the 1990s

From its exclusive focus on premarriage education, CRE has diversified and occurs in a wide range of formats and settings, with many of these offerings not being explicitly labeled as relationship education For example, antenatal care often includes some mention of couple relationships, though participants report they think much more couple focus is needed in education preparing couples for parenthood (Nolan, 1997) A range of school curricula address interpersonal relationships and often include some focus on couple relationships (Simons & Parker, 2002) In Australia and the United States defense force community service programs preparing military families for overseas deployments include some CRE (Simons & Parker, 2002; Stanley et al, 2005) Learning about couple relationships is embedded in programs as diverse as those assisting grandparents to care for their grandchildren, training carers for patients with Alzheimer's disease, and assisting people to address sexuality after traumatic brain injury (Simons & Parker, 2002)

Inventories

Two general approaches to relationship education are evidence-based and reasonably widely adopted: assessment with feedback and curriculum-based education In current practice most assessment with feedback uses one of three inventories: PREmarital Preparation And Relationship Enhancement (PRE-PARE; Olson, Fournier, & Druckman, 1996), the Facilitating Open Couple Communication Understanding and Study (FOCCUS; Markey & Micheletto, 1997), or RELATionship Evaluation (RELATE; Busby, Holman, & Taniguchi, 2001) When using any of these three inventories each partner separately completes the self-report inventory All three inventories assess a broad range of couple functioning dimensions and the couple is provided with systematic feedback about the results of that assessment (Larson, Newell, Topham, & Nichols, 2002) In current practice the feedback sometimes is supplemented with skill-training activities, although the skill training is not a systematic or central part of the inventory approach (Simons & Parker, 2002) Inventories are widely used in a number of Western countries including Australia, the United Kingdom and the United States (Larson et al, 2002)

Table 21 summarizes some key characteristics of the three most widely used relationship assessment inventories As is evident from the table, the inventories have a number of common characteristics Each takes approximately an hour for each partner to complete The content assessed has similarities, with each of the inventories assessing many of the known predictors of relationship satisfaction and stability described in Chapter 1 Computer-aided scoring is available for all three inventories, which is desirable given their respective lengths Each inventory provides a summary report that identifies a couple's areas of relationship strengths and vulnerabilities Moreover, the authors of each of the inventories have developed manuals that provide guidance to relationship educators on how to interpret the reports and structure the provision of feedback to couples Additional training is available to educators on use of each of the inventories

There are several important strengths common to the widely used inventories of FOCCUS, PREPARE, and RELATE First, each has well-established psychometric properties and they all have adequate reliability, content validity, and construct validity (Larson et al, 2002) Second, each inventory predicts the trajectory of relationship satisfaction in the early years of marriage (Fowers & Olson, 1986; Holman, 2001; Larson & Olson, 1989; Williams & Jurich, 1995) Thus, each inventory assesses factors relevant to relationship outcomes Third, the inventories provide the opportunity for couples to assess their relationship profiles concerning risk and resilience factors As noted earlier, there is a large research literature that allows couples' relationship profiles to be defined based on replicated predictors of relationship outcomes Fourth, there is structured training on the use of these inventories (eg, Olson, Dyer, & Dyer, 1997) The structured approach to use of the inventory, and the training available, may at least partly explain the widespread adoption of inventory-based relationship education

There are some noteworthy differences between the three inventories RELATE is available via the Internet, and is structured so that couples can receive a computer-generated report with or without the involvement of a relationship educator For busy couples this option can be appealing In contrast, PREPARE and FOCCUS are only available to couples in printed form, and the assessment and feedback is designed to be delivered only with the involvement of a relationship educator RELATE has more items, and is more comprehensive than the other inventories It takes longer to complete than FOCCUS, but its layout on the Web allows partners to complete the inventory in about the same time it takes to complete PREPARE, even though PREPARE has 84 fewer items than RELATE

The fundamental weakness of inventories is that, to my knowledge, there has been no published systematic evaluation of the long-term effects of inventory administration and feedback on relationship outcomes Some previous critiques of inventories (eg, Silliman, Stanley, Coffin, Markman, &

TABLE 21 Key Characteristics of Three Widely Used Couple Relationship Assessment Inventories

Title	Authors	No of items, time to complete	Scales; content	Scoring; report
FOCCUS	Markey, Micheletto, & Becker (1997)	156, about 50 minutes	19 scales; personality, activities and friends, communication, shared religious and other values, family-of-origin experiences	Computer or by hand; report identifies areas of relationship strength and vulnerability, vague or conflicting expectations
PREPARE	Olsen (1996)	195, about 60 minutes	20 scales; current relationship satisfaction and functioning; personality, activities, and friends; shared religious and other values; relationship and role expectations; family-of-origin experiences	Computer; report identifies areas of relationship strength and vulnerability, vague or conflicting expectations, classifies the couple into one of four categories
RELATE	Holman et al (1997)	271, about 60 minutes	20 scales; current relationship satisfaction and functioning; personality, activities, and friends; shared religious and other values; relationship and role expectations; family-of-origin experiences; conflict management patterns; psychological problems	Computer; report identifies areas of relationship strength and vulnerability, vague or conflicting expectations, key problem areas

Jordan, 2002) argue that identification of partner differences or relationship weaknesses may actually be counterproductive unless couples are helped to deal effectively with the issues identified For example, feedback on divergent expectations may lead to profitable discussion, but couples lacking conflict management skills may be unable to resolve these differences

Three recent studies have evaluated the immediate effects of assessment and feedback on couple relationships The first was a quasi-experimental study by Knutson and Olson (2003), who found that assessment and feedback using the PREPARE inventory program significantly improved premarital couples' relationship satisfaction A randomized controlled trial showed feedback using the Internet-based RELATE inventory increased relationship satisfaction relative to a wait-list control (Larson, Vatter, Galbraith, Holman, & Stahmann, 2007), though the maintenance of these effects was not evaluated Busby, Ivey, Harris, and Ates (2007) found that feedback based on the Internet-based RELATE inventory plus six sessions of skill training significantly enhanced relationship satisfaction relative to a guided reading control, and that this higher relationship satisfaction was sustained for at least 6 months However, it is not possible to disentangle the effect of the assessment and feedback from the skill training provided Whether the promising immediate effects of assessment and feedback found by Larson and colleagues (2007) are maintained over the long term is as yet untested Each of the samples of couples in these three studies were well educated and in early-stage committed relationships (long-term dating or engaged), and the generalizability to couples who are less educated or in longer, more established relationships is untested Furthermore, whether the effects of assessment and feedback are maintained beyond a month or two is unknown

A second weakness of inventories is their exclusive reliance on self-report assessment Self-report may not accurately identify some key risk factors For example, poor conflict management is a predictor of deteriorating relationship satisfaction in early marriage (Karney & Bradbury, 1995), but self-reports of couple communication in early-stage relationships often do not reflect subtle communication deficits that are detectable with observational assessment (Sanders et al, 1999) However, self-report is cost-effective and assessments are easily accessible to couples and educators via printed forms and the Internet

Curriculum-Based Education

Curriculum-based education typically has a focus on active training of key relationship skills, although curriculum-based approaches usually also include significant emphasis on building awareness and cognitive change (Stanley, 2001) Examples of curriculum-based training programs include the Relationship Enhancement (RE) program (Guerney, 1977, 1987), the Prevention and Relationship Enhancement Program (PREP) (Markman, Floyd, Stanley, & Storaasli, 1988), the Couple Commitment And Relationship Enhancement (Couple CARE) program (Halford, Moore, Wilson, Dyer, & Farrugia, 2006a, 2006b; Halford et al., 2006c), the Couples Communication Program (CCP; Miller, Miller, Nunnally, & Wackman, 1992), and Couples Coping Enhancement Training (CCET; Bodenmann & Shantinath, 2004) These programs have a number of content areas in common For example, skills training in positive communication, conflict management, and positive expression of affection are included in RE, PREP, Couple CARE, CCP, and CCET There also are significant variations For example, in PREP there are multiple foci of intervention, but most time is devoted to prevention of destructive conflict, as this is considered to be central to the prevention of relationship problems (Markman et al, 1988) In RE the development of partner empathy receives strong emphasis (Guerney, 1977), whereas this receives less emphasis in PREP Individual and conjoint coping with life stress is a major component of CCET that receives little attention in most other programs, though Couple CARE does include some content on this topic In Couple CARE the development of relationship self-regulation, involving each partner identifying and implementing personal change plans, is a core focus that is not part of the other programs

A major strength of the curriculum-based approach is that training is focused on variables that predict relationship outcomes In particular, teaching couple communication is a key focus of all skill-training approaches, and observed effective communication in engaged couples predicts sustained relationship satisfaction, at least over the first 5–10 years of marriage (Gottman et al, 1998; Markman, 1981; Pasch & Bradbury, 1998) However, as described in Chapter 1, there are important caveats to the research on the association of couple communication with relationship satisfaction Specifically, particular communication skills have not been shown to cause future couple relationship satisfaction, and there is considerable controversy about which communication skills to teach However, on balance, our best guess at this point is that promoting effective couple communication enhances maintenance of relationship satisfaction, at least for some couples

THE EFFECTS OF RELATIONSHIP EDUCATION

The most important research question to be addressed in evaluating marriage and relationship education is: Does education enhance long-term couple relationship outcomes? In particular, it is important to establish whether CRE can prevent the erosion of relationship satisfaction, separation, and divorce

To demonstrate an impact of CRE on relationship satisfaction, studies need extended follow-up assessments because the erosion of average relationship satisfaction in initially satisfied couples tends to be gradual To illustrate, in a recent longitudinal study of newlywed couples, Halford, Lizzio, and colleagues (2007) reported mean declines in newlywed couple relationship satisfaction over the first 4 years of marriage of 4 SD for men and 5 SD for women on the widely used Dyadic Adjustment Scale of relationship satisfaction Even if relationship education prevented half of any decline in satisfaction, then after 4 years this would show up as a small effect in comparison to the Halford, Lizzio, and colleagues sample Any shorter follow-up than 3 or 4 years in a sample of newlywed couples, and the effects of education would be so small that they would only be detectable with a sample of thousands of couples Thus, studies need to have extended follow-ups of years to have adequate power to detect effects of education

Detecting any effects of CRE on separation and divorce is even harder than detecting effects on relationship satisfaction About 3–4% of couples separate each year across the first 10 years of marriage (Glenn, 1998) If relationship education was successful in preventing half of the separations that otherwise would have happened, then after 4 years there would be about 12–16% of separated couples in a control condition and 6–8% in the education condition This is a very small effect detectable only with thousands of couples in each condition (Cohen, 1992)

One way to enhance the power of studies to detect effects of CRE is to focus on couples at high risk for deteriorating relationship satisfaction Media outreach for participation in relationship education tends to recruit couples with more relationship distress, and with other characteristics that place them at higher risk for relationship problems than more representative samples of couples (Rogge et al, 2006) For example, Halford and colleagues (2001) included statements in media outreach that family-of-origin parental divorce or violence put couples at risk for future relationship problems, and found that strategy yielded high proportions of couples presenting for CRE with those risk factors The more rapid decline in relationship satisfaction in high-risk relative to low-risk couples allows easier detection of education effects in the high-risk couples For example, Halford and colleagues demonstrated an effect size of $d = 10$ for relationship education over 4 years in a high-risk sample of couples, with the high-risk control samples showing a decline of 09 SD on relationship satisfaction over the 4 years compared with a slight (nonsignificant) increase for the couples who received CRE In contrast, the low-risk control sample in the Halford and colleagues study showed no significant decline in relationship satisfaction over the 4 years, making demonstrating any prevention effect with this group impossible

Another strategy to enhance detection of the effects of CRE is to focus on couples experiencing life stresses that put them at risk for relationship deterioration For example, given the previously described rapid declines in relationship satisfaction often associated with the transition to parenthood, relationship education at this time seems both appropriate and likely to demonstrate if there is any positive effect of education

Efficacy Studies

Many research studies have evaluated CRE, and there have been numerous reviews and meta-analyses of that evidence (eg, Bagarozzi & Rauen, 1981; Dyer & Halford, 1998; Giblin, Sprenkle, & Sheehan, 1985; Guerney & Maxson, 1990; Hahlweg & Markman, 1988; Hawkins, Blanchard, Baldwin, & Fawcett, 2008; Sayers, Kohn, & Heavey, 1998; van Widenfelt, Markman, Guerney, Behrens, & Hosman, 1997) There is a general finding that most couples that complete competently run premarriage education programs report high satisfaction with the programs (Harris, Simons, Willis, & Barrie, 1992) This high satisfaction is evident across programs that include various mixes of awareness, feedback, cognitive change, and skills training (Halford et al, 2003; Halford & Simons, 2005) When given comprehensive programs with all these components, participants rate the communication skill training as the most helpful (Stanley et al, 2001) Although high consumer satisfaction is desirable and participant perceptions of the value of various components are informative about face validity, neither of these outcomes demonstrate that CRE has any effect on relationship outcomes

Almost all controlled trials of CRE have been with curriculum programs that have a strong skill-training focus Two notable exceptions were a quasi-experimental study (Cordova et al, 2001) and a randomized controlled trial (Cordova et al, 2005) of a "relationship checkup" The relationship checkup consisted of two sessions of structured assessment including completion of self-report measures, and communication tasks involving discussing an area of disagreement in the relationship In a third session the results of the assessments were discussed with the couple, and potential relationships change goals negotiated An assumption of this approach is that, once the goals are identified, the partners will be able to successfully self-implement any needed changes In both studies the relationship checkup produced significant gains in relationship satisfaction that were maintained for at least 12 months Both these studies were with couples who had low relationship satisfaction, but were not clinically distressed Although neither study used any of the three widely used inventories, the studies do suggest that relationship education consisting of assessment with feedback can be helpful, at least for mildly distressed couples

Turning now to the much more comprehensively researched curriculum approaches to CRE, the pioneering studies of Guerney and colleagues, and Miller, Wampler, and associates, established by the mid-1980s that skill-based relationship education produces large improvements in relationship skills immediately after programs (Giblin et al, 1985; Hahlweg & Markman, 1988) Immediate, modest improvements in relationship satisfaction also were reported in some studies, though many studies found no immediate impact on relationship satisfaction (Giblin et al, 1985; Hahlweg & Markman, 1988) Building on the very important early studies, subsequent research from the mid-1980s to the mid-1990s showed that changes in how couples communicate and handle conflict persist over time (for reviews, see Silliman & Schumm, 2000; Silliman et al, 2002; van Widenfeldt et al, 1997) Reviews of the large number of studies conducted up till the early 2000s showed that it was studies with a high proportion of couples with low initial relationship satisfaction that showed some short-term improvement on relationship satisfaction (Silliman & Schumm, 2000) The lack of short-term effects of CRE on the relationship satisfaction of highly satisfied couples likely reflects ceiling effects That is, relationship satisfaction initially was so high it was difficult to raise it further This further underscores the importance of assessing the long-term effects of CRE across years to establish whether education prevents erosion of relationship satisfaction in initially highly satisfied couples

Description of Relationship Education Trials with Follow-Up Assessments

I conducted an extensive literature search of controlled trials of CRE that included at least a 6-month follow-up assessment Table 22 summarizes 21 published controlled trials of CRE that involved couples in committed relationships As shown in the table, 11 trials were with couples in early-stage couple relationships, either engaged, recently married, or recently cohabiting Six trials were with couples having their first child Four trials were with couples who had been together for a number of years (means of between 8 and 11 years) Most (14 of 21) trials were universal prevention applied to all couples irrespective of their relationship risk profile Three of the studies targeting long-established couples were with couples who sought relationship enhancement, and substantial proportions of the samples showed mild relationship distress (Bodenmann, Pihet, Shantinath, Cina, & Widmer, 2006; Braukhaus, Hahlweg, Kroeger, Groth, & Fehm-Wolfsdorf, 2003; Kaiser, Hahlweg, Fehm-Wolfsdorf, & Groth, 1998) Four studies targeted couples currently high in relationship satisfaction but who were at high risk of future relationship problems: the Bouma, Halford, and Young (2004) study involved couples in which at least one partner drank at hazardous levels, the Nicholson and colleagues (2007) study focused on stepfamily couples, and the van Widenfelt, Hosman, Schaap, and van der Staak (1996) study targeted couples in which at last one partner's parents had divorced The Halford, Wilson, and colleagues (2010) study was universal, but had a substantial representation of high-risk couples The Halford and colleagues (2001) study stratified their sample into high- and low-risk groups High-risk was defined as a history of family-of-origin parental divorce in the female partner or family-of-origin parental violence in the male partner

The intensity and mode of delivery of CRE varied substantially between trials In 18 of the 21 studies CRE consisted of face-to-face sessions, delivered to groups of couples in all except the Bouma and colleagues (2004) study, which provided face-to-face education to individual couples Fourteen of the 18 face-to-face programs consisted of 6–8 weekly sessions of 2–3 hours per session Four studies provided 2-day weekend workshops (Bodenmann et al, 2006; Braukhaus et al, 2003; Kaiser et al, 1998; Shapiro & Gottman, 2005) Two of the studies provided very brief interventions of an extra 10 minutes per session (Hawkins, Fawcett, Carroll, & Gilliland, 2006), or one extra session (Matthey, Kavanagh, Howie, Barnett, & Charles, 2004), attached to existing antenatal education for expectant couples Three studies made use of flexible delivery of relationship education (Halford, Moore, Wilson, Dyer, & Farrugia, 2004; Halford, Petch, & Creedy, 2010; Halford, Wilson, et al, 2010) rather than just face-to-face delivery The Halford and colleagues (2004) and Halford, Wilson, and colleagues (2010) studies evaluated Couple CARE, which consists of six units Each unit involves the couple watching a DVD segment, completing couple exercises described in a guidebook, and receiving coaching from a psychologist via a telephone call Halford, Petch, and Creedy (2010) evaluated Couple CARE for Parents, an adaptation of Couple CARE for couples expecting their first child, which included one face-to-face workshop for groups of couples, two face-to-face home visits, and three units provided through flexible delivery The level of time commitment for couples was similar across most face-to-face and flexible delivery programs, about 12–15 hours Notable exceptions were two of the programs for couples becoming parents, which ranged from very brief interventions of just an hour or two (Hawkins et al, 2006; Matthey et al, 2004), to the extensive Cowan and Cowan (1992) program, which had about 50 hours of face-to-face contact in regular monthly group sessions across 2 years for couples becoming parents

(text resumes on page 52)

TABLE 22 Promotion of Relationship Satisfaction: Summary of Controlled Trials with 6-Month or More Follow-Up

Authors	Participants	Intervention	Measures	Key findings
Early-stage relationships				
Avery, Ridley, Leslie, & Milholland (1980); Ridley, Jorgensen, Morgan, & Avery (1982)	54 couples	Guerney Relationship Enhancement (RE) program	Self-report of relationship satisfaction and relationship quality; OBS (for 37 couples only)—audiotape of couple "request for change" interaction	RE couples improved in communication and relationship adjustment from pre- to posttest Increases in communication skills maintained at 6-month follow-up No follow-up data reported on perceived relationship adjustment
Bagarozzi, Bagarozzi, Anderson, & Pollane (1984)	18 couples planning marriage	Premarital Education and Training Sequence (PETS)	Self-reported relationship satisfaction, irrational beliefs, and relationship commitment; observed couple communication before and after education and at 3-year follow-up	PETS was associated with a short-term decrease in irrational beliefs and an increase in relationship commitment, but these effects were not maintained at 3-year follow-up NB: The sample may have been too small to detect effects
Bouma, Halford, & Young (2004)	37 couples in early-stage relationships with at least one partner drinking at hazardous levels	Controlling Alcohol and Relationship Enhancement (CARE), a six-session skill training couple program with brief intervention to promote safe, controlled drinking	Self-reported relationship satisfaction, contemplation of separation, and alcohol consumption; observed couple communication Assessment at pre- and posteducation and at 6-month follow-up	CARE enhanced couple communication, reduced contemplation of relationship dissolution, but had no effect on relationship satisfaction Both CARE and an assessment and reading control condition reduced problem drinking
Halford, Sanders, & Behrens (2001)	83 engaged couples stratified into high- and low-risk groups based on parental divorce or violence	Self-PREP, a six-session group program compared to an awareness control condition	Self-report of relationship satisfaction, observed couple communication	High-risk couples showed sustained gains in communication to 1-year follow-up; low-risk couples showed no sustained effect of Self-PREP on communication High-risk couples receiving Self-PREP showed higher satisfaction at 4-year follow-up than high-risk control

46

				couples Low-risk couples did not benefit from Self-PREP
Halford, Moore, Wilson, Dyer, & Farrugia (2004); Halford & Wilson (2009)	59 couples in early-stage committed relationships	Couple CARE, a six-unit, flexible delivery, skill-based program, versus a wait-list control	Self-report of relationship satisfaction, relationship self-regulation, and observed couple communication	Couple CARE produced immediate increases in relationship satisfaction and stability, and increased relationship self-regulation for women but not men; there were no changes in couple communication Couples' maintenance of satisfaction to 4-year follow-up was predicted by their relationship self-regulation NB: This randomized controlled trial provided Couple CARE to the wait-list control couples after the post-assessment, so there was no control at follow-up assessments
Halford, Wilson, et al (2010)	60 newlywed couples	RELATE assessment plus feedback versus RELATE assessment plus feedback followed by Couple CARE	Self-report of satisfaction at pre- and postintervention and 12-month follow-up, observed couple communication at pre- and post-intervention	RELATE + Couple CARE couples improved in couple communication more than couples who undertook RELATE alone after CRE, and also better sustained high relationship satisfaction to 12-month follow-up
Hahlweg, Markman, Thurmaier, Engl, & Eckert (1998)	81 couples	EPL (German PREP) plus segment on Christian marriage	Self-report of relationship satisfaction OBS—videotape of couple problem-solving interaction	EPL couples improved in communication skills and nonverbal positivity from pre- to posttest and maintained gains at 1 1/2-, 3-, and 5-year follow-ups No differences between groups on relationship satisfaction at posttest, but EPL couples demonstrated significantly higher relationship satisfaction at 3- and 5-year follow-ups NB: Participants were not randomly assigned to conditions

(cont)

TABLE 22 *(cont)*

Authors	Participants	Intervention	Measures	Key findings
Markman, Floyd, Stanley, & Storaasli (1988); Markman, Renick, Floyd, Stanley, & Clements (1993); Stanley, Markman, St Peters, & Leber (1995)	114 couples	PREP	Self-report of relationship satisfaction Videotape of couple problem-solving interaction	PREP couples showed significant gains in communication at posttest; these maintained to 15- and 3-year follow-ups PREP couples' relationship satisfaction was greater at 15- and 3-year follow-ups Males maintained higher relationship satisfaction through 4- and 5-year follow-ups, but effects had attenuated by 10-year follow-up NB: Participants were not randomly assigned to conditions
Nicholson, Phillips, Whitton, Halford, & Sanders (2007)	60 couples in early-stage stepfamily formation, with at least one child from a prior relationship aged between 4 and 12 living with them at least 3 days per week	Step PREP, six sessions of group communication training, parent training, and managing stepfamily-specific issues Control was a reading and discussion group	Self-report of relationship satisfaction, relationship stability, child adjustment, and observed couple communication assessed to 5-year follow-up	Step PREP had no detectable effects on any of the outcome measures
Stanley et al (2001); Laurenceau, Stanley, Olmos-Gallo, Baucom, & Markman (2004)	217 couples planning to marry	PREP delivered by either religious organizations (RO-PREP), or by Denver University staff (U-PREP) versus naturally occurring education in the religious organizations (NO)	Observed couple communication, self-reported relationship satisfaction, at pre- and postintervention and 1-year follow-up	RO-PREP produced an increase in positive communication, and both RO-PREP and U-PREP produced decreases in negative communication relative to NO No effects of PREP on relationship satisfaction at postassessment or 12-month follow-up
Wampler & Sprenkle (1980)	52 couples	Minnesota Couple Communication Program	Self-report of relationship quality	MCCP couples improved in communication skills significantly more than

48

			OBS	
		(MCCP)	OBS—audiotape of couple problem-solving interaction	attention-only and control couples, and increased in perceived relationship quality Increases in perceived relationship quality were maintained at 6-month follow-up, but improvements in communication skills were not maintained

Long-established relationships

Bodenmann, Pihet, Shantinath, Cina, & Widmer (2006)	118 couples: 59 seeking relationship enrichment, 59 matched volunteers for a couple assessment study	Couple Coping Training, a weekend workshop focused on conjoint coping with life stress	Relationship satisfaction and couple coping at pre- and postworkshop, and at 6-month, 1-year, and 2-year follow-up	Enhanced relationship satisfaction and coping, though effects were most marked up to 1-year follow-up and attenuated after that
Braukhaus, Hahlweg, Kroeger, Groth, & Fehm-Wolfsdorf (2003)	62 couples seeking couple enrichment	EPL (German PREP) delivered as a weekend workshop versus EPL plus two booster sessions	Relationship satisfaction and observed couple communication assessed at pre- and postassessment, and at 4- and 12-month follow-ups	Both conditions resulted in enhanced couple communication and relationship satisfaction, with the booster session enhancing long-term outcomes
Kaiser, Hahlweg, Fehm-Wolfsdorf, & Groth (1998)	67 couples together at least 3 years (M = 11 years), seeking relationship enrichment	EPL (German PREP) delivered as 2-day workshop, compared with a wait-list control	Self-reported relationship satisfaction and problems, and observed couple communication	EPL produced significant improvements in couple communication and relationship satisfaction at 1-year follow-up
van Widenfelt, Hosman, Schaap, & van der Staak (1996)	67 couples with history of parental divorce	Dutch PREP plus family-of-origin session	Self-report of problem intensity, problem-solving efficacy, and relationship satisfaction at pre- and postintervention and at 2-year follow-up	All couples deteriorated over time on all measures; no evidence of effect of PREP

(cont)

49

TABLE 22 *(cont)*

Authors	Participants	Intervention	Measures	Key findings
Transition to parenthood				
Cowan & Cowan (1992); Schulz, Cowan, & Cowan (2006)	72 couples expecting their first child, 24 couples not expecting a child	24 weekly group sessions focused on parental relationship, parenting expectations; no treatment control; only postassessment control; 24 couples not expecting children as comparison group	Relationship satisfaction, couple separations up to 5 years after intervention.	Program enhanced maintenance of relationship satisfaction relative to no-treatment control; childless comparison couples experienced less decline in relationship satisfaction than the control couples who became parents.
Halford, Petch, & Creedy (2010)	71 couples expecting their first child	Couple CARE for Parents (CCP), a six-unit program running from 2 months before birth to 6 months after; control was standard antenatal and postnatal care	Self-reports of relationship satisfaction, observed communication, and parenting satisfaction and competence before the program and 12 months after the child's birth.	CCP significantly enhanced couple communication and prevented the deterioration in relationship satisfaction observed in control condition women.
Hawkins, Fawcett, Carroll, & Gilliland (2006)	155 pregnant couples INT 1 = 51; INT 2 = 55; Control = 50% uptake Attrition 24% at follow-up	INT 1 = five weekly antenatal classes with relationship education homework activities INT 2 = same as INT 1 delivered as self-paced education	Self-report of relationship adjustment, strengths and satisfaction, parenting adjustment; 9-month postpartum follow-up.	No effects of intervention

Study	Sample	Intervention	Measures	Outcomes
Matthey, Kavanagh, Howie, Barnett, & Charles (2004)	268 pregnant couples INT 1 = 78; INT 2 = 89; Control = 101 78% uptake Attrition 27% at follow-up	INT 1 = extra antenatal class, information, and group discussion on couple adjustment INT 2 = extra antenatal class, information, and education on baby play	Mental health, partner and social support, parenting competence, self-esteem, partner awareness; 6-month postpartum follow-up.	At 6 weeks INT 1 women with low self-esteem, relative to controls, reported more positive mood, higher parenting competence, and greater satisfaction with partner support, but effects were lost by follow-up.
Midmer, Wilson, & Cummings (1995)	70 couples having their first child	Antenatal couple communication and values clarification versus a control condition	Self-reported relationship satisfaction, trait anxiety, and postpartum adjustment in the second trimester, and at 6 weeks and 6 months postpartum.	Enhanced relationship satisfaction, adjustment, and reduced anxiety in new parents in the intervention condition.
Shapiro & Gottman (2005)	38 couples expecting their first child	Couples randomly assigned to a couple-focused workshop plus five home visits or a wait-list control The intervention consisted of information and skill training on couple communication, positive interaction, and infant care	Self-reported marital satisfaction, self-reported depression in the woman, and observed couple communication assessed before birth, 3 months after birth, and 12 months after birth	Relationship satisfaction declined and depression increased in the control group; satisfaction was sustained and depression declined in the intervention group Couple negative communication (hostility) increased in the control condition and declined in the intervention condition NB: Means and standard deviations not presented, effect sizes are unclear

Note PREP, Prevention and Relationship Enhancement Program

In 17 of the 21 trials couples were randomly allocated to CRE or a comparison condition One trial randomly allocated couples to relationship education with or without booster sessions (Braukhaus et al, 2003) The remaining three trials were quasi-experimental, with couples self-selecting into conditions (Bodenmann et al, 2006; Hahlweg et al, 1998; Markman et al, 1988), which makes interpretation of the findings from these studies problematic In nine of the 17 randomized controlled trials the control condition was a wait-list or no-education condition In eight studies, skill-based relationship education was compared with a comparison intervention The comparison was guided reading and discussion without active skills training in three studies (Bouma et al, 2004; Halford et al, 2001; Nicholson, Phillips, Whitton, Halford, & Sanders, 2007), relationship assessment and feedback in one study (Halford, Wilson, et al, 2010), usual relationship education provided by religious organizations in one study (Laurenceau, Stanley, Olmos-Gallo, Baucom, & Markman, 2004), infant care education in one study for expectant parents (Matthey et al, 2004), and standard antenatal and perinatal care for couples having their first child in three studies (Halford, Petch, & Creedy, 2010; Hawkins et al, 2006; Shapiro & Gottman, 2005)

The duration of follow-up varied from the minimum of 6 months required to be included in the current analysis, to 10 years (Stanley, Markman, St Peters, & Leber, 1995) Only eight of the 21 studies included follow-up assessments more than 1 year after the CRE, and a number of these longer term follow-up studies have significant limitations Three studies were not randomized controlled trials (Bodenmann et al, 2006; Hahlweg, Markman, Thurmaier, Engl, & Eckert, 1998; Markman et al, 1988) In one other study only the immediate assessment of outcome was controlled, as couples in the wait-list control condition received CRE before follow-up assessments were conducted (Halford & Wilson, 2009) Thus, there are only five true randomized controlled trials evaluating relationship outcomes for more than 1 year (Halford et al, 2001; Kaiser et al, 1998; Nicholson et al, 2007; Schulz, Cowan, & Cowan, 2006; van Widenfelt et al, 1996)

Substantive Findings on the Long-Term Effects of Relationship Education

Six of the 21 studies did not assess couple communication skills (Bagarozzi, Bagarozzi, Anderson, & Pollane, 1984; Hawkins et al, 2006; Matthey et al, 2004; Midmer, Wilson, & Cummings, 1995; Schulz et al, 2006; van Widenfelt et al, 1996) As shown in Table 22, 13 of the 15 studies in which communication was assessed replicated earlier work that communication skills are acquired through relationship education Two studies failed to find any effect of education on communication skills (Halford et al, 2004; Nicholson et al,

2007) In both these studies there seems to have been a floor effect in that preeducation levels of negative communication were very low Several studies extended earlier work showing that communication skills acquired through CRE are maintained for 1 year or more (Hahlweg et al, 1998; Kaiser et al, 1998; Laureanceau et al, 2004; Markman et al, 1993) However, one study found that the effect of CRE on communication had attenuated by 6-month follow-up (Wampler & Sprenkle, 1980) Another study found that communication skills only showed sustained improvements in couples at high risk for future relationship problems, and that the couples had higher initial levels of negative communication than low-risk couples (Halford et al, 2001) The longest duration follow-up study found that attenuation of training effects occurred over a 5- to 10-year period (Stanley et al, 1995) In summary, there is a consistent finding that curriculum-based CRE reduces negative communication in couples that show at least modest levels of negativity initially, and that such changes persist for some years

PREP is a skills-based CRE program developed by Markman and colleagues, which has been evaluated for its long-term effects in more trials than any other CRE program In two of the earliest studies with follow-ups of more than 12 months, PREP was associated with enhanced relationship satisfaction 2 and 5 years after marriage (Hahlweg et al, 1998; Markman et al, 1993) The Markman and colleagues (1993) study also found that across the 3-, 4-, and 5-year follow-ups, the intervention couples reported significantly fewer instances of spousal physical violence than control couples However, they randomly assigned couples to either be offered or not offered PREP and only about one-third of couples offered PREP agreed to participate In the Hahlweg and colleagues (1998) study, couples chose whether to undertake a German version of PREP named EPL or a standard church-provided relationship education program Thus, there was self-selection into PREP in both the Markman and colleagues and Hahlweg and colleagues studies, and self-selection might account for the observed differences between conditions in these two studies

In a third study using a Dutch version of PREP, no intervention effects were evident at 2-year follow-up (van Widenfelt et al, 1996) The lack of effect of PREP in that study fails to replicate the positive long-term effects of PREP found in the Markman and colleagues (1993) and Hahlweg and colleagues (1998) studies This lack of replication could mean that the effects of PREP in both studies were artifacts of couples self-selecting into the experimental condition Alternatively, the 2-year follow-up period for the van Widenfelt and colleagues (1996) study might have been inadequate to detect effects of PREP In the Hahlweg and colleagues and Markman and colleagues studies, which showed long-term benefits of PREP, some of these effects (on satisfaction and divorce rates) became evident only after 4–5 years

Another trial evaluated a variant of PREP intended to assist couples forming a stepfamily (Nicholson et al, 2007) This program incorporated the standard PREP content, and added parenting skills and discussion of stepfamily challenges The intervention had no detectable effect on couple relationship satisfaction or stability over a 5-year period Recent research has highlighted that the challenges specific to stepfamily couples, such as failing to develop a strong sense of stepfamily identity and agreement about the role of the stepparent in parenting, predict risk of relationship deterioration for stepfamily couples (Nicholson et al, 2008) Nicholson and colleagues (2007) suggested that their program might not have adequately addressed these crucial stepfamily issues

One other study found that PREP enhanced relationship satisfaction over a 12-month period for couples in long-established relationships who were suffering mild relationship distress (Kaiser et al, 1998) In another study, the PREP enhancement of satisfaction in couples in long-established couple relationships suffering mild relationship distress was strengthened by adding a booster session that assisted these couples to continue to apply the skills learned in PREP (Braukhaus et al, 2003)

The largest study evaluating PREP is an ongoing, randomized controlled trial delivered in religious settings, which is where most couples who marry are already receiving services (Stanley et al, 2001) At 1-year follow-up the couples who receive usual non-PREP relationship education deteriorate on observed couple communication, whereas those who receive PREP improve No effects of PREP on relationship satisfaction or stability exist at the 12-month follow-up, and further follow-ups are required to establish whether there are reliable long-term benefits of PREP in preventing erosion of relationship satisfaction

Aside from PREP, another widely evaluated couple relationship education program is Couple CARE, developed by Halford and colleagues (2006a, 2006b, 2006c). Couple CARE has some similar content to PREP, with communication skills training, and enhancement of couple commitment and positive interaction It also has some distinctive content with a strong focus on enhancing relationship self-regulation, facilitating self-directed learning processes, and helping couples manage life change and stress Halford and colleagues (2001) conducted a randomized controlled trial of an early version of Couple CARE, labeled Self-PREP Couples were stratified into high- and low-risk groups for relationship problems on the basis of negative family-of-origin experiences (parental divorce or interparental violence) At the 4-year follow-up, couples who completed Self-PREP had significantly higher relationship satisfaction than couples in a control condition, but this effect was only evident for couples at high risk of relationship problems In a subsequent randomized controlled trial of Couple CARE, a modified version of Self-

PREP adapted into a flexible delivery mode significantly increased short-term relationship satisfaction (Halford et al, 2004), and the extent of relationship self-regulation after the program predicted sustained relationship satisfaction 4 years later (Halford & Wilson, 2009) The most recent study evaluating Couple CARE found that it was more effective than assessment and feedback based on the RELATE inventory in enhancing couples' communication and sustaining relationship satisfaction over 12 months (Halford, Wilson, et al, 2010)

Couple CARE content has been adapted to address the needs of couples in which at least one partner drinks at hazardous levels; this variant has been labeled the Controlling Alcohol and Relationship Enhancement (CARE) program In a small-scale randomized controlled trial, CARE significantly decreased negative couple communication and contemplation of relationship dissolution, and this effect persisted at the 6-month follow-up (Bouma et al, 2004)

Only one published study has evaluated the Couple Coping Enhancement (CCE) program (Bodenmann et al, 2006) This quasi-experimental study found that completing CCE was associated with sustained relationship satisfaction over 2 years, though effects attenuated somewhat between the 1- and 2-year follow-ups

Six studies have evaluated the effects of CRE in assisting couples with the transition to parenthood Two studies assessed changes in couple communication skills, and each found sustained reductions in negativity (Halford, Petch, & Creedy, 2010; Shapiro & Gottman, 2005) Four studies reported enhanced relationship satisfaction at the longest available follow-up, which ranged from 6 months (Midmer et al, 1995) to 7 years (Schulz et al, 2006) after the birth of the child Two studies found no significant intervention effects, but these studies had very brief interventions (Hawkins et al, 2006; Matthey et al, 2004) Collectively the four studies with at least 10 hours of intervention provide evidence of the benefits of this intensity of CRE for couples undertaking the transition to parenthood All four studies were randomized controlled trials, and there are consistent findings across all four studies

Conclusions

There is substantial evidence for the efficacy of CRE, but only for interventions of sufficient intensity and duration Very brief interventions of just a few hours have failed to produce detectable effects (eg, Hawkins et al, 2006; Matthey et al, 2004), or have shown weaker effects than more extensive interventions (eg, Halford, Wilson, et al, 2010) Adequate intensity of interventions still only produces consistent effects for some couples under some circumstances There is no convincing evidence that CRE provided universally to all couples prevents deteriorating relationship satisfaction The studies that have found evidence of a universal effect either had very short follow-up assessments, or were not randomized controlled trials Those studies that did find long-term effects of CRE found effects in couples at high risk for relationship problems In some studies high risk was attributable to characteristics of the couples, such as a history of negative family-of-origin experiences (Halford et al, 2001; Halford, Wilson, et al, 2010), at least one partner who drank heavily (Bouma et al, 2004), or the couple already had somewhat low relationship satisfaction (Kaiser et al, 1998) In other studies it was the life stage of the couples that defined high risk All four randomized controlled trials of CRE of at least 12 hours duration found that it enhanced relationship satisfaction across the transition to parenthood, known to be a particularly high-risk time for onset of relationship problems

Not all randomized controlled trials of CRE with high-risk couples produced positive effects (Nicholson et al, 2007; van Widenfelt et al, 1996) As noted, a longer follow-up with the van Widenfelt and colleagues (1996) study might have detected effects, but the lack of effects after 5 years in the Nicholson and colleagues (2007) study is striking This is the only randomized controlled trial of a program for stepfamilies, and greater attention to the special challenges confronting stepfamilies might produce more powerful effects of CRE

The lack of compelling evidence for a universal benefit of CRE does not mean that there is no benefit The sample size in most existing studies has been modest, limiting the power to detect effects of CRE Halford, Wilson, and colleagues (2010) did find sustained benefits for couples 12 months after completing Couple CARE, though their sample seemed to have a substantial representation of high-risk couples The ongoing trial by Stanley and colleagues (2001) and other large-scale research could detect benefits for relationship satisfaction where it is not yet detected Furthermore, beyond the effects of CRE on skills and maintenance of relationship satisfaction, there are a number of potential benefits that have been suggested for relationship education Stanley (2001) proposed that CRE might promote increased commitment to work on the relationship and facilitate early presentation for couple therapy should relationship problems develop While these actions are often encouraged in CRE, there is no evidence to date to suggest that relationship education facilitates these outcomes Further research is needed in order to test the possible benefits of CRE

How Does Couple Relationship Education Work?

Recently, numerous studies have attempted to test the mediators of the effects of curriculum-based CRE As described in Chapter 1, communication has been argued to be a significant influence on couple relationship satisfaction For example, Markman and colleagues (1993) argued that negative communication and ineffective conflict management erode relationship satisfaction, and they include the teaching of active listening techniques in PREP to inhibit negative communication However, this view is controversial Gottman and Notarius (2000) dispute the value of teaching active listening, arguing that active listening skills do not predict the trajectory of relationship satisfaction Stanley, Bradbury, and Markman (2000) countered this argument, suggesting that active listening skills can inhibit the use of negative, destructive communication

Schilling, Baucom, Burnett, Sandin-Allen, and Ragland (2003) were the first to attempt to directly test how CRE works They found that, as proposed by Markman and colleagues (1993), reductions in male negativity associated with completing PREP predicted sustained male relationship satisfaction However, in an unexpected finding, reduction in women's negative communication was associated with *lower* female relationship satisfaction In a second paper with a sample of couples undertaking a German adaptation of PREP, it was found that women who made the largest reductions in negative communication, and the highest increases in positive communication, had deteriorating relationship satisfaction over the next 5 years (Baucom, Hahlweg, Atkins, Engl, & Thurmaier, 2006) However, the unexpected finding that declining female negativity predicts deteriorating relationship satisfaction was not replicated in two separate samples of couples in the third study (Stanley, Rhoades, Olmos-Gallo, & Markman, 2007)

One likely explanation for the inconsistent findings regarding the association of changes in couple communication after CRE and future relationship satisfaction is that the effects of change depend on how negative a couple is before CRE Some couples prior to CRE have high rates of negative communication, rates that make them likely to experience deteriorating relationship satisfaction (Bradbury & Karney, 2004) The extent to which CRE reduces negativity in these initially negative couples would be expected to predict future high relationship satisfaction However, other couples have low rates of negative communication, rates that make them likely to sustain high relationship satisfaction (Bradbury & Karney, 2004) Reducing initial low negativity seems unlikely to mediate any benefit from CRE In fact, Schilling and colleagues (2003) suggest that their CRE attempts to reduce already low levels of negative female communication might inadvertently have promoted avoidance of difficult relationship issues, and that such avoidance might account for deteriorating relationship satisfaction Collectively these studies point to the conclusion that reductions in negative communication are likely to be helpful only to some couples, those couples that are high in negativity

Change in communication is almost certainly not the sole mechanism for the effects of CRE on relationship satisfaction Halford and colleagues (2004) reported increases in relationship satisfaction without changes in couple communication We know from the evidence reviewed in Chapter 1 that couples have a diverse array of risk and resilience factors in their relationships It therefore would seem likely that the mediator of any association between relationship education and sustained relationship satisfaction will depend on the risk factors that a couple brings to CRE That is, any given couple is likely to benefit from reductions in risk factors that are elevated for them, and from enhancement of resilience factors that are low for them For example, as noted in Chapter 1, problem drinking is a risk factor for relationship problems In couples in which at least one partner drinks heavily, then moderation of problem drinking might well predict future relationship satisfaction However, change in alcohol consumption after CRE is, for the majority of couples who do not drink heavily, not likely to be relevant to their future relationship satisfaction

One possible common pathway for the influence of many relationship risk factors is relationship self-change (also termed *relationship self-regulation*) Halford, Lizzio, and colleagues (2007) suggest that increases in relationship self-change mediate the effects of CRE Within this framework, working at your relationship by reflecting on how things are going, setting personal goals to improve your behavior within the relationship, and putting in effort to be a loving partner will help promote the long-term maintenance of relationship satisfaction It is possible that partners who are assisted through CRE to maintain this relationship focus, and to work on their relationship effectively, might overcome the effects of relationship risk factors Relationship self-change has been shown to predict relationship satisfaction (Halford, Lizzio, et al, 2007; Wilson et al, 2005); CRE can increase relationship self-change (Halford & Moore, 2002); and the extent of self-change after CRE predicts future relationship satisfaction (Halford & Wilson, 2009)

Relationship self-change might occur in one of at least two different ways It is possible that the act of committing to undertake CRE, and being prompted through that to be reflective about your relationship, might prompt self-change Alternatively, self-change might be specifically promoted within CRE programs Since no research studies have compared CRE that teaches self-change with a program that simply encourages reflection on the couple relationship, it is not yet clear what mechanism promotes self-change The Couple CARE program, which is a central focus of this book, is predicated on the assumption that promoting self-change is important In Chapter 5 I discuss the details of how self-change is promoted in that program

Progress in providing effective CRE is likely to be assisted by future research elucidating the mechanisms of the effects of relationship education Two potential mediators of positive change are alterations in individual risk profiles and changes in relationship self-change

Effectiveness Studies

Almost all CRE efficacy research has been conducted within universities Usually the educators are highly trained in the specific programs being evaluated and deliver the programs in those research settings Education provided in a research setting usually is delivered following written manuals, with predefined content being covered in sessions In addition, the delivery of education is often individually supervised and carefully monitored Moreover, the couples in research settings must agree to the conditions of research For example, couples usually must agree to be randomly assigned to conditions In efficacy research the assessment of individual partners is extensive, and couples have to agree to this assessment before entering the study

Each of the characteristics of efficacy studies is intended to maximize the internal validity of the research, allowing a clear test of whether the CRE produces sustained relationship satisfaction and stability At the same time, these characteristics might limit the generalizability of research efficacy findings to effectiveness in routine service delivery For example, efficacy studies all require participants to complete substantial numbers of questionnaires as part of the evaluation, which can be daunting for people with low levels of formal education Perhaps this is why almost all of the efficacy research is carried out with samples of middle-class, highly educated, white couples (Carroll & Doherty, 2003; Rogge et al, 2006) It is unclear from the efficacy research alone if existing evidence-based programs address the needs of less educated, poor couples, or are generalizable to nonwhite populations Therefore it is important to consider effectiveness studies as well as efficacy studies

Four studies have evaluated the effects of premarriage CRE, when it is routinely and widely delivered, on relationship satisfaction or stability Sullivan and Bradbury (1997) conducted a longitudinal study assessing relationship satisfaction across the first 4 years of marriage in a large sample of newlywed couples They found no effect of reported attendance of premarriage education on the trajectories of relationship satisfaction

Schumm, Resnick, Silliman, and Bell (1998) surveyed over 18,000 military couples and found an association between reported attendance of premarriage education and high relationship satisfaction in the wives However, this study did not control for possible differences between those attending premarriage education and those not attending Given that those attending premarriage education tend to be at somewhat lower risk for relationship problems than couples not attending premarriage education (Halford, O'Donnell, et al, 2006), these results might reflect a selection effect

Birch and colleagues (2004) did not directly assess the effects of CRE, but rather the implementation of community marriage initiatives These initiatives are broad in scope and emphasize promoting the importance of marriage and supporting marriage The particular community marriage initiative they evaluated focused on encouraging clergy to promote the importance of marriage and to increase the availability and scope of CRE Birch and colleagues found that the mean longitudinal trajectory of divorce rates in 122 different counties' districts declined after the introduction of the community marriage initiatives compared with the trajectory before the initiatives Furthermore, the downward shift in trajectory in these districts did not occur in comparison counties that had not introduced community marriage initiatives, suggesting that the downward shift did not reflect broader social trends

In a survey of a large ($N = 2,323$) representative sample of adults in four midwestern U.S. states, having participated in premarital education was associated with high marital satisfaction, high marital commitment, low marital conflict, and low rates of marital separation (Stanley et al, 2006) The magnitude of the effects were generally small: marital satisfaction was 15 standard deviations higher in married people who received premarriage education than in those who did not Among people receiving premarriage education, 10% experienced a marital separation in the first 5 years of marriage, compared with 14% of people who did not attend premarriage education However, if these small differences exist across the entire population of marrying individuals, this would have enormous public health significance

In Stanley and colleagues' (2006) sample, not attending premarriage education was associated with low religiosity, being black, low education, and receiving welfare (public assistance) As described in Chapter 1, these characteristics are associated with high risk for future marital problems Stanley and colleagues found that the association of premarriage education with high relationship satisfaction and commitment was still evident after statistically controlling for these variables However, the effect of premarriage education on reducing risk of marital separation was only evident in couples with higher levels of education; couples with low education did not show reduced risk for separation through completing premarriage education By including the number of years of marriage as a covariate, Stanley and colleagues demonstrated that the effects of premarital education were most evident in the early years of marriage, and tended to dissipate over time

These effectiveness studies do have significant limitations First, the absence of random assignment makes it very difficult to demonstrate causal effects for CRE Even with sophisticated statistical procedures like those used by Birch and colleagues (2004) and Stanley and colleagues (2006), correlates of attending CRE still might explain the association of marriage duration and relationship outcomes, rather than better outcomes resulting from CRE

A second weakness of effectiveness studies is that the CRE provided is often not clearly described, so it is unclear what sort of relationship education might be having an effect The Stanley and colleagues (2006) study found that CRE of at least 10 hours duration had a stronger association with positive relationship outcomes than briefer education, but CRE programs that were longer than 10 hours duration seemed to provide no incremental benefit Stanley and colleagues also reported that most CRE that was provided was brief, with the modal duration of education reported as being 2 hours This suggests that the magnitude of effects of premarriage CRE might be substantially increased by providing 10 hours of relationship education However, none of the effectiveness studies were able to test whether a particular approach to marriage education was effective

Despite the methodological limitations of the effectiveness studies, the three studies with large samples all found an association of premarriage education with marital satisfaction or stability In combination with the efficacy research, the weight of evidence supporting the effectiveness of CRE is substantial Moreover, the efficacy and effectiveness research is consistent in pointing to a minimum duration of 10 hours of CRE to achieve a reliable effect on relationship satisfaction and stability

IMPLICATIONS OF EFFECTIVENESS RESEARCH FOR RELATIONSHIP EDUCATION

The huge costs and suffering associated with couple relationship distress and separation have focused attention on CRE as a means of helping couples sustain mutually satisfying relationships The research evaluating marriage and relationship education is still at an early stage of development and more research is needed to address what we do not know There is a tension between wanting more definitive answers on what works before we act, and responding to the demands to address the current social problem of high rates of relationship distress and separation There is a substantial body of evidence that guides the offering of relationship education For example, inventory- and skill-based CRE each show considerable promise as interventions to enhance couple relationship outcomes Below I propose best practice guidelines based on existing research, although these guidelines will likely need to be revised as our knowledge expands

Enhance the Reach of Marriage and Relationship Education

As noted previously, in the United States and Australia less than half of marrying couples participate in CRE, and rates of attendance are even lower for cohabiting couples There are limited data on the attendance of relationship education by different socioeconomic and ethnic groups, but available data in both the United States (Ooms & Wilson, 2004) and Australia (Halford

& Simons, 2005) suggest that couples of low socioeconomic status and from minority groups are underrepresented Enhancing the reach of CRE is crucial if it is to impact upon rates of relationship distress and dissolution

The barriers to couples attending CRE are many and varied Couples often report that they do not perceive a personal need for relationship education, see relationship education as being for couples with problems, and are concerned that relationship education might raise problems where none currently exist (Australian House of Representatives Standing Committee on Legal and Constitutional Affairs, 1998; Simons et al, 1994) Couples who do not attend CRE often report a view that relationships are private, and that relationship education groups are too intrusive (Simons et al, 1994) Many countries have tried through marketing campaigns to promote the view that attending CRE is helpful and socially normative For example, in Australia the federal government uses a variety of initiatives including marketing CRE to civil marriage celebrants, subsidizing the costs of CRE by accredited providers, and providing Internet-based resource materials that promote CRE as socially normative and desirable (Simons & Parker, 2002) Systematic evaluation of these initiatives is lacking, and it is unclear whether these approaches alone increase utilization of existing CRE programs

Integrating the offering of CRE with other services, and promoting the value of quality marriages, seems to show more promise in enhancing engagement with CRE For example, there has been an extensive statewide initiative in Oklahoma to enhance marital commitment and quality (Johnson et al, 2002) In this initiative, statewide surveys identify the extent and costs of marital distress and the results are used to promote the importance of marriage to the community As the work of Birch and colleagues (2004) shows, community marriage initiatives do seem to increase the use of CRE and reduce divorce rates Such initiatives can promote evidence-based CRE programs being widely offered to the population in an effort to reduce the statewide prevalence of relationship problems For example, Stanley and colleagues (2001) reported on a large-scale dissemination of evidence-based CRE in which local religious leaders were trained to deliver PREP In a different example, in ongoing work my colleagues and I (Halford, Petch, et al, 2008) have worked with midwives to provide Couple CARE for Parents through a range of maternity hospitals In another initiative, PREP was offered to armed service personnel through clergy (Stanley et al, 2005) Ooms and Wilson (2004) suggest that providing access to CRE through agencies that service the poor and disadvantaged, such as those providing financial assistance, could enhance accessibility of relationship education to disadvantaged groups

Expanding the range of formats in which CRE is offered could enhance the accessibility of such education Most existing relationship education programs are offered in face-to-face sessions (Halford et al, 2003) Although this format appeals to some couples, the majority of marrying couples do not participate (Simons et al, 1994) Many adults prefer to access psychological education through self-directed programs that can be undertaken at times and places that suit participants, rather than through face-to-face programs (Christensen & Jacobson, 1994) For example, there are substantial numbers of people who prefer the Internet, DVDs, and the like to face-to-face contacts when seeking psychological information (Emmelkamp, 2005) There is increasing evidence that people might be more willing to disclose about sensitive issues like relationship functioning with Internet- or computer-based assessment than with face-to-face or written assessment (Kaltenthaler, Parry, & Beverly, 2004) At least some couples might prefer the flexibility and convenience of accessing CRE through Internet-based or other self-directed programs Moreover, in geographically large countries like the United States, Canada, and Australia, distance can make attendance of face-to-face programs difficult, and flexible delivery programs might help overcome this barrier Examples of evidence-based flexible delivery relationship programs are the RELATE Internet-based assessment and feedback, and the Couple CARE skill training program Each of these programs allows couples to complete education at home, in their own time

Combining the Strengths of the Inventory and Skill-Based Approaches to Education

Inventories and skill-based relationship education each have their strengths and weaknesses as approaches Combining the strengths of the two approaches is likely to enhance relationship education effectiveness, and hence that is the approach recommended in this book Inventory-based assessment and feedback provides couples with an individualized profile of their relationship strengths and vulnerabilities Such assessment allows identification of whether skill-based relationship education is inappropriate For example, a RELATE assessment that could detect severe relationship distress or violence in a couple might suggest couple therapy to be most helpful, rather than relationship education

Inventory assessment of a couple's risk profile might also guide the couple as to whether intensive skill-based CRE is necessary Couples with many relationship strengths and few risks might receive that information via a brief feedback session, and be encouraged to focus on sustaining their current positive patterns of interaction For couples with a higher risk profile, the assessment also might promote the tailoring of any skill-based education to address particular challenges the couple faces For example, if one partner was drinking at hazardous levels, CRE could incorporate brief education and intervention to promote safe drinking, as done by Bouma and colleagues (2004) As a second example, couples forming stepfamilies could receive education tailored specifically to address the challenges unique to stepfamilies

Curriculum-based CRE significantly extends the insights provided in inventory approaches, and provides couples with the chance to develop new knowledge and skills For example, Couple CARE for Parents provides information to prospective parents on the demands of infant care, and helps the couple to develop realistic and shared expectations and roles with respect to child care Currently curriculum-based education programs tend to be applied with relatively fixed curricula, but incorporating inventory assessment would allow tailoring of curricula to the relationship needs of particular couples

In conclusion, we have substantial data that suggest that inventory-based assessment can usefully identify couples' relationship education needs Curriculum-based relationship education seems to help couples sustain relationship satisfaction, though these effects might be restricted to couples at high risk for future relationship problems Extending the reach of CRE and combining the strengths of the inventory- and skill-based approaches can enhance the effectiveness of relationship education In Chapter 3 I describe an approach to marriage and CRE that reflects these evidence-based principles of effective practice of relationship education The approach uses inventory assessment to determine the need for curriculum-based CRE, and also uses the assessment to guide tailoring the curriculum to individual couples' needs

Assessment in an Evidence–Based Approach to Couple Relationship Education

This chapter provides an overview of a stepped approach to the provision of CRE, one that is well supported by empirical evidence. The initial step is an inventory-based assessment of a couple's current relationship strengths and challenges, which is used to help the couple define specific goals for relationship enhancement. This statement of goals is used to negotiate with the couple whether participation in curriculum-based relationship education is to be undertaken. I recommend the RELATE assessment for the inventory-based assessment, as it is available via the Internet at *www.relate-institute.org*, is self-scoring and interpreting (Busby et al., 2001), and has been adapted to integrate with the curriculum-based Couple CARE program that I will describe in more detail later (Halford, Wilson, et al., 2010). While the major focus of this chapter is on how to conduct the RELATE assessment, the described approach to assessment could be utilized with other widely available inventories like PREPARE or FOCCUS. In order to use PREPARE or FOCCUS, professionals must complete a training program; information on the training and accessing the inventories is available at *www.prepare-enrich.com* and *www.foccusinc.com*.

The curriculum-based CRE described in later chapters of this book is Couple CARE, which has evidence of its effectiveness either when provided face to face with couples (Halford et al., 2001) or when completed by couples at home (Halford et al., 2004; Halford & Wilson, 2009; Halford, Wilson, et al., 2010). The current book provides the necessary information to allow educators to deliver Couple CARE face to face to either groups or individual couples.[1]

THE STEPPED MODEL OF RELATIONSHIP EDUCATION

Most curriculum-based CRE programs such as Couple CARE, PREP, and Couple Coping Enhancement have a basic curriculum intended to address the needs of many couples. However, as previously discussed, couples differ greatly in their profiles of relationship strengths and challenges. Some couples have so many strengths and so few challenges in their profiles, it is questionable whether they need intensive, curriculum-based CRE. Other couples have moderate-to-high elevations of challenge factors; these couples seem especially likely to benefit from curriculum-based relationship education. A third group of couples who seek CRE have substantial individual or relationship problems, and seem likely to benefit from therapy rather than from CRE.

In order to evaluate whether curriculum-based relationship education is appropriate for a given couple, it is advisable to conduct an assessment of the couple's relationship before they begin CRE. The assessment report needs to be discussed with the couple, helping them to identify goals they might have for strengthening their relationship and negotiating whether skill-based relationship education is appropriate. Providers of CRE rarely ask couples to complete a relationship assessment before undertaking curriculum-based relationship education. My recommendation to conduct assessment is a significant departure from current practice. I think that the benefits of such assessment warrant changing current practice.

The general approach recommended is depicted in Figure 3.1. In essence, this is a stepped approach to CRE. It is "stepped" in the sense that the educator negotiates with couples one of three possible steps of increasing intensity of CRE, or if the couple are distressed in their relationship the educator might recommend couple therapy.

---

[1] When couples complete Couple CARE at home they need access to the Couple CARE resources. These materials consist of a DVD, partner guidebooks, and an educator's manual, which are available through *www.couplecare.info*. In flexible delivery couples complete much of the work independently by themselves, by watching the DVD, and by undertaking exercises described in the guidebook. Their educator assists them by reviewing their progress and coaching as required. The Couple CARE resources are also useful to assist with program delivery in the face-to-face mode. For example, the DVD has an explanation and demonstrations of key communication skills that can be shown in a group. However, educators can use a mixture of live demonstrations and lectures to make the same points when providing the program face to face with couples.

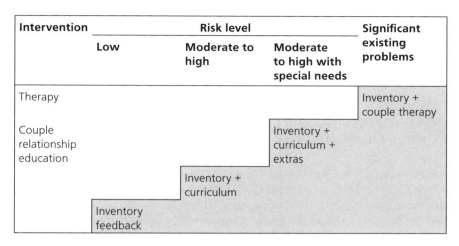

FIGURE 3.1. The stepped model of couple relationship education.

As depicted in Figure 3.1, couples with low-risk profiles are probably best served with a brief program of inventory-based assessment, feedback, and goal setting. Low-risk couples are likely to sustain high relationship satisfaction without further CRE. A single session reviewing and affirming their relationship strengths, and identifying some areas of the relationship that might benefit from minor fine-tuning, is all that is required. Couples with moderate- to high-risk profiles are likely to benefit from curriculum-based CRE, which is intended to help partners negotiate realistic, shared relationship expectations with one another, and to develop their relationship knowledge and skills. In this case the assessment feedback session identifies the couple's relationship strengths and challenges, and the educator explores with the couple how the CRE curriculum content relates to their relationship goals. If the couple has special needs not covered in the standard curriculum (e.g., a stepparent needs parenting education, or the couple are about to have their first child and need guidance on the special challenges of parenthood), then the standard curriculum can be supplemented as necessary. As another example, if one partner is drinking too much, an intervention to promote safe drinking might be added to CRE, as described by Bouma and colleagues (2004). Couples with significant relationship distress are unlikely to benefit from CRE alone. Such couples are more likely to benefit from couple therapy that might include the use of Couple CARE content as part of the therapy.

The stepped model of CRE provides only as much relationship education as is necessary for a couple to receive. This has the advantage of managing the time demands on couples, and focusing costly professional educators' time where it is likely to do the most good. It also allows those who fund relationship education (which can be any combination of religious and other community organizations, government, and the couples themselves) to make it widely available while still containing the costs of providing CRE.[2]

GOALS OF ASSESSMENT
IN RELATIONSHIP EDUCATION

Assessment of the couple relationship before curriculum-based relationship education serves three very important purposes. First, it begins the relationship education process by encouraging partners to reflect upon the strengths and challenges each brings to their relationship. For some couples with many relationship strengths and few relationship challenges, the couple and the educator might decide that the discussion of the assessment results is sufficient relationship education. Second, for couples with more relationship challenges, the assessment can assist the couple and the educator to focus education on the aspects of the relationship that are of particular importance to the couple. For example, if this initial assessment shows that the partners have difficulties managing conflict, or share relatively few positive activities, then CRE can address those challenges.

The third important purpose of assessment is to determine whether or not CRE is appropriate. A substantial proportion of couples who seek CRE are experiencing significant relationship distress (De Maria, 2005). Sometimes it can be difficult to address the needs of a highly distressed couple with CRE, particularly in a group context. Therapy rather than relationship education might be more appropriate. In other couples individual difficulties, such as depression, alcohol abuse, or other problems might need to be addressed through therapy. This is not to say that the content covered in Couple CARE is not useful to distressed couples. I regularly use the Couple CARE content

---

[2]To illustrate the effect of the stepped approach to CRE on costs, consider the following cost projections. At the time of writing it costs about five times as much to deliver RELATE plus Couple CARE across seven sessions as it does to provide a single session providing assessment and feedback based on RELATE alone. Thus focusing the use of the more intensive and extensive program on the approximately 50% of couples at moderate to high risk of future relationship problems substantially reduces the overall costs of providing a universal service.

A typical course of couple therapy as described in the research literature of 20 1-hour sessions costs three to four times that of providing RELATE plus Couple CARE. Effective dissemination of CRE should reduce the need for costly couple therapy. Moreover, when couple therapy is needed, the use of Couple CARE relationship education materials can make therapy more efficient, and briefer therapy of 10 sessions could potentially reduce the total cost of professional fees by 50%.

in my couple therapy, but often the content needs to be supplemented. For example, I conducted an assessment of a recently married couple aged in their early 70s who presented requesting relationship education. The assessment found that the couple had severe levels of violence, especially by the woman toward the man. The man was quite frail, and this constituted a significant risk to his health. I worked with the couple in a face-to-face mode. Therapy combined individual and couple sessions. There were five individual treatment sessions for the woman, who had long suffered from posttraumatic stress disorder consequent to her being raped as a young woman. These individual sessions were interspersed with seven couple sessions, the first two focusing on the violence reduction and anger management strategies for couples described by Heyman and Schlee (2003), and the remaining sessions using the Couple CARE content to help the couple enhance their relationship.

RELATE ASSESSMENT

As described in Chapter 2, assessment of couple relationship strengths and vulnerabilities has been used to provide couples with systematic feedback designed to allow them to select aspects of their relationship they wish to change (Larson et al., 2002). Three inventories have been widely used to assess couple relationship strengths and challenges as part of relationship education: FOCCUS, PREPARE, and RELATE (Larson et al., 2002). Each of these inventories predicts the trajectory of relationship satisfaction in the early years of marriage (Holman, 2001; Larsen & Olson, 1989; Williams & Jurich, 1995), and any of the three inventories provides an evidence-based and useful assessment of couples. I prefer to use RELATE, and focus the detailed description of how to conduct couple assessment with RELATE.[3] However, almost all the guidelines and suggestions could be applied to use of the other inventories.

---

[3]There are four key reasons why this book focuses on the RELATE assessment. First, RELATE is the most comprehensive of the three inventories. For example, it assesses patterns of conflict management, which are important but are not assessed in the other inventories. Second, RELATE is unique in being accessible via the Internet, and feedback can be provided from a computer-generated report. Third, I have worked closely with the developers of RELATE to integrate the strengths of RELATE and Couple CARE (Larson & Halford, in press), and the RELATE assessment directly informs the delivery of Couple CARE. Finally, in the only randomized controlled trial of using a couple assessment inventory with feedback, RELATE assessment and feedback produced short-term increases in relationship satisfaction (Larson et al., 2007). Although the long-term effectiveness of assessment and feedback with RELATE is unknown, it is the only inventory for which there is evidence that assessment and feedback alone improve couple relationship satisfaction.

When a couple first expresses interest in CRE, it is helpful to do an initial review with them to get to know them a little, and to explore their ideas about relationship education. This interview can be done face to face or by telephone. Figure 3.2 sets out a semistructured interview that reviews the couple's conjoint and individual ideas about participation in CRE. Having the couple describe how they met, and what attracted each to the other, helps the educator understand a little about the couple, and develops rapport. The questions about prior couple and individual therapy alert the educator to potential difficulties that might need to be addressed in therapy rather than in CRE. Speaking with each partner individually is highly advisable, as there are sometimes issues people might not raise in front of their partner— particularly issues about domestic violence or individual problems that might impact on the relationship.

The questions on interpartner violence are worded in a particular way to maximize the chance of accurate reports about such violence. The initial statement about how disagreements occur for all couples is true, and it seeks to normalize the idea that we need to discuss how this couple manages conflict. The suggested questions on violence in Figure 3.2 ask about specific behaviors, citing hitting, pushing, and slapping as these are the most common behaviors that occur in interpartner violence. The question deliberately avoids asking questions like: "Have you been a victim of domestic violence?" or "Have you been subjected to abuse by your partner?" Terms like *abuse* and *domestic violence* can be interpreted very differently. For example, I had a man who had lifted his partner over his head and dropped her onto a concrete floor comment that "I am not a violent man, I don't beat her or anything, I just lost my temper." His spouse had earlier reported to a colleague that she was "not a victim of wife abuse," even though she later described multiple episodes of pushing, slapping, and shoving, several incidents of being held down forcibly, as well as the incident of being dropped onto the floor. The research is very clear that people are much more likely to report violence when asked about particular behaviors, rather than when asked about the occurrence of "abuse" or "domestic violence."

Table 3.1 summarizes the content of the RELATE measure. There are 271 items in total. In the items on personal characteristics and some aspects of the current relationship people rate their own and their partner's behavior, which makes it possible to compare the two partners' perceptions. It typically takes people about 1 hour to complete the assessment. Educators can have couples access the website, complete the assessment, and access the report themselves. Alternatively, educators can register with the RELATE Institute and have the couple's report sent to them. The report is presented as a downloadable file, which can be printed either in color or in black and white.

(text resumes on page 75)

Names: Partner 1: _____ **Partner 2:** _____

Date: _____

1. **GOALS OF PARTICIPATION**

What are you hoping to get from taking part?

Partner 1: _____

_____

_____

_____

Partner 2: _____

_____

_____

_____

2. **CURRENT RELATIONSHIP**

a. Can you tell me how you met? _____

_____

_____

_____

_____

_____

_____

b. What attracted you to each other?

Partner 1 to Partner 2: _____

_____

_____

_____

Partner 2 to Partner 1: _____

_____

_____

_____

(cont.)

FIGURE 3.2. Couple intake interview.

c. What do you see as the strengths of your relationship?

Partner 1: _____

_____

_____

_____

Partner 2: _____

_____

_____

_____

d. All relationships have their less positive aspects. Are there any areas you'd like to work on to make sure things work out the way you'd like?

Partner 1: _____

_____

_____

_____

Partner 2: _____

_____

_____

_____

e. This might sound like a bit of a funny question to ask, but we ask it because it does happen. Has there ever been a time in your relationship for either of you, when you've left the house for more than 24 hours and you weren't sure you would come back?

Partner 1:   Yes / No

If yes, how long were you apart for?   _____

Partner 2:   Yes / No

If yes, how long were you apart for?   _____

f. Sometimes when a couple disagrees things can get heated. This can result in one or both partners slapping, pushing, or hitting the other. Have you ever hit, pushed, or slapped your partner?

Partner 1:   Yes / No   **Partner 2:**   Yes / No

Has your partner ever done this to you?

Partner 1:   Yes / No   **Partner 2:**   Yes / No

g. Have you ever had problems in your current relationship for which you have sought professional help?   Yes / No

(cont.)

FIGURE 3.2. *(cont.)*

If yes, give details including the nature of problem, treatment sought, length and dates of treatment, what helped/didn't help, and outcome of treatment from your perspective.

_____

_____

_____

_____

_____

_____

_____

_____

3. **INDIVIDUAL PSYCHOLOGICAL PROFILE**

Have you ever sought help for any psychological or psychiatric problem?

Partner 1:	No	0
	Depression	1
	Anxiety disorder	2
	Posttraumatic stress disorder	3
	Bipolar disorder	4
	Psychotic disorder	5
	Alcohol/substance abuse/dependence	6
	Other	7

If yes, clarify nature of problem, including the number of episodes, treatment sought, length and dates of treatment, what helped/didn't help, and if problem is ongoing or not.

_____

_____

_____

Partner 2:	No	0
	Depression	1
	Anxiety disorder	2
	Posttraumatic stress disorder	3
	Bipolar disorder	4
	Psychotic disorder	5
	Alcohol/substance abuse/dependence	6
	Other	7

If yes, clarify nature of problem, including the number of episodes, treatment sought, length and dates of treatment, what helped/didn't help, and if problem is ongoing or not.

_____

_____

_____

(cont.)

FIGURE 3.2. *(cont.)*

4. HOPES/EXPECTATIONS OF THE PROGRAM

a. What does each of you hope to get from the program? (Clarify goals.)

Partner 1: _____

_____

_____

_____

_____

Partner 2: _____

_____

_____

_____

_____

b. Do either of you have any concerns about doing the program?

Partner 1: _____

_____

_____

_____

_____

Partner 2: _____

_____

_____

_____

_____

c. Is there anything else either of you want to discuss about your participation?

_____

_____

_____

_____

_____

_____

FIGURE 3.2. *(cont.)*

TABLE 3.1. Content of the RELATE Assessment

Area assessed	No. of items	Key content
Demographics	7	Age, occupation, education, religion
Individual characteristics of partners	61	Ratings of own and partner's personality, reports on substance abuse
Personal values	41	Beliefs about religion, importance of marriage, gender roles, work–family balance, individual autonomy, sexuality, children
Family background	55	Family-of-origin parental divorce or violence, experience of child abuse, parental relationship satisfaction, parental patterns of communication, current relationship with parents
Current relationship	107	Relationship history, satisfaction, stability, communication, areas of problems, expectations, conflict patterns, violence, sexuality

The RELATE Report

The report generated for the RELATE assessment is quite detailed, but also easy to follow. As noted previously, couples can access the RELATE website, complete the assessments, and review the computer-generated report on their own. However, many couples report that having a relationship educator guide them through the report is helpful (Larson et al., 2007). In my experience most couples can complete RELATE and interpret it on their own, but a proportion of couples report they have conflict about the answers. For example, partners can be surprised and disappointed when their spouse reports lower relationship satisfaction than them, or reports concerns about an area of the relationship. Some couples with elevated challenge profiles state that the report confirms or strengthens concerns held about their relationship, and they feel the need for assistance to resolve those concerns.

The RELATE report consists of a set of instructions to the couple on how to interpret the report, information about each of the areas assessed, a summary relationship profile, and some suggested discussion questions for the couple to discuss their report. The RELATE website also lists a range of resources and agencies that can provide further relationship education or counseling. This information is a useful resource for couples living in the United States, but has limited utility for couples living elsewhere.

The RELATE report includes a brief description of nine different areas assessed by RELATE, and a graph that shows the ratings each partner made in that area. The nine areas covered in the report are relationship satisfaction, relationship stability, kindness/caring, effective communication, flexibility, conflict, conflict style, sexual intimacy, and problem areas. An example of a graph for the area of relationship communication is presented in Figure 3.3. The graph illustrates each partner's rating both of him- or herself and of his or her partner. When printed in color, the background is divided into green, white, and red areas. When printed in black and white, as shown in Figure 3.3, these areas appear as different shadings. The colored (or shaded) areas show the scores that represent relationship strength (green at the top), neutral (white in the middle), and challenge (red at the bottom) areas.

The scores that define each area are based on research examining which RELATE scores are correlated with relationship satisfaction. The cutoff point for the green zone is the level on each scale where 90% or more people reporting that score also reported that they were satisfied with their relationship. The white zone is the level where 70–89% of couples typically report being satisfied, and the red zone indicates the level where less than 70% of partners report being satisfied with their relationship. For example, if the green zone

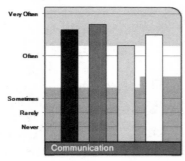

Effective Communication

The **Effective Communication scale** measures your and your partner's levels of empathy, listening, and ability to send clear messages.

Strength Area (Green/Top Area): People who score in the Green/Top Area area of this scale see themselves and/or their partners as being high in empathy, listening, and in sending clear messages.

Challenge Area (Red/Bottom Area): People who have effective communciation scores in the Red/Bottom Area area are more likely to be in relationships that are less satisfying. People rating themselves and/or their partners in the challenge area on this scale may want to evaluate their ways of interacting to see how they can increase empathy and understanding between partners, and how they can send and receive the communication of needs, concerns, and desires more effectively.

RELATE Institute Findings: In research with couples, higher levels of effective communication have been shown to be associated with higher relationship quality.

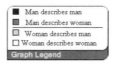

FIGURE 3.3. RELATE summary report graph of relationship communication. Reprinted with permission from Dean Busby, School of Family Life, Bingham Young University.

for a scale begins at a score of 4.50, it means that more than 90% of partners who rated themselves or their partner at or above that level also reported that they were satisfied with their relationship.

Apart from the first two areas of relationship satisfaction and relationship stability, all the areas included in the RELATE report have both partners' ratings of their own behavior and their ratings of their spouse's behavior. However, individuals are not asked to rate their spouse's relationship satisfaction or stability. The inclusion of both partners' ratings of each other makes it possible to compare the self- and partner ratings in particular areas, which can be a useful prompt for discussion.

A summary profile of the couple relationship is provided on the final page of the report. This shows the overall level of various relationship strengths and challenges. This can be very useful for integrating the findings during discussion of the report with a couple.

The RELATE report is focused on particular scales and is deliberately designed not to include a number of things assessed in RELATE. For example, the report does not include the ratings by the partners of prior experience of abuse or parental violence. The educator can assess and review the partners' responses to these items, which can be useful information for the educator to know. However, the report is focused on those scales that assess potentially changeable aspects of the couple's current behavior within the relationship. The report also does not include ratings by the partners of violence in the current relationship. This is an important but potentially delicate issue to discuss with couples; the designers of RELATE have deliberately left these ratings out of the report so that the educator can determine the best way to discuss the problem of violence with couples, where it is relevant.

DISCUSSING ASSESSMENT RESULTS WITH A COUPLE

The procedure in conducting the assessment feedback process has two phases. First, there is the relationship educator and couple preparation done *before* the feedback session. This includes the educator reviewing the couple's report, developing ideas about areas that warrant exploration, and evaluating the couple's overall level of relationship strengths and challenges. It also includes each partner reading their report. Second, there is the feedback session itself, which involves reviewing and discussing the report, exploring the likely impact of current relationship strengths and challenges, identifying relationship goals, and then developing self-change goals for each partner to enhance the relationship. It also involves negotiation of the approach to be taken, including discussion of whether curriculum-based relationship education (e.g., Couple CARE) is appropriate. If curriculum-based relationship education is appropriate, then the educator discusses the association of the couple's stated relationship goals to the content of the CRE program.

Preparation for the Session

Figure 3.4 is a useful note sheet for the educator to structure his or her preparation for a feedback session, and for taking notes during the session. In preparation for the feedback session it is important for the educator to read the couple's RELATE report, take notes on areas of relationship challenges and strengths, and identify the areas of agreement and disagreement in the partners' ratings. It can be useful to identify some open-ended questions to encourage the couple to explore their overall understanding of the report and their perceptions of their relationship in each area, which are discussed as you guide the couple through the pages of the report.

Some open questions that often are useful to pose to a couple to explore their overall understanding of the report are listed below. The aim is to encourage the couple to be active in the feedback session, thinking about what they make of the assessment report.

- "What, if anything, surprised you about the report?"
- "Which aspects of the report, if any, confirmed your beliefs about your relationship?"
- "On which RELATE scales were you and your partner most similar in your answers?"
- "On which scales were you least similar in your ratings?"
- "What do you see as the most important strengths in your relationship?"
- "How do you think those strengths might help your relationship?"

After the educator has talked with the couple about their overall impressions, it is useful to explore each of the areas of strengths and challenges. For example, for each of the areas of strength it can be helpful to ask questions like "What do you do that makes this an area of strength?," "What do you see your partner doing?," and "What effect do you think this area of strength has on your relationship?" Similarly, if one of the partners scores in the red zone (challenge area) on kindness/caring, list follow-up questions to help them understand their scores such as, "*When* do you see your partner acting unkindly?" and "How does that affect you and your relationship?"

In areas where there are large differences in perceptions (which is quite common), prepare some open-ended questions that help the partners better understand each other. For example, if Robert perceives Melissa to be a poor communicator while she rates herself as a good one, ask questions like,

Names: Partner 1: _____ **Partner 2:** _____

Date of review session: _____

Educator: _____

1. EDUCATOR-IDENTIFIED COUPLE PROFILE

Couple strengths: _____

_____

Couple challenges: _____

_____

Areas of couple agreement and disagreement: _____

_____

2. QUESTIONS TO EXPLORE COUPLE UNDERSTANDING OF THEIR PROFILE

Open questions to put to couple on overall understanding: _____

_____

Open questions to put to couple on strengths: _____

_____

_____

Open questions to put to couple on challenges: _____

_____

_____

Their answers: _____

_____

_____

3. EXPLORING PLUSES AND MINUSES OF STATUS QUO

What strengths are important to sustain? How will you sustain them? ____

_____

_____

What challenges do you think are most important? _____

_____

_____

(cont.)

FIGURE 3.4. Providing feedback to a couple on their RELATE assessment.

What will happen if you change nothing about those challenges? _____

_____

_____

What goals might you like to see in your relationship (sustaining strengths, changing challenges)? _____

_____

_____

4. INDIVIDUAL PARTNER ACTION GOAL SETTING

Partner 1:

What can you contribute to enhance your relationship? _____

_____

How would you go about doing that? _____

_____

Partner 2:

What can you contribute to enhance your relationship? _____

_____

How would you go about doing that? _____

_____

5. RELATIONSHIP OF PARTNER GOALS TO COUPLE CARE CONTENT _____

_____

_____

_____

6. ANY SPECIAL AREAS NEEDING ADDITIONAL INPUT _

_____

_____

_____

7. OTHER ISSUES OR QUESTIONS

_____

_____

_____

_____

_____

_____

FIGURE 3.4. *(cont.)*

"What do you think might lead you to disagree with Melissa on her ability to effectively communicate?" and "What have you seen or heard that leads you to that conclusion?"

In preparation for the feedback session it can be useful for the educator to identify the units of Couple CARE and the sections within particular units that are most relevant to addressing the couple's areas of identified challenges. However, the discussion with the partners often modifies the educator's and the couple's perceptions of their relationship education goals and needs.

Conducting the Session

The feedback session has four steps. First, I suggest that the educator sets some ground rules for the session. Setting clear ground rules maximizes the usefulness of the session to the couple. Second, the educator uses a mix of open-ended and clarifying questions to guide the couple to develop a constructive understanding of their assessment report. Third, the educator helps the couple integrate their understanding of the report, identify relationship goals they wish to pursue, and specify individual self-change goals that would help achieve those relationship goals. Finally, the educator and the couple discuss the appropriateness of Couple CARE versus other options.

Establishing the Session Ground Rules

It is a good idea to begin the session explaining that the overarching goal of the session is to help the couple discuss relationship strengths and challenges, to consider personal goals for change that could enhance their relationship, and to identify how the Couple CARE program can assist them to achieve these goals. The session typically lasts about 1 hour. Explain that experience suggests the following guidelines are useful in making the most of interpreting RELATE and undertaking Couple CARE:

1. Couple CARE is a self-directed learning program in which the partners select the goal they wish to work on to strengthen and enrich their relationship. RELATE provides a broad initial assessment of their relationship to assist them in selecting goals, and to help them decide if Couple CARE is appropriate for them.
2. At the end of the session the aim is to define a preliminary set of goals. These goals often are revised as a couple works their way through Couple CARE.
3. The goal of taking RELATE is to gain a *better understanding* of each other and the relationship. RELATE predicts patterns of relation-

ship outcomes across couples but it is *not* a crystal ball and cannot predict if any individual couple will have a happy relationship.

4. Some results may surprise the couple. Encourage them to *try to be open* rather than defensive about the new feedback RELATE provides.

5. Stress that they should *be honest* in communicating how they feel about their results.

6. Encourage them to *listen closely* while their partner speaks. Empathize with their thoughts and feelings expressed during the interpretation.

7. Suggest that they *be kind* when their partner admits to a challenge. Take an attitude of helpfulness and supportiveness when a partner's challenge is discussed or when he or she discloses sensitive information.

8. *Develop a spirit of collaboration*—for example: "How can we work together to celebrate our strengths and work on our challenges to make our relationship better?"

9. Explain if some results do not make sense, as they may have misinterpreted an item on the questionnaire or made an error when marking their answer (e.g., marked "rarely" when they meant "often").

10. Explain that the purpose of RELATE is to provide ideas and to foster couple communication about the relationship; it does not provide absolute truths. It can guide but not define possible goal setting for change to enhance the relationship.

Exploring the RELATE Report

In this step it is important to be collaborative with the couple in interpreting their results, and to focus on exploring what the results mean to *them*. Invite each person to ask questions about his or her results and how he or she interprets his or her results. Emphasize the importance of adding the test information to other information the couple already has about themselves. For example, a common response from couples is, "We knew we often had misunderstandings but with the RELATE results now we know why: neither of us are good listeners."

While the major focus in the discussion of the RELATE report is on the partners' understandings about their relationship, there are a few discussion points that the educator should make about the nature of the assessment and the report.

1. There are two key limitations to self-report tests like RELATE. First, the accuracy of each graph depends on the levels of insight and honesty each

person had when he or she responded to the RELATE questions. Second, the RELATE results are like a snapshot of a relationship on the day the couple took it, and perceptions of relationships can change over time. Explain that the Couple CARE program provides extra information and learning opportunities (e.g., to assess their communication more precisely) that will help them to refine their understanding of their relationship.

2. Explain how the scores for the graphs are calculated. The strength and challenge zones on the couple profile graphs were calculated using a large, national sample of couples in the United States. The cutoff points between zones were determined by comparing scale scores with partners' reports of relationship satisfaction.

3. Explain how the couple's scores are related to RELATE Institute findings for each chart, and how this is integrated in the final summary profile.

The educator uses the open-ended questions identified in preparation for the session to assist the couple in clarifying their understanding. Here are three useful tips for making this process flow well. First, try to promote an approximately equal level of contribution from each partner. If necessary, address questions to the quieter partner by name. Second, try to explore each area in sufficient detail that partners have identified specific behaviors that might form the basis of change goals in the case of challenges, or the focus of efforts to sustain relationship strengths. For example, many couples say, "We communicate really well." It is important to probe such global comments to elicit specific behaviors with question such as, "When you say 'communicate well,' what does your partner (or do you) do that you think is good communication?" Third, try to prevent the couple from getting bogged down if they disagree about some aspect of their relationship. It is important to emphasize that the goal of the discussion is not to have an absolutely accurate or agreed-upon view of the relationship. If they disagree about something, it is sufficient to note that disagreement, and to explain that undertaking Couple CARE will provide the opportunity of gathering more information and building skills to address that area.

Integrating Results and Setting Goals

In this section you assist the couple to integrate the results of the RELATE assessment, set goals, and understand the links between their goals and the content of Couple CARE. Usually the process of discussion modifies and clarifies the partner's and the educator's perceptions of the relationship. Some useful questions to help couples summarize their views are as follows:

- "What do you see as the most important challenges in your relationship?"
- "How might those challenges show up in your relationship?"
- "Are there aspects of your relationship that you think are important that were not covered in the report?"
- "Overall, after reviewing the report, how would you summarize the strengths and challenges in your relationship?"

The educator should integrate all this by providing a summary of the two partners' views. The next step uses an adaptation of Miller and Rollnick's (2002) motivational interviewing process in an effort to increase the partner's motivation for change. As summarized in Figure 3.4, I suggest that the educator uses a series of open-ended questions that explore the advantages and disadvantages of the current relationship functioning, culminating in a statement by the couple of their relationship goals. Develop a list of goals for improvement based on challenges identified in the report. The educator should help the couple focus on listing between two and four of their most important goals, as more than four goals seem to be too complex for people to remember or work on. Examples of commonly selected goals include continuing to have lots of quality time together, making sure the couple keeps talking about areas of disagreement, improving communication skills, enhancing individual stress management, broadening the range of positive shared activities, resolving differences in key values, and resolving family background problems.

Each partner is then encouraged to identify specific self-change he or she could undertake to help achieve the selected relationship goals. This can be explored with questions like: "How would you go about making the change?," "What will you do and when will you do it?," and "How would you know if the changes that occur have the desired effect on your relationship?"

Negotiating about Couple CARE Appropriateness

It is important to explain to the partners that Couple CARE (or any form of CRE) is not appropriate for all couples. Some contraindications for CRE, particularly education offered in a group format, are presented in Table 3.2. Each of these areas is assessed by RELATE, and can provide guidance to the educator about the advisability of CRE. If one or both partners report low relationship satisfaction (in the red challenge area on the RELATE relationship satisfaction graph), then the educator should discuss the option of the partners attending couple therapy.

Many distressed couples have significant difficulties with conflict management, which often shows up as rapid negative escalation when discuss-

TABLE 3.2. Contraindications for Group Couple Relationship Education

Indicator	Impact on relationship education	Intervention required
Low relationship satisfaction	Low commitment to enhancing relationship, sometimes associated with ambivalence about the future of the relationship; high conflict in sessions can disrupt educational process, particularly in group delivery format.	Thorough clinical assessment of relationship and individual functioning; motivational enhancement through structured and empathic process of identifying short-term relationship goals.
Individual psychological disorder	Significant depression, alcohol abuse, or other major disorder can impair one or both partners' capacity to engage with or utilize the program.	Thorough clinical assessment of relationship and individual functioning; negotiation of therapy that might include individual and/or couple therapy.
Violence in the current relationship	If individual partners feel unsafe to discuss the relationship openly, without fear of coercion or threat, then education is ineffective; management of safety of partners is very difficult within a group relationship education setting.	Thorough clinical assessment of severity and impact of violence; negotiation of a safety plan, which can include leaving the relationship when risk of injury is high.
Sexual dysfunction	If a partner is suffering from a significant sexual dysfunction, this is difficult to manage well in a group setting.	Thorough clinical assessment of relationship and individual functioning; negotiation of therapy that might include individual and/or couple therapy.

ing areas of relationship challenge. The answers the partners give to the RELATE conflict style scale provide information on whether the couple perceives problems with escalation. Furthermore, conducting the RELATE feedback discussion gives the educator a sample of how the partners discuss their relationship challenges. If partners are hostile and critical toward each other, do not listen effectively, and become angry or distressed, then this suggests that couple therapy rather than CRE is appropriate. On the other hand, there are some mildly distressed couples who do not evidence severe negative escalation when discussing challenges; such couples can benefit from CRE.

RELATE does not directly assess individual psychological disorder. The intake interview presented in Figure 3.2 can help identify individual problems that might be affecting the couple relationship. In addition, people with a psychological disorder often score in the challenge area on the RELATE scales assessing flexibility and kindness/caring. If someone does score in this challenge range, I ask him or her about his or her current mood and feelings, and whether he or she feels that inhibits his or her capacity to enjoy and strengthen his or her relationship with his or her partner. The crucial issue in determining the suitability of CRE is whether a disorder in either person is likely to inhibit his or her effective participation. The most common individual problems that present difficulties for relationship educators are depression, severe anxiety disorders, alcohol or drug abuse, and problem gambling. A prior history of suffering from such problems is not a barrier to participation, but currently suffering these problems can be.

The suggested intake interview asks each partner individually about inter-partner violence. As mentioned previously, there are questions about inter-partner violence in RELATE that deliberately do not appear in the RELATE report. However, the educator can access that information and then explore the issue of violence. A key issue when violence is detected is assessing the level of current risk to safety for each partner, and the appropriateness of CRE. The most common form of interpartner violence is reciprocal, of low severity and frequency, and often reflects ineffective conflict management. If the violence is restricted to one or two acts of aggression, and has not resulted in injury, then CRE might assist the couple to manage conflict more effectively. In contrast, more severe and frequent violence, which predominantly is perpetrated by men and often is associated with injury and/or intimidation of the woman, has not been shown to improve in response to CRE. The focus in instances of severe violence needs to be on protecting the safety of the victim(s), which also can include any children in the house.

The treatment of sexual dysfunction is difficult to manage effectively within group CRE. Sexual dysfunction includes male impotence, retarded ejaculation, female painful intercourse and failure to achieve orgasm, and low sexual desire by either partner. Each of these conditions can be influenced by medical conditions (e.g., diabetes can damage the small blood vessels in the penis or clitoris, and produce sexual dysfunction). Effective treatment requires careful and detailed clinical assessment that is beyond the scope of what is usually thought of as CRE. If, however, the relationship educator has the required professional expertise, then working with the individual couple on treating the sexual dysfunction within the context of CRE to enhance their relationship can be appropriate.

One specific area of sexual difficulty worth mentioning is low sexual desire. If either partner reports an almost total lack of sexual desire in an otherwise satisfying relationship, then regarding this as a sexual dysfunction is appropriate. However, differences in desire between partners are quite common, and low desire if there is some dissatisfaction with the relationship also is common. In these instances, CRE might well help the couple to enhance their sexual relationship.

If Couple CARE is contraindicated, it is important for the educator to discuss what aspects of the couple relationship would not be well addressed by relationship education, and to provide alternative suggestions of how the couple could get assistance. The educator might see the couple in therapy (I am a clinical psychologist by training, and often do couple therapy), or the educator might refer the couple to other services if that is more appropriate. It is important for relationship educators to know the available services for individual and couple therapy in their region, so that they can make referrals when appropriate.

Negotiating the Focus of Couple CARE

Assuming that there are no strong contraindications for Couple CARE, the educator should describe the content of the units in Couple CARE that are most relevant to addressing the couple's identified relationship goals and self-change goals. It can be useful to show the couple the program content (presented in Table 4.1 in the next chapter) and relate the content to their goals. For example, suppose one couple has identified being more supportive of each other as their goal, and another couple has identified managing conflict as their goal. For the first couple you could state, "Unit 3 on intimacy and caring includes a section on types of partner support, how to evaluate what you each do to support each other at the moment, and how to work out what you could do differently." For the second couple the educator could make the following comment: "I suggest Unit 4 on managing differences might be particularly useful given the challenges you report with conflict. It has suggestions on how to assess and improve your communication when discussing conflict topics as well as reviewing specific strategies for preventing destructive arguments." Note that in these examples the educator illustrates how the Couple CARE content might assist the couple.

Some couple relationship and self-change goals might not be addressed in Couple CARE. For example, there is no parenting education in Couple CARE. If a couple has difficulties with parenting a child (a child of the current or a past relationship), then it might be important for the couple to access parenting education. Parenting education might be undertaken instead of, or as a complement to, undertaking Couple CARE. For example, I have offered an additional session or two to couples who are forming a stepfamily to discuss issues specific to stepfamily life, like negotiations about parenting roles and the relationship with former partners.

Some couples with many relationship strengths and few challenges might be able to implement the identified self-change goals without further assistance. Other couples with more relationship challenges, or who are really struggling with a key challenge, are likely to benefit from the chance to complete Couple CARE. It can be useful to ask each partner to describe his or her reaction to the idea of completing Couple CARE, and how this might advance achievement of the couple's stated relationship goals. The educator can complement the couple's perceptions with his or her own observations and negotiate what the couple will do.

Adapting Assessment for Different Modes of Delivery

As described earlier in the chapter, there are a variety of modes for delivering CRE. Assessment can be conducted via telephone or in face-to-face sessions (with face to face being with one couple or in groups). The procedure just described for conducting the feedback session works well in either face-to-face or telephone mode. When feedback is conducted over the telephone I add three extra points to the 10-point guidelines already described for the assessment feedback session. These extra points are useful general guidelines for conducting all telephone-based CRE sessions.

11. Both partners need to be able to speak and hear, which requires either a speaker telephone or two handsets. Most households have either a land line or cell phone (mobile) with hands-free speaker function. In our research we lend speaker telephones to the small proportion of couples who do not have access to one.
12. The telephone call is treated the same as any other appointment: the start and finish time is negotiated ahead of time.
13. The telephone call works best if both partners are free from distractions. It is best to schedule the call when the couple is unlikely to be disturbed. Also, it is important not to have music or the television on, not to answer other telephone calls (e.g., on a partner's cell phone), and not to have reading material or other distractions around.

The other adaptation the educator needs to make when working over the telephone is to work without nonverbal cues. This necessitates spelling out process issues more clearly. For example, regulating who is to speak next is often done nonverbally in face-to-face sessions, whereas the educator often needs to address questions to a specific partner by name during telephone calls. Also, the absence of nonverbal cues can make it harder for the educator to monitor the emotional reactions of the partners to the discussion, and it is important to ask each partner about his or her response to what is being said on a regular basis.

Assessment feedback can be conducted in a group session as well as with one couple at a time. When a number of couples are reviewing their RELATE assessment report simultaneously, the process focuses more on the couple being given the prompt questions, and then discussing the issues together.

The educator can circulate among the couples, ask each couple to summarize their discussion, and add comments and suggestions as required. Conducting assessment feedback sessions in groups of couples where at least one couple has significant relationship problems can be challenging. It is important that the educator has reviewed each couple's RELATE report before the session and identified couples who might require special assistance in interpreting their reports.

Common Challenges in Discussing Assessment Results

A number of common challenges occur when discussing assessment results. This section offers suggestions for managing these challenges. Ensuring that the ground rules are discussed and understood before reviewing the assessment reduces the frequency of these challenges. One challenge is if the balance of talk time between partners becomes markedly uneven. It is important to restate that it is vital to hear the views of both partners, and you can note that one partner is speaking noticeably less than another. Directing questions specifically by name to the undertalking partner is useful, especially when the discussion is occurring over the telephone ("Jess, what do you see as some key relationship strengths?"). It also is important for the educator to thank partners for their thoughts, to summarize, and be encouraging of any contributions made ("Thanks, Jess, that is really helpful to know, you see the communication as working well"). Talk can also be unbalanced when one partner is overtalkative. It can be useful to specifically encourage people to be brief, and to highlight that brevity often helps clarity: "Lesley, let me interrupt you for a second. I am getting a little lost in detail here. Can you briefly tell us what is the most important relationship weakness in communication?"

A second common challenge is if a partner wants to debate the "truth" about his or her relationship, and disagrees with either his or her spouse or the assessment results. In the former instance, exploring how the two partners might develop different views can be useful: "So it seems Jess sees your communication as good, whereas Lesley feels it is not good. Let's see if we can understand that difference. Jess, what do you feel is good about the communication?" The educator can then look for areas of agreement about communication (or whatever the topic might be at the time), as well as any specific identified areas of different viewpoints. In the case of disagreement with the assessment results, it is useful to restate the ground rules that emphasize that the assessment is a basis for suggestions to be considered. I point out that the answers someone gives on a particular day can be influenced by a range of factors like mood, what has happened during the day, or how the person interprets the question at the time.

A third common challenge is if someone is reacting negatively to his or her spouse's comment(s). Defensive and negative reactions to a partner's comments can be reduced if we help partners express their concerns about the relationship in positive ways, ways that make it easier for the spouse to respond constructively. Often there is a positive motive lurking underneath a criticism. For example, "He is a terrible communicator" and "He does not listen to me" often reflect that the complaining partner desperately wants and values positive communication with his or her spouse. Similarly, comments like "We never have fun anymore" and "She is never happy with anything we do" often reflect a desire for fun. The educator can try to reframe complaints by asking questions that probe for the underlying positive motivation.

> EDUCATOR: Geraldine, what do you see as the major challenges you face?
>
> GERALDINE: Well, Chao is very unemotional, you know, he never really says what he is feeling.
>
> EDUCATOR: So, you really value, want to know how Chao feels?
>
> GERALDINE: Well, how can we be close when he never shows me any affection, or talks about anything important?
>
> EDUCATOR: This seems really important to you Geraldine. Help Chao and me to understand what makes it important to you. What does it do for you if Chao expresses positive feelings toward you?
>
> GERALDINE: It doesn't happen.
>
> EDUCATOR: And you are saying you would like this, so if Chao looked you in the eyes, smiled, and told you he loved you, or if he reached out and held your hand and said he was proud to have you as his partner, what would that do for you?
>
> GERALDINE: (*with a tear in her eye*) I would feel secure, know that I really was still loved.
>
> EDUCATOR: That would feel really special, really warm?
>
> GERALDINE: Yes.
>
> EDUCATOR: Chao, Geraldine is saying something pretty important here. What is it that is important to her about you expressing affection?

It is important to note that the educator persists in trying to be empathic with what Geraldine is saying, as well as seeking out the positive motivation underlying the complaint. In addition to helping people to express concerns positively, the educator needs to highlight negative reactions, and encourage receptiveness to the spouse's concerns: "Lesley, it seems you disagree with

Jess here. There will always be some areas where any couples will not agree, and this might be one. At the same time, it is really important that you and I make sure we understand Jess. Jess, can you tell me more about . . . ?"

A fourth challenge is if a partner finds it difficult to specify a self-change goal. One common reason for this challenge is that the person believes the relationship currently is functioning well, and finds it hard to identify a relationship-enhancing change. In that case I would ask the person to be as precise as possible about what are the most important strengths of the relationship, and explore how the person could ensure that these strengths are maintained or built upon, as illustrated in the transcript below.

> EDUCATOR: Terri, what would you like to do to strengthen your relationship with Brian?
>
> TERRI: Uh, well . . . things seem to be pretty good right now.
>
> EDUCATOR: So, is there anything that you want to fine-tune? Make even better?
>
> TERRI: Not that I can think of right now.
>
> EDUCATOR: So what do you think is going right?
>
> TERRI: Well, like we discussed, we have fun together, we communicate well, we support each other.
>
> EDUCATOR: Terrific. Those are important parts of a great relationship. Tell me about having fun together. What do you do to help the two of have fun?
>
> TERRI: We both like martial arts, we go to karate together, we encourage each other.
>
> EDUCATOR: Great, so you support Brian and he supports you in the karate?
>
> TERRI: Yeah.

At this point the educator could highlight the need to keep reinventing fun things to do together (remember the information on the importance of novelty in relationships to sustain passion?), and explore what new things they might want to do together and how Terri could contribute to that. The educator also could explore under what circumstances having fun might get less frequent (e.g., pressure at work, sick relatives needing care, having children to care for), and how the couple could manage to sustain fun under times of pressure. The goal is to have partners think about how to sustain and build on their relationship strengths, if they do not see any major challenges they wish to address.

A second reason for partners' difficulty in defining a self-change goal is if they find it hard to think in concrete behavioral terms. The educator can help the partner refine any vague goals (e.g., to be nicer to each other, to have more fun) and make them more specific (e.g., to make requests for change of each other politely, to arrange specific fun activities so they can spend quality time together). Questions like, "Specifically what would you like to do and when?" and "If I had a camera recording you doing this what would I see?" can help people to be more concrete.

A third reason for failing to define self-change goals is that one or both partners is distressed in the relationship. Distressed couples often need substantial structure and time during the assessment process to reach a point where they are willing to identify specific actions they personally can take to enhance the relationship (Halford, 2001). If a couple scores low on current relationship satisfaction, and struggles to define self-change goals, then couple therapy rather than CRE is likely to be more helpful. In essence the RELATE feedback session provides the educator with a sample of the couple's readiness to change, reflected in their capacity to identify relationship strengths, to discuss constructively the challenges that are identified, and to develop realistic self-change goals. If there is low readiness to change, then further assessment and interventions other than CRE are indicated.

The key criteria for readiness to change using CRE are that at the end of the feedback session, the educator and the couple have jointly identified the couple's relationship strengths and challenges, the couple has developed a statement of relationship goals, and each partner has identified some preliminary self-change goals he or she wishes to work on. If the couple has moderate or high risk for future relationship problems, but there are no contraindications for CRE, then Couple CARE is likely to be the agreed-upon means by which the couple will work on their relationship. The remaining chapters of this book detail how to deliver Couple CARE in face-to-face sessions.

CHAPTER 4

Couple CARE

Program Overview and Tips for Implementation

This chapter provides an overview of the content covered in the Couple CARE program and the learning processes used in the program. It also provides some practical tips for delivering the program in a variety of modalities, including face-to-face groups, face-to-face sessions with a single couple, and flexible delivery mode.

COUPLE CARE PROGRAM CONTENT

Couple CARE consists of six units that are designed to address the needs of most couples. Couple CARE emphasizes that there is no one right way to have a great relationship. Each couple is assisted to define how they want to relate. This approach involves the couple being provided information and undertaking experiential exercises to clarify their beliefs about what constitutes a good relationship, and to develop shared and realistic expectations for their relationship (described in Couple CARE as the "relationship vision"). Couples also are assisted in developing their relationship skills, self-evaluating their current behavior in the relationship, and self-selecting personal changes intended to help realize their relationship vision.

Couple CARE does not prescribe particular ways of relating. Instead the emphasis is on relationship self-change. This self-change focus encourages each partner in the relationship to take active responsibility for sustaining and enhancing the relationship. Couple CARE covers those areas identified in the research reviewed in Chapter 1 as predicting future relationship satisfaction, and in Chapter 2 as the components of effective CRE.

Table 4.1 summarizes the content covered in the Couple CARE program. (In Chapter 10 I describe how to modify the content in Table 4.1 to address the special needs of particular couples.) Unit 1, Self-Change, has two key aims: (1) to help the couple set goals about the sort of relationship they want, and (2) to understand the role of self-change in achieving those relationship goals. The content on relationship goals includes introducing the concepts of standards (how relationships should be) and expectations (how this relationship will likely be in the future); and having partners clarify their standards and expectations in key areas like gender roles, communication, and power and control. In Couple CARE, structured exercises provide the opportunity for each partner to explore how his or her life experiences have influenced his or her current relationship expectations, discuss these ideas with his or her partner, and then develop a shared relationship vision based on the ideals and values that are important to them. Couples are encouraged to identify specific behavioral markers that will indicate when they are achieving their vision.

The first unit also introduces a process of self-change. Each partner is asked to develop and implement self-change plans in each of the units of Couple CARE. In Unit 1 we introduce a five-step process of relationship self-change that is used in all subsequent units: (1) *describe*, which involves defining a relationship area for focus; (2) *focus*, which is identifying current behavior and evaluating the strengths and weaknesses of that current behav-

TABLE 4.1. Content of the Couple CARE Program

Unit	Title	Content
1	Self-Change	Relationship expectations; relationship goals; self-change to achieve goals.
2	Communication	Model of communication; speaking and listening; self-evaluation of communication; emotional bids; self-change of communication.
3	Intimacy and Caring	Expressions of caring; balance of individual, couple, and other activities; mutual support; self-change of intimacy.
4	Managing Differences	Value of individual differences; effective communication during conflict; conflict management guidelines; self-change of conflict management.
5	Sexuality	Sexual myths; sexual preferences; communication about sexuality; self-change to enhance sexuality.
6	Looking Ahead	Anticipating change; planning for change; early identification of relationship problems; maintaining a relationship focus; self-change for managing the future.

ior; (3) *goal*, that is, defining clear behaviorial self-change goals; (4) *act*, which is implementing the self-change; and (5) *evaluate*, which is reviewing whether the desired self-change was achieved, and if so evaluating the effects of that change.

Unit 2, Communication, involves presentation of a model of good communication that includes clear speaking and active listening. There is demonstration of what good communication looks like, as well as how to self-assess communication. The couple completes specific discussion exercises, which include partners providing constructive feedback to each other on their communication. In addition, the concept of emotional bids is introduced, which refers to subtle ways in which partners communicate their desire for emotional intimacy. Each partner is assisted in developing individual self-change plans to enhance their communication.

In Unit 3, Intimacy and Caring, there are three major foci: (1) partner support, (2) showing caring, and (3) balancing individual and couple activity. There is a description and demonstration of different forms of partner social support, and explanation of how support needs can vary from situation to situation. Through structured exercises, partners are encouraged to reflect on what sorts of support are helpful to them in various situations. The unit also describes the importance of showing caring in sustaining happy couple relationships, and how partners vary widely in their preferred ways of expressing caring. Partners are encouraged to experiment with different acts of caring and to monitor their partner's response to their offerings of caring. Finally, there is discussion of the importance of individual time and couple time, and the need to balance time use. Couples complete structured tasks to discuss how they support each other and how they express caring, They also reflect on their current mix of individual and couple activities, and are given suggestions for new individual and couple activities. The partners identify and implement self-change to help them enhance their relationship in these key areas.

In Unit 4, Managing Differences, it is suggested that differences are a normal part of any relationship that, when well managed, benefit both partners. The application of effective communication (as described in Unit 2) to help manage and resolve differences is demonstrated, as are a range of strategies for managing conflict. Finally, the unit includes a review of how people can recover after conflict and prevent it from having major long-term negative consequences. Structured exercises encourage partners to discuss an area of difference using the communication skills developed in Unit 2. The partners self-assess their communication and develop self-change plans to enhance their communication about differences. The couple is also encouraged to review a range of conflict management strategies, and to select the strategies that they think might be useful for them as a couple. Finally, each partner reviews how he or she typically responds after conflict, and suggests ways in which that approach could be improved. As in previous units, each partner develops and implements a self-change plan.

In Unit 5, Sexuality, the major focus is on enhancing couples' communication about sexuality. The content educates partners about the strong association between sexual satisfaction and relationship satisfaction, and demonstrates the role of effective communication in fostering sexual satisfaction. There also is discussion of how partners do not always feel like having sex at the same time, and how differences in sexual desire can be managed. There is also a description of how changing life circumstances, such as stress and having children, can impact on sexuality. Finally, the nature of common sexual problems is described. Readings describe and challenge some common myths that may lead to unrealistic sexual expectations (e.g., "sex is all about achieving orgasm"). Partners are invited to discuss these myths, aspects of their current sex life that they do and do not like, and how they communicate about their sexuality.

The sixth and final unit, Looking Ahead, focuses on helping couples adapt to life changes, sustain their commitment to their long-term relationship goals, and maintain a relationship focus as a central life priority. The unit introduces the ideas of how changing life events impact on couples, and how to anticipate and prevent the potential negative effects of such changes. The content also addresses how to sustain a relationship focus and celebrate the relationship. In structured exercises couples are asked to identify life changes that are likely to occur, to anticipate the relationship consequences of those changes, and to develop a plan to maximize positive and minimize negative relationship effects. The couple is invited to review and update the relationship vision they developed in Unit 1 and discuss how they will maintain that vision. Couples also are encouraged to plan ahead to celebrate their relationship regularly as a means of enhancing satisfaction. Finally, there is discussion of the early warning signs of emerging relationship problems, and what help is available should a partner believe problems are developing in the relationship.

MODES OF DELIVERING COUPLE CARE

In order to enhance accessibility of CRE, it is useful to consider what modes of delivery are attractive to couples. Table 4.2 is a summary of some of the possible modes of delivery of CRE, and the advantages and disadvantages of these various possibilities. Many providers of CRE offer it in a range of delivery modes, recognizing that different delivery modes are likely to appeal to different couples. Surveys of relationship education providers show that face-to-face delivery, either with individual couples or with groups of couples,

TABLE 4.2. Some Possible Formats of Skill-Based Couple Relationship Education

Format	Advantages	Disadvantages
Regular weekly face-to-face sessions for couple groups; six 2-hour sessions	Group members can learn from each other; information can be presented efficiently; leader can reach many couples at once; spaced sessions allow couples to practice skills between sessions.	Scheduling multiple couples to attend sessions at a fixed time on a regular basis can be challenging; some couples dislike groups; challenging to tailor content to individual couple needs; if a couple misses one or more sessions this can be difficult to manage.
Intensive couple face-to-face workshop; typically 14 hours of face-to-face contact spread over 2 days	Group members can learn from each other; information can be presented efficiently; leader can reach many couples at once; short but intense time commitment from couples can be easier for couples to manage than weekly sessions.	Scheduling multiple couples to attend at a fixed time can be challenging; some couples dislike groups; challenging to tailor content to individual couple needs; requires attention to logistics like meals and possibly accommodation; intense format does not allow couples time to practice skills at home.
Regular weekly face-to-face sessions of about 1 hour for an individual couple over 6 weeks	Content can be tailored to accommodate individual couple needs; duration of education can be negotiated to meet couple's needs; spaced sessions allow couple to practice skills between sessions; couples who value privacy and confidentiality value this format.	Can be an expensive process for the couple; travel and time commitments can be substantial.
Flexible delivery to individual couples; takes couples about 2 hours per week over 6 weeks	Couple complete programs in their own time, in privacy; educators can use their time efficiently as the couple do much of the work themselves; reaches couples who cannot access face-to-face sessions; can utilize Web, DVD, and other audiovisual media to make an interactive experience; couples who value privacy and confidentiality value this format. Some forms can be highly cost-effective, such as Web-based couple assessment.	Requires well-developed educational materials; requires couples to have access to relevant technology (e.g., Web access, DVD player); some couples like face-to-face contact; educators need to develop their skills in sustaining couple engagement through telephone- or Internet-based contact.

is the most common method of providing CRE (Halford & Simons, 2005; Stanley et al., 2006). However, couples are increasingly seeking information about their relationship via the Internet, and CRE via flexible delivery is becoming more popular (Halford & Casey, 2010).

When running Couple CARE with groups of couples the ideas are introduced and the couples do exercises in the sessions, and this process allows use of the group processes to enhance learning. The content of each of the units can be covered in a 2-hour group session. This book will focus predominantly on this group mode of delivery, but also suggests ways that the procedures can be adapted for other modes of delivery. In group delivery mode couples usually complete the RELATE assessment in preparation for the first session. Feedback and discussion of those assessment results are best done with the couples before the first group session, in either face-to-face or telephone-based discussion, but it is also possible to do a group-based review of the RELATE assessment.

Couple CARE can also be delivered in an intensive 2-day workshop. For example, Couple CARE can be delivered as a weekend retreat with about 14 hours needed for covering the content. Combining this modality with a weekend accommodation package in a romantic location is an attractive option for couples with the money to afford this sort of experience. It is possible to add fun and romance to the experience by including in the weekend couple activities like wine tasting, cooking lessons, or instruction in massage.

After weekend retreats I give couples the option of having a follow-up session. This option has proved popular with many couples as it gives them the chance to review their application of the learning from the weekend, and to fine-tune any further relationship changes they wish to make. The follow-up can be done face to face or by telephone. The follow-up session is used to review the ideas covered in the units and anything else the couple wishes to focus on.

Couple CARE can also be delivered in face-to-face mode in weekly sessions with one couple. In this mode completing one unit per week over 6 weeks seems to work well. In working face to face with an individual couple it is possible to work through the same ideas and tasks as with the group delivery format.[1]

---

[1] I usually provide the Couple CARE resource materials to the couple and suggest that the partners watch the unit DVD segment and do the exercises in the guidebook prior to our session. This allows the face-to-face session to be focused on reviewing the couple's understanding of the ideas, acquisition of skills, and implementation of their self-change plans. Some couples struggle to regularly complete the tasks before sessions. When that is a persistent problem, an option is to have the couple book a 90-minute session, and they spend the first 45 minutes watching the DVD and doing the exercises together. Then the educator joins them and assists the couple to complete the tasks and apply the ideas and skills.

When Couple CARE is provided in flexible delivery mode, couples complete the program at home, and need access to the Couple CARE materials. In this modality I have couples complete an initial RELATE assessment and then suggest they aim to complete one unit per week over 6 weeks. Following this schedule, the typical weekly time commitment for couples is 15 minutes to watch the DVD, 60 minutes to do the individual and couple exercises, and 45 minutes for the telephone call with the educator. The flexible delivery mode does allow the couple to negotiate whether they want to complete the program more quickly, or space out units over a more extended period. However, weekly completion of units provides most couples with reasonable time to complete the various tasks, while limiting the duration of time they are committing to working on the program. It also encourages the partners to establish a routine for completing units, such as setting aside a particular evening each week.

CRE can make use of different combinations of the modes of delivery to enhance accessibility and cost-effectiveness. For example, the Couple Care for Parents program (CCP; Halford, Petch, & Creedy, 2010) involves six learning units delivered in a mix of face-to-face groups, home visits to a single couple, and flexible delivery. A full-day face-to-face workshop is provided to groups of couples when the expectant mother is about 6–7 months pregnant. Many couples are keen to access CRE at that time, and willing and able to set aside time to attend a full-day session. The group session allows couples to learn from other couples about the diversity of expectations and approaches couples take to sharing parenthood.

In CCP, couples complete the final prebirth and all four postbirth units at home, avoiding the inconvenience of travel when in advanced pregnancy or when caring for a young infant. There are two home visits by a relationship educator, one in the last month before the birth and the second about a month after the birth of the child. The visits give the educator an opportunity to observe the home environment, which provides information on how the couple is managing. For example, if the home is very untidy with few safe places for the infant to explore, then education and assistance can be provided to develop a safe and stimulating environment for the child. The last three units of CCP are done in flexible delivery mode and involve the couple watching a section of a DVD, completing structured exercises together, and having a telephone call with an educator. The flexible delivery is cheaper and easier to implement than the home visits, as it does not involve travel for the educator, and allows couples to complete the program in their own home and at times that suit them.

It is possible to use a mix of modes of CRE delivery in the same program for different couples, depending on their preferences. For example, I run a weekend relationship enrichment program for couples. I use the Web-based RELATE assessment with couples who attend this workshop, asking them to complete the assessment before coming to the workshop. This allows each partner to complete the initial assessment at a time and place that suits him or her. Once both partners have completed the assessment, I can access the report that is computer-generated and then discuss that report with the couple. However, if one or both partners do not have access to the Web, or dislike the idea of Web-based assessment, I can provide the assessment as a written questionnaire.

LEARNING PROCESSES IN COUPLE CARE

A distinctive characteristic of Couple CARE is that it offers an active, skill-focused approach to CRE. This means the sessions focus on having the couples try out new ways of relating, and having spouses talk to each other about their relationship. There is some didactic input from the educator (or the DVD, when the program is provided in flexible delivery mode), but face-to-face sessions are structured primarily around couple-based activities. These activities always lead partners toward defining changes they wish to implement in their relationship between sessions.

A second distinctive characteristic of the Couple CARE program is that it seeks to promote relationship self-regulation, which is a metacompetence (learning to learn) rather than a skill. In the adult education literature, self-regulated learners are characterized as setting realistic and meaningful goals for themselves based on accurate self-assessment, implementing change to achieve those self-selected goals, self-evaluating their progress toward their goals, planning and trying new strategies, and persisting in the implementation of strategies (Purdie, Hattie, & Douglas, 1996). Relationship self-regulation is being able to self-guide required learning about one's relationship, and self-manage the relationship change process. In developing Couple CARE the aim was to empower partners to enhance their long-term relationship by developing relationship self-regulation.

The learning processes in Couple CARE incorporate two key principles of adult learning, principles that facilitate self-directed learning and enhance the acquisition of metacompetencies like relationship self-regulation. First, Couple CARE is designed to reflect Kolb's (1984) experiential learning cycle. Second, it provides repeated opportunities to practice the components of the metacompetence (relationship self-regulation), as has been recommended by Kember, Jenkins, and Ng (2003) and Laurillard (1992, 2002).

Kolb's cycle has wide currency in adult education. Significant empirical support indicates that it does describe how people learn from experience (Lizzio & Wilson, 2004). Kolb (1984) describes the learning process as an iterative four-stage cycle: (1) a concrete experience followed by (2) observation

and reflection, leading to (3) the formation of abstract concepts and general-
izations, leading to (4) hypotheses to be tested and applied in future action,
which in turn leads to new experiences. In essence, this means people often
learn from experiences and reflections on those experiences. It is necessary to
provide didactic input (e.g., lectures, videotape demonstrations) to introduce
abstract ideas (e.g., a model of good communication). However, experiences
that prompt people to be reflective around issues related to the idea (e.g., seeing an example of poor communication and being asked to reflect on what
makes it poor communication) often enhances receptiveness and understanding of the abstract idea. Furthermore, once the idea is introduced, adults are
unlikely to apply it without experiences that prompt them to apply and then
reflect on the idea (e.g., communicate with their partner and then use the
model to self-evaluate their own communication).

The experiences in each Couple CARE unit reflect Kolb's (1984) experiential learning cycle. Each unit in Couple CARE begins with an experience
to prompt reflection, followed by an input of ideas, and modeling of key
relationship skills. The presentation is structured to prompt further reflection
on the personal relevance of the ideas and skills. For example, in the group
format the Couple CARE unit on communication begins by eliciting comments from different couples about what constitutes good communication
and the importance of communication in a couple's relationship. Each couple
is invited to reflect on the different ideas offered by a variety of other couples.
This is followed by modeling of good communication, and description of a
model of effective communication.[2] Partners then talk together, reflecting on
the strengths and weaknesses of their communication. In face-to-face delivery
(with groups or individual couples) the educator can model the key relationship skills via a demonstration.

Exercises in each unit of Couple CARE enable couples to relate the ideas
and skills introduced in the program to their relationship. The exercises are
a mixture of partners working independently and together, with each person
self-appraising his or her own behavior and personal history in relation to a
particular relationship topic (e.g., communication, caring, and support); setting his or her own goals for a desired self-change with the aim of improving
their relationship; developing realistic strategies for implementing and monitoring the change; and seeking feedback on the progress and effectiveness of
their change efforts. The learning for each unit is completed with a written
self-change plan that helps each partner to both consolidate and apply his

[2] Alternatively, the educator can show the relevant segments of the Couple CARE DVD.
In the flexible delivery mode, the modeling of skills is provided primarily through the
DVD, though this can be supplemented by demonstrations by the educator during tele-
phone-based review sessions.

or her learning. The program provides a structure that combines individual reflection with opportunities for couples to progressively share, discuss, and negotiate ideas and behaviors as they work through the tasks in each unit. Thus, consistent with Kolb's learning cycle, the program is structured to give couples experiences and prompt reflection on those experiences.

In group face-to-face delivery the exercises completed by the couple are complemented with group discussion. For example, in the first unit couples are asked to reflect upon what constitutes a great relationship. I often have each couple talk about a couple they know who they think has a great relationship, and what behaviors they notice in the partners that lead them to classify it as a great relationship. I then ask each couple to tell the group a key relationship behavior they have identified as characteristic of a great relationship, and we write the behaviors each couple identified up on the board. Having couples discuss what they think are the most important behaviors highlights that there often are behaviors important to most couples, and also behaviors that are important to only some couples. (Later chapters provide examples of group exercises for each Couple CARE unit.)

After couples have completed the exercises, the educator's role is to prompt and support couples through the program. In particular, the educator reviews the concepts introduced by the lectures or discussion in face-to-face mode, and the exercises completed by the couple.[3] The educator focuses on promoting self-directed learning by shaping and modeling self-change skills. For example, in Unit 2, Communication, the educator listens to a sample of the couple's communication and then asks each partner to self-appraise his or her own communication. These self-appraisals are shaped by the educator to ensure that each partner has developed realistic and concrete ideas about specific strengths and weaknesses, which can be used to generate self-change goals. It is important to note that self-directed learning does not mean there is no input from the educator, but rather that the educator helps the partners to clarify and define their learning goals.

The research in adult education shows that interaction with an educator is often vital to learning (Rourke & Anderson, 2002). Specifically, learners often report the need for such contact to sustain engagement with the programs of learning, and feel they need to receive meaningful feedback quickly in order to guide future performance (Carmichael, 2001). The RELATE assessment is available to couples over the Internet, but there is no convincing evidence that couples can benefit from receiving an assessment and interpreting it themselves. In my experience couples who access such reports and have poor conflict management skills often find the report to be

---

[3] In flexible delivery mode the DVD and partner guidebooks introduce the content to be reviewed.

a source of disagreement. Even though Couple CARE can be completed in large part by couples at home if they have access to the program materials, the program was not designed to be a self-help program for couples. It has not been evaluated for its efficacy without an educator, and for that reason the program materials are only made available to educators rather than to couples.

The skills required of the educator are similar whether the program is provided in face-to-face or flexible delivery mode. The educator needs to have the content knowledge about the major influences on couple relationships, to be able to demonstrate the core skills covered in the program, and to have the teaching skills to assist couples through the program. Figure 4.1 summarizes the core educator skills that are important for delivering Couple CARE effectively. The figure is formatted such that you can self-evaluate your current skills, or ask a colleague who knows your work well to give you an honest evaluation. Scores range up to maximum of 116, and a score of at least 60 is a minimum skill level needed to deliver the program adequately.[4]

HOW TO RUN GROUP SESSIONS OF COUPLE CARE

There are four issues that you need to consider before starting to run CRE groups. The first is the number of couples to include in group sessions. This might be influenced by the rate of couples expressing interest in your program. I usually run group sessions for between four and six couples. Any less than four couples and it can be hard to develop an effective group process. To maintain active skill training and attention for each couple, which is central to the Couple CARE approach, about one educator to every four couples is desirable. Groups with more than six couples can be run effectively, but require more than one educator to be present. If you have more than one educator, having an educator of each gender present is an advantage.

A second consideration is the venue. You will need a large enough room to comfortably seat all the couples in movable seats, and to allow the couples to space themselves out from each other when they are doing couple exercises. The spacing provides some privacy, and prevents the noise of others from being too distracting. Arrangement of seats into a half circle is helpful, as it allows the participants to see and talk to each other, while being able to see and hear the educator(s) when they are at the front.

---

[4]Individuals who would like further training in delivering CRE can e-mail *couplecare@ psy.uq.edu.au* for information on training in Couple CARE, visit *www.prepinc.com* for information on training in the PREP relationship education program, or review the *www.smartmarriages.com* website, which promotes a range of training opportunities.

Please rate your current level of knowledge and skill in each of the areas listed below, using the following key:

0	No skill
1	Some skill
2	Adequate skill level
3	Good skill level
4	Excellent skill level

KNOWLEDGE AREAS

1. Summarize and analyze key psychological influences on couple relationship satisfaction and stability.
2. Analyze marriage and relationship education outcome research.
3. Describe key risk indicators and risk factors that put couples at risk for marriage and relationship problems.

COUPLE CARE DELIVERY SKILLS

1. Assess the couple's relationship education needs and goals, and determine if the Couple CARE program is appropriate.
2. Describe the key dimensions of couple relationship expectations, and the role of family of origin and other learning experiences on development of those expectations.
3. Introduce the importance of relationship goal setting to couples.
4. Help partners identify the key aspects of their relationship visions and discuss how these relate to setting relationship goals.
5. Demonstrate key listening and speaking skills.
6. Describe and give examples of emotional bids in couple communication.
7. Help partners self-assess and set goals for communication enhancement.
8. Help couples understand the need for self-assessment and goal setting in both the social-support and acts-of-caring areas.
9. Help partners self-assess both their social support and acts of caring, then help them set goals for enhancement in these areas.
10. Help partners identify changes to their shared/individual activities that would enhance their relationship, and offer suggestions for change where appropriate.

(cont.)

FIGURE 4.1. Couple CARE leader knowledge and skills.

11. Describe key conflict patterns, guidelines for managing conflict, and ground rules for managing conflict.

12. Help partners self-assess and set goals for using guidelines and ground rules for managing conflict, and provide appropriate suggestions for change/fine-tuning to meet couples' needs where necessary.

13. Discuss with partners the importance of *experimenting* with guidelines and ground rules, noting that it may take some fine-tuning and ongoing review to find the combination that suits them best.

14. Help partners identify strengths and weaknesses in their current communication in relation to sex.

15. Help partners set goals for enhancement of their sexual relationship.

16. Describe the common changes occurring in couples' lives in the early years of their relationship, and the adaptations couples need to make.

17. Help couples to self-assess likely changes in their future, identify the likely effects of those changes, and develop plans for adapting to those changes.

18. Assist couples in identifying ways they can self-assess and maintain their relationship skills over time and set goals for future development.

RELATIONSHIP EDUCATION PROCESS SKILLS

1. Provide clear instructions on the content and process of couple activities and facilitation activities.

2. Identify blocks to learning for one or both partners and assist them to problem-solve to overcome those barriers.

3. Respond positively and negotiate appropriately with partners who respond negatively to activities or input.

4. Fully engage both partners in activities and discussions.

5. Provide empathic support to partners in their efforts to enhance their relationship and assist partners to problem-solve barriers in the relationship.

6. Review barriers to completion of program tasks for partners who do not engage in more than half the tasks/activities and negotiate appropriate future engagement with couples.

7. Present ideas in an engaging manner with appropriate use of examples, humor, and interaction with partners.

8. Develop an appropriate balance of unstructured and structured discussion so that discussion of the couple's concerns/issues can be balanced with completion of tasks.

FIGURE 4.1. *(cont.)*

Equipment is a third consideration. Couples and the educator(s) will need to write. Providing clipboards for the participants allows them to complete written exercises without desks or tables acting as barriers to interaction. A whiteboard or flip chart is essential for the educator(s) and group members to write up comments and key points during the session. If the group is larger, with more than six couples, it can be very helpful to have a radio microphone (to allow moving around the group) and an amplifier for the educator(s), so they do not have to strain to project their voices in order to be heard. Women, who typically have softer voices than men, might want to use a microphone even in smaller groups.[5]

The fourth issue is the most difficult. Child care can be a very useful service to provide if you seek to engage couples with young children, particularly if you are working with couples with low income who find paying for child care a hardship. Establishing child care facilities is an important responsibility and needs to be worked out well ahead of scheduling sessions. It is important to make clear to couples well ahead of time whether child care is available.

One other issue you might want to consider is how you will manage if a couple, or a partner, misses a session. You might want to offer the chance of an extra session for the couple (with a fee attached) to catch up on the material that they missed. Alternatively, you might give the opportunity to make up a missed session with flexible delivery, and provide the couple with self-directed materials to allow them to complete the work in their own time.

Sending couples a letter (or e-mail) ahead of the first session is useful. I send a letter that welcomes the couple to the program and congratulates them on their decision to invest time in enhancing their relationship. The letter provides people with directions on how to get to the center, with a map and clear directions for public transport and parking. In the letter couples are encouraged to arrive at least 5 minutes before the scheduled starting time. I indicate that the sessions will start promptly at the designated time, and we will complete the sessions at the specified time. Providing these key pieces of information can help get the first session off to a good start.

---

[5] If you plan to make use of DVD clips from the Couple CARE materials, you will also need a data projector, screen, and computer at the front of the room. In larger groups you will need a sound system to make sure the DVD can be heard.

CHAPTER 5

Unit 1
Self-Change

This chapter describes how to provide the first unit of Couple CARE to a group of couples. Because it is the first session, it is the first time a group of couples comes together. Some attention needs to be paid to developing a constructive group process; this chapter starts with a description of how to go about creating this process. The rest of the chapter focuses on how to provide the content of Unit 1, which is summarized in Table 5.1.

The overall aim of Unit 1 is to help couples clarify and refine their relationship goals, and to apply the process of self-change to enhance their relationship. The unit begins by inviting the partners to reflect on what they

TABLE 5.1. Overview of Unit 1: Self-Change

Topic and aim	Exercise(s)
Establishing positive group process	An-ice breaker exercise.
Clarifying source and nature of relationship expectations	Reflections on general relationship expectations; educator introduces dimensions of relationship expectations; individuals and couples reflect on impact of prior relationship experiences on relationship expectations.
Developing a relationship vision of shared and realistic relationship expectations	Educator introduces ideas of realistic relationship expectations; individual and couple reflect on relationship expectations.
Self-change	Educator introduces idea of self-change; individuals develop self-change plan to enhance their relationship.

think constitutes a great, long-term relationship. To develop these ideas further, couples are provided with a way of describing relationship expectations. They are then asked to describe their current relationship expectations, and how these expectations might have been shaped by their family of origin and other relationship experiences. The partners are also asked to consider which of their current expectations are likely to be helpful in sustaining their relationship, and whether any expectations might be unhelpful. Initially, the partners reflect on their relationship expectations individually. Next, the couple discusses their individual expectations and identify areas of similarities and differences concerning their expectations. Each partner individually develops a written statement of his or her relationship vision, and then they jointly develop a written statement of their shared relationship vision. The importance of self-change focus is explained, the steps involved in self-change are described and demonstrated, and then each partner is assisted in developing a personal self-change plan. The aim, by the end of this session, is for each partner to identify a specific action he or she wishes to make to enhance the couple relationship.

BEGINNING THE FIRST GROUP SESSION

When a couple arrives I show the partners into the room and make a point of introducing myself to each couple and asking a couple of questions to get them talking. I then introduce each couple to at least one other couple. I make sure to start the first session on time.

Ground Rules for Group Couple CARE

When conducting group sessions of Couple CARE it is helpful to establish some basic ground rules for group sessions, which maximize the advantages of that format. Table 5.2 lists some ground rules that are useful to review. Three guidelines should be emphasized at the start of the first session. You could introduce the ground rules with words something like the following:

> "Welcome everyone, it is great to see you all. Congratulations on taking a really important step to having the very best relationship you can, by putting aside time to focus on your relationship and come to this group. Great relationships don't just happen, partners need to nurture and care for them. We will work with you to help you nurture your relationship.
> "There are a few ground rules I want to mention about how we run the group sessions that seem to make them work better for everybody.

TABLE 5.2. Suggestions for Group Ground Rules

Ground rule	Rationale
The sessions are about making good relationships stronger, even better, and helping them to stay strong for the long run.	Almost all couples aspire to a lifelong, quality relationship, but only about half achieve this. Learning what you are doing that is helpful is important—so you can keep doing it—and learning what you can change to make your relationship even better is good too.
There is no one right way to have a great relationship; each couple will find their own way.	It is important that differences in beliefs and values are respected both within a relationship and between couples.
Sessions begin and end at the scheduled time; the leader makes sure we stick to time. Please come 5 minutes early to sessions, so we can start promptly.	This is fair to everyone and prevents wasted time.
What is said in the sessions is confidential and is not to be repeated outside the group.	People need to feel free to discuss issues in the group that are important to them.
Respect is important to relationships. Listen to your partner and to other people; do not interrupt.	Everyone needs to be able to state his or her opinion.
Some aspects of a couple relationship are private, and the staff and group members should respect a couple's right not to talk about some aspects of their relationship.	The educator needs to help each couple find a balance of sufficient self-disclosure to benefit from the program without feeling pressure to disclose what they regard as private.
A balance of work and fun makes the group go well.	It should be enjoyable, but also task-focused.
If you are having problems, speak to the leader.	Even if couples are assessed carefully before the group sessions, it is still possible for a couple to struggle with ideas or to uncover challenges in their relationship that are of concern.
If a couple must miss a session we cannot go over material for them in the group. A couple can make up the content with an individual session or by doing the unit at home, but has to pay for the extra educator time involved.	This prevents group sessions repeating material, which is unfair to couples who attend each session. At the same time it allows couples to keep up if they have an unavoidable scheduling problem.

First, after 25 years of running sessions, I now am confident that there is no one right way to have a great relationship. These sessions are not about telling you what to do. The whole point of the Couple CARE program is to help each of you define as a couple how you want your relationship to be, and for you to be in charge of shaping your relationship. Second, respect for the views and opinions of others—your partner and other group members—is really important. Let people finish what they are saying. Do not immediately disagree with someone. Instead, think about what you hear, and be open to new ways of doing things. Third, some bits of your relationship are private. There are some things that happen between my wife and me that only she and I know about, and we like it that way. Different couples will have different boundaries about what they want to discuss in a group like this. A lot of the work we do will involve you talking with your partner. We will invite you to discuss things with the rest of the group, but you should feel free to say: 'I would rather not talk about this to the group'—and that is fine."

One goal in the first group session is to help the group members get to know each other a little, and to feel comfortable talking with each other. A common method of breaking the ice is to have people introduce themselves to the group. That works satisfactorily most of the time, though for people who are less comfortable in groups that can be a slightly daunting way to start. Table 5.3 describes four different possible ice-breaker exercises that focus on couple relationships, but also provide a comfortable way for couples to talk together. Any of these exercises can be effective, so you might like to experiment to find what works best for you and the couples with whom you work.

RELATIONSHIP EXPECTATIONS

Engaging Couples in Thinking about What Makes a Great Relationship

As noted in Chapter 1, realistic shared expectations are a strong predictor of couples sustaining high relationship satisfaction. Therefore, Couple CARE begins by aiding couples to clarify their expectations. The aim is to help couples develop an understanding of the dimensions of relationship expectations; to reflect on their current expectations and how those expectations might have developed; and to negotiate shared, realistic expectations with their partners.

The first step is to engage couples in reflecting on what constitutes a great relationship. A very useful exercise is to have couples reflect on what behaviors contribute to a great long-term relationship. One way to do this is

TABLE 5.3. Possible Ice-Breaker Exercises for Couple CARE Groups

1. Have the couples talk together in pairs of couples for 5 minutes, telling each other their names, how long they have been together, and one thing they really enjoy doing as a couple. Each couple then briefly introduces the couple with whom they spoke to the group.

2. Have the couples talk together in pairs of couples for 5 minutes, telling each other their names, and discussing together at least two possible romantic ways to spend an anniversary. Each couple introduces themselves to the group, and reports on one of the ideas they generated for a romantic anniversary celebration.

3. Have the couples talk together in pairs of couples for 5 minutes, telling each other their names, with each couple describing one really romantic experience they have shared as a couple. Each couple introduces the other couple to the group and describe the romantic experience of that couple.

4. Play the Couple CARE DVD opening scene of a 30th wedding anniversary. The educator then asks the couples to imagine they are gathered at such a party. The educator states that she or he is going to continue the speech about the couple by stating one thing she or he believes the couple might do if they have a great 30-year marriage. The educator then suggests a specific behavior, such as they always listen to each other, always have fun, have a wide range of friends they each relate well to, and so on. The educator then invites other people to stand up, state their name, and describe a behavior the couple might have done that helped them have a great relationship.

to ask each couple to identify a couple they know (1) who has been together at least 10 years, and (2) whom they each regard as having a really good relationship. The partners are asked to make a list of behaviors that the successful couple does that they associate with their great relationship. The couples can be asked to report these ideas to the group, and the educator can write the ideas on a whiteboard.

A second possibility is to ask the group to imagine they are gathered for a couple's 30th anniversary, and that the couple has had a wonderful 30 years together. Group members can be asked to imagine they are close to the couple and have been asked to take just a minute or two to share an impression or anecdote that conveys something about how this special couple interacts together. The couples in the group each make a brief speech describing the couple of honor. We then talk about what people said, and how that relates to what constitutes a truly strong long-term relationship.

A third option for having couples reflect on what constitutes a great couple relationship is to play the first section of Unit 1 of the Couple CARE DVD, which depicts a party for a couple's 30th wedding anniversary. The couple's daughter is making a speech about her parents' relationship. The narrator invites viewers to consider what they would like family members and friends to say about their relationship with their spouse at their own 30th wedding anniversary. In particular, the narrator asks viewers to reflect on what observable behaviors help to build a great long-term relationship. The DVD segment can be used as a trigger to encourage couples to reflect on what they believe constitutes a great couple relationship.

Most groups of couples identify some combination of the following as constituting a great couple relationship: good communication, respect in how the partners speak to each other, provision of mutual support to cope with difficult life stresses, positive expression of affection, having fun together, having a sense of humor and laughing together, and shared decision making. If any of these key areas are omitted, the educator should raise them. It is also helpful to ask participants to give examples of observable behaviors that reflect each of these positive couple qualities. For example, what does good communication actually consist of? Aside from promoting discussion, the answers to these questions give the educator a sense of how easy each of the participants finds it to be behaviorally specific when discussing a couple relationship. The skill of being behaviorally specific is an important element of effective self-change.

It is also useful to pose the following question: "Are there behaviors that are private, that likely only the couple knows about, that are important in couple relationships?" Most groups will identify sexual behaviors as one such private area. There are also most likely some other private intimacies. The use of certain pet names is one example. Many couples also have private signals to communicate key ideas (e.g., some couples have a key word or gesture to signal when they want to leave a social event). Since many couple relationships include these private aspects, they might see talking about these intimacies with other people as a significant violation of trust.

One aspect of successful couple relationships is often overlooked by couples that the educator can usefully raise: the commitment to the relationship. *Commitment* is the extent to which each partner feels that being in the relationship is important, the idea that once you decide to be with someone, you stick to that commitment. Commitment might be based on religious ideas, though many nonreligious people also express strong relationship commitment. Commitment can be related to being married, though many couples who cohabit also report strong commitment to each other.

In talking about commitment I note to couples that surveys suggest that soon after marriage almost all couples expect and hope to be with their partners for the rest of their lives. At the same time studies of couples show that almost all couples have at least one difficult period in their relationship, when the sense of intimacy and love is not as strong. For example, when couples have very young children, the opportunity for the couple to have fun together often erodes, and a loss of interest in and enjoyment of sex is common. Across a lifetime ill health, job stress, financial difficulties, and disagreements with family and friends are all likely to be issues that impact on the couple relationship. A strong commitment to the relationship involves accepting that a loving life together will sometimes require some effort to renew the relationship if it becomes strained. Commitment means thinking about how to improve the relationship when things are not going so well. In contrast, low commitment is often associated with responding to relationship strains by thinking about leaving or fantasies about a relationship with someone else.

Relationship commitment does not mean staying in a really bad relationship. When violence, drug abuse, affairs, or other serious problems arise, considering whether to leave is very reasonable. Leaving a marriage that has severe problems might well be a very sensible choice. However, about half of all marital separations emerge from relationships that do not have severe problems like violence or affairs. Rather, many separations occur when the partners feel somewhat distant from each other. It is essential to mention that how to sustain relationship commitment is a key focus of the final unit of Couple CARE.

Exploring Couple's Relationship Expectations

Dimensions of Relationship Expectations

To assist couples in exploring their expectations about their relationship, it is useful to give them some guidance on important types of relationship expectations. The research on couple relationships has identified at least five dimensions of relationship expectations that are reliably associated with relationship satisfaction and relationship stability. Baucom and colleagues (1996) identified three dimensions of relationship expectations: boundaries, power and control, and personal investment in the relationship. In addition, expectations of gender roles and conflict management were identified by Eidelson and Epstein (1982) as closely associated with relationship satisfaction. Table 5.4 summarizes these dimensions.

In a group the relationship educator can give a minilecture based on the content of Table 5.4, illustrating the extremes of each dimension. Alternatively, Unit 1 of the Couple CARE DVD presents the relationship dimensions. Showing couples this segment can introduce the ideas. The relationship expectations described in Table 5.4 are not exhaustive, but they do reflect those expectations identified in the research literature as influencing a couple's relationship. When asking couples to reflect on their relationship expectations, encourage them to identify other expectations they believe are important. Additional expectations couples often commonly raise include having children together, the amount of time spent with friends and extended family, the extent of involvement in religious practices, and how finances will be managed.

It is important to emphasize to couples that there are no specific expectations that inevitably lead to a good or bad relationship. The goal of exploring expectations is not to arrive at a set of "correct answers," but rather to help the partners clarify what they want from their own relationship. At the same time, some research shows that holding extreme views on some of the expectations described in Table 5.4 can be unhelpful to a relationship. Specifically, an expectation that any form of disagreement is destructive, and conflict is to be avoided if at all possible, is associated with low relationship satisfaction (Eidelson & Epstein, 1982). Often such a belief indicates that prior experiences of severe destructive conflict have made the person uncomfortable with disagreement. A more realistic and helpful expectation than "any disagreement is destructive" is "disagreements are inevitable and we need to develop ways to manage our disagreements and prevent destructive conflict."

A second potentially unhelpful relationship expectation is strong adherence to traditional gender roles, which can reduce the flexibility of couples to manage life circumstances. For example, suppose the man focuses exclusively on paid employment and attends little to household chores or child care. If the woman develops a serious illness that prevents her from doing her usual tasks, the man is ill-prepared to take up the slack with child care and

TABLE 5.4. Dimensions of Relationship Expectations

Dimension	Anchor point 1	Anchor point 2
Boundaries	*Low*: Couples should spend all their time together, and share all their innermost thoughts and feelings.	*High*: Independence is vitally important; partners should sustain their own interests and friends.
Investment	*High*: Relationships require work; each partner needs to make the relationship a priority and commit him- or herself to making the relationship stronger.	*Low*: Great relationships happen naturally; the outcome of your relationship is largely determined by whether or not you selected the right partner.
Power and control	*Even*: Decision making should be shared, with both partners having an equal say on all decisions.	*Selective*: Some or all decisions should be made by a particular partner.
Gender roles	*Nontraditional*: Men and women are essentially similar in what they want in relationships, and most of the tasks they do in the relationship should be shared.	*Traditional*: Men and women are fundamentally different; they have different abilities and interests, and need to divide the tasks based on those abilities and interests.
Communication and conflict	*Any disagreement is destructive*; it is best to avoid conflict, and when you are unsure, stay quiet.	*Disagreement is inevitable*; conflict needs to be managed, and opinions and ideas need to be communicated.

housework. He likely has limited understanding of what is involved. Another challenge of such a traditional division of gender roles is that if the woman has not been in paid employment, then if the male loses his job or becomes ill the couple could experience severe financial difficulties. This is not to say that adhering to traditional gender roles is not a viable choice, but there are particular challenges that a very rigid adherence to such roles imposes on the couple relationship.

The third expectation that can be associated with poor relationship outcomes is that "good relationships happen naturally." In fact, increasing evidence indicates that couples need to work at their relationship, at least at certain crucial points, if they are to sustain relationship satisfaction. As described in Chapter 1, considerable evidence indicates that an accumulation of stressful life events can erode relationship satisfaction (Story & Bradbury, 2004). It seems likely that couples need to work at their relationship at these times. One critical point in a couple's relationship lifespan is the early years of marriage or cohabiting, when the partners are establishing their patterns of how they will live together as a partnership. Other key critical points are the transition to parenthood, when a partner or child has a serious illness, a change in job for either partner, relocation to a new place to live, or a change in circumstances of extended family members. All of these life events require the couple to adapt and develop new ways of being together, and at such times attention to the relationship and how to nurture it are important.

Some people find the idea of needing to work at their relationship difficult, and feel they should just "let things happen." I find the analogy of canoeing on a river helpful to explain how I see working at relationships. At times the river might flow smoothly and you can sit back, relax, and enjoy the flow. At other times rapids will appear with sudden changes of direction, and you need both people in the canoe to pay attention and work together as a team to get through the rapids safely.

Exploring How Relationship Expectations Are Learned

Encourage each partner to reflect individually on the couple relationships they have experienced, and how these earlier relationships might have shaped their current relationship expectations. Often these influences are subtle, but lead to strongly held but often unexplored views about the "right way to do things." Here is one fun group exercise that can introduce this point. String up two parallel lines of cord heavy enough to hang washing on (like a clothes line) at the front of the room. Have two baskets of socks, shirts and pants, and underwear available, along with some clothespins. Get four couples to stand up, with the couples at the two lines facing in opposite directions with their backs toward the couples on the other line. (Two couples face toward the front wall of the room and two toward the back wall.) Ask each couple to *quickly* hang up the washing, making sure each couple has at least two pairs of socks, and two pairs of underpants, a shirt, a pair of pants, and a bra each. As the couples do the hanging up of the clothing, note how the partners work together.

Once the clothing is hung up, ask each couple who hangs out the washing most often in their household, and whether the partners ever disagree about how to hang out washing. Select the couple that has the biggest differences on how to hang out the washing and have that couple examine and comment on the different modes of hanging out the washing the other couples have used. Once the couples have completed the task ask the partner who most often hangs out the washing to comment on how the other couples have hung out their washing. What usually emerges is that people often have strongly held but different views about how to hang out washing. For example, some people insist underwear is hung with the waistband uppermost, while others do not. The differences can be used to illustrate that we often learn a variety of expectations about how we should go about things, without necessarily being aware that we have different views to others.

One very important relationship that influences most people's expectations about their own relationship is how their mother and father related to each other (Conger, Cui, Bryant, & Elder, 2000). It is useful to have each partner individually reflect on the relationship between their parents. Figure 5.1 sets out a form that I have partners complete. The form asks people to individually jot down some general impressions of their parents' relationship, and then to write down specific descriptions of the relationship on each of the dimensions of relationship expectations previously introduced. Those people who were not raised by two parents are asked to focus on the close relationship(s) of those adults who cared for them when they were growing up, or if raised by a single parent what were the messages given about couple relationships.

The individuals are also asked to consider any committed relationships they experienced prior to the current relationship (i.e., any previous cohabiting or married relationship). It is important to remember that a high proportion of marriages are second marriages for at least one partner. For example, in the United States and Australia about 40% of marriages are remarriages for one or both partners (Australian Bureau of Statistics, 2003; U.S. Census Bureau, 2003). Furthermore, an increasing proportion of partners marrying for the first time have previously cohabited with at least one other partner. Some people find it difficult to hear about their current partner's former relationships. It is important to emphasize that the focus when reflecting on past

(text resumes on page 120)

MY RELATIONSHIP EXPERIENCES

On your own, reflect on and write down what you saw in your parents' (or other carers') relationship when you were growing up. What was their relationship like? (For example, did they argue a lot? Were they affectionate with each other?) If you grew up in a single-parent family, what was your mother or father's relationship like, in general, with other people who were close to her or him?

My parents' or carers' relationship: What was it like? _____

_____

_____

_____

_____

Let's get more specific now. What was your parents' (or other carers') relationship like when it came to the following?

Boundaries (For example, did one or both partners believe they should be very close as a couple? Did one or both partners believe that partners should maintain very independent lives?) _____

_____

_____

_____

_____

Power and control (Did one partner make most of the decisions, or was decision making shared equally?) _____

_____

_____

_____

_____

Investment (For example, how much time and effort did they invest in their relationship? Did one partner "give" more?) _____

_____

_____

_____

_____

(cont.)

FIGURE 5.1. Relationship experiences and expectations.

Gender roles (For example, in your family of origin did the women tend to do traditional "female" jobs such as cooking and cleaning? Did the men tend to do "male" jobs such as gardening and taking out the garbage? Were they able to be flexible?) _____

_____

_____

_____

_____

_____

_____

_____

Communication and conflict (For example, did they talk a lot or not much at all? Did each person speak respectfully to the other, or did they put each other down? When dealing with conflict did they give each other the silent treatment, store up resentments, or did one partner always give in?) _____

_____

_____

_____

_____

_____

_____

Other relationships. Are there any other relationship experiences that you think are important? It might be other relationships you have seen, or relationships you have been in. Write down the relationship(s), and what you noticed about this relationship or relationships. (For example, you might have been with a dating partner who drank too much, or was aggressive. Or you might have friends who are very loving in how they talk to each other.) _____

_____

_____

_____

_____

_____

_____

(cont.)

FIGURE 5.1. *(cont.)*

MY RELATIONSHIP EXPECTATIONS

On your own . . . You have looked at the relationship patterns in your family of origin and in other relationships. How do you think these relationship experiences have influenced you in your relationship now? What effect have they had on your *expectations* about how relationships should be? _____

_____
_____
_____
_____
_____
_____
_____
_____
_____
_____

Some of these expectations could have a helpful effect on your relationship. Other expectations may be unhelpful. (For example, if your parents argued a lot, you may avoid discussion of difficult issues.) Write down your thoughts below.

My expectations that *help* my relationship include: _____

_____
_____
_____
_____
_____
_____

My expectations that *do not help* my relationship include:

_____
_____
_____
_____
_____
_____

FIGURE 5.1. *(cont.)*

relationships is on the individual identifying any influences of that relationship on their expectations or behavior in the current relationship. It is not necessary to discuss the details of past relationships with a spouse to achieve this aim.

The next step is to have individuals reflect on how their prior exposure to relationships might have shaped their current relationship expectations. For example, a common theme in many people's reflections is that they seek to include positive aspects of their parents' relationship in their own relationship, or to avoid replicating negative aspects. When people are reflecting on negative behaviors that they do not want to emulate, it is important to prompt them to attend to what they want to do instead. It is more effective to enact a decision to do something positive than it is to just resolve not to do something negative. For example, Mitch mentioned he did wish to be like his father, whom Mitch saw as being preoccupied with work to the exclusion of family life. After discussion Mitch framed this desire as wanting to be active in parenting his children, which included picking them up after school on at least some days of the week, helping them with homework, attending some of their sporting and other activities, and having a family holiday each year.

Negative aspects of a partner's prior relationship also can have substantial impact on relationship expectations and behavior in the current relationship. One common theme for people who have been divorced is that they see conflict as a problem in a past relationship. After experiencing the pain of destructive conflict and separation, people understandably often seek to avoid destructive conflict in their current relationship, which sometimes can lead to unproductive behavior like avoiding discussing difficult issues. For example, stepfamily couples avoid discussing difficult family issues more than first-marriage couples (Afifi & Schrodt, 2003; Halford, Nicholson, & Sanders, 2007), often in the hope that ignoring such issues will prevent destructive conflict. However, the more stepfamily couples report avoiding talking about difficult issues, the lower their reported relationship satisfaction (Afifi & Schrodt, 2003). The desire to avoid destructive conflict is understandable, but avoidance of talking about difficult issues means they never get resolved. It is important to help partners develop realistic expectations, and to clarify what they want to do. It is simply not possible to have a long-term relationship and not discuss contentious issues: all couples have some issues about which they disagree. Hence the educator needs to remind the partners to focus on what is realistic (e.g., learn effective means to manage differences) rather than setting the goal of avoiding arguments. This focus on positive goals can be prompted by a question like: "Given that all couples will disagree some times, what might you do to manage these differences and avoid *destructive* conflict?"

The next step in the process of exploring relationship expectations is to ask each individual to consider which of his or her current expectations might be helpful for the current relationship, and which might be unhelpful. This step is important as it focuses the person on two key messages. First is the implicit message that expectations are learned, that they are—at least in part—a result of prior relationship experiences. The second message is that some relationship expectations might need to be revised. Implicitly this also suggests that, just as people learned their current relationship expectations, they also can learn new expectations to replace any expectations that are seen as unhelpful. Helping individuals to shape specific, realistic relationship expectations often requires the educator to be active in reinforcing positive expectations and to gently challenge less helpful expectations.

In a group setting the leader should circulate among the partners as they are writing, discussing with them what they are discovering and helping them clarify ideas. This process is illustrated in the following conversation, in which Dora reflects on her past relationship with Jon, and what she thinks it means for her current relationship with Mike.

DORA: Look, this is man number three for me. I got two kids under 8, and I don't want them going through any more dramas with a father disappearing. So, number one: I am going to look after myself better. I got really down for a couple of years there, stuck on weight. I know I wasn't much fun to be around. I like being around me more now.

EDUCATOR: So you feel an important lesson from your past is to take care of Dora, keep her feeling good, and then the relationship might work out better?

DORA: Yeah, when I was depressed I was rotten—I was tired, irritable all the time. I thought of leaving me about when Jon decided to disappear. (*Laughs.*)

EDUCATOR: So what do you need to do to avoid going down—into depression—again?

DORA: Time for me, keep seeing my friends like I do now, I got interests.

EDUCATOR: OK, so a big lesson is make sure Dora has time for seeing her friends, doing things that interest her. Any other lessons from the past?

DORA: Yeah, Jon and I argued about my kids. He was always on about me being too soft on them. But, like Mikey, Jon had no kids of his own—he wasn't really cut out to be a dad. I reckon I need to look after the kids and keep Mike and the boys out of each other's way.

EDUCATOR: So as you see it, the parenting is down to you?

DORA: I've been doing it on my own, I figure I can just keep going.

EDUCATOR: So, Dora, I can see making sure things work for your boys is really important to you. Tell me how this would work. Mike is home with the boys. You've just gone out shopping. The boys start arguing, what should Mike do?

DORA: Nothing, I'll fix it when I get home.

EDUCATOR: What if they're doing things kids sometimes do, throwing stuff around and maybe one of the boys is hitting the other?

DORA: If they really get out of hand, he'll do something, just keep it under control till I get back.

EDUCATOR: What do you think is OK for Mike to do? Can he send them to their room? Give them a smack?

DORA: No hitting. Their dad used to hit them, that's mainly why I left him. Nah, if I thought Mike would ever hit them it would be all over.

EDUCATOR: Dora, it seems to me like you're saying you have some pretty strong views on what you think should happen between Mike and your boys. You think you're the best one to do most of the parenting, but also sometimes you think Mike needs to be an adult in the house, making sure your kids are safe and behaving. Have you and Mike talked about how *you* expect the parenting to go?

DORA: No, no . . . , not really. See, Jon and I argued so badly over the kids, I . . .

EDUCATOR: . . . find it hard to bring it up?

DORA: Yeah, I want this one to work, I don't want to argue with Mike over the boys.

EDUCATOR: So, if we can find a way that you and Mike can talk without fighting, talk about your kids, and how the four of you can get along under the same roof, is that what you want?

DORA: Gotta talk to him about it, don't I?

EDUCATOR: Yeah, I think you do. And we can work to make it a good talk.

After each partner has identified his or her individual relationship expectations, the couple then talks together about these individual reflections and the partners seek to understand each other's expectations. The discussion should cover areas of expectations that the partners think are strengths brought to the current relationship. For example, one strength reflected in the preceding dialogue is Dora's implicit commitment to making the relationship with her partner Mike work long term for both of them. The discussion should also cover any expectations that might be challenges for their relationship. For instance, Dora's lack of clarity about how much she wants Mike to be involved in parenting her children may pose a relationship challenge.

Figure 5.2 is a useful handout that couples can use for completing the exploration of their relationship expectations. *Strengths* are relationship expectations that are shared and realistic. *Challenges* are unrealistic, relationship-undermining, or discrepant relationship expectations. In the group setting each couple can be invited to describe some of the relationship expectations shared by both partners, and any relationship expectations that might create challenges. The educator can write up the relationship expectations that couples describe. After listing a wide range of ideas, the educator can prompt the partners in the group to talk to each other about any expectations other couples raised that they like or think are important. Another useful topic is to discuss areas that might create relationship challenges, and how such challenges could be managed.

Developing a Relationship Vision

Ask individual partners to write down some ideas describing their vision for their relationship. Start this experience by referring back to the ideas of what constitutes a great relationship that were discussed earlier in the session and inviting people to list things they would like in their relationship. Next, ask the couple to discuss together their relationship expectations and the sources of those expectations. Then ask the couple to develop a joint statement of their relationship vision, defined as the shared goals and expectations they have. It is important to emphasize that the partners do not have to agree on every aspect of their relationship vision. In fact, it would be surprising if they agreed on everything. Discrepant ideas about their relationship vision can be identified and explored in more depth across the course of the program. For example, point out to couples that Unit 4 is about managing differences, and explain that this unit will provide a good opportunity to further discuss differences in individual partners' ideas about their relationship vision.

Educator Guidelines

The educator has an important role in assisting the partners to clarify their relationship expectations and relationship vision. Some potentially useful

As a couple, discuss your answers to the following questions.

1. What relationship patterns from your parents' relationships do you want to transfer to your own relationship? Which patterns would you like to avoid?

2. How do you think your relationship with each of your parents has influenced your emotional health as an adult?

As a couple, discuss your answers to the exercise you just completed, "My expectations that help . . . " and "My expectations that don't help. . . . " Write down what you see as your joint **strengths and challenges** in terms of relationship expectations. There are two sorts of expectation challenges. The first is expectations that you agree might undermine your relationship (e.g., both our sets of parents divorced, and we are both a bit doubtful about whether relationships can really last). The second is when you have quite different expectations, such as one person wanting to have children and the other not.

As a couple we think our joint strengths are:

_____

_____

_____

_____

_____

_____

_____

As a couple we think our potential challenges are:

_____

_____

_____

_____

_____

_____

_____

FIGURE 5.2. Our relationship experiences and expectations.

questions for the educator are presented in Table 5.5. In group sessions the educator can circulate among the couples as they talk, and use these questions to help partners clarify their expectations. In telephone or face-to-face sessions with one couple, these questions can form the basis of a review of the work the couple has already done together.

A common challenge in helping couples to clarify their relationship expectations is that some people are vague about their relationship expectations and vision. Being concrete and detailed in the analysis of their relationship is an important skill for the partners to develop. For example, George (46, a plumber) and Lyn (47, a nurse) had married about 1 year before undertaking Couple CARE. It was the second marriage for both of them and each was very keen to "avoid the mistakes made last time around," but George initially found it hard to be clear about what went wrong in his first marriage and what he wanted to do differently.

EDUCATOR: So, George, what do you think you learned from the last marriage?

GEORGE: The divorce made a mess of things for me and the kids—

TABLE 5.5. Some Useful Questions for Exploring Relationship Expectations and Vision

Domain	Suggestions
Relationship expectations	*What are the key impressions you had of your mother and father's relationship as you grew up?* Probe as required to relate impressions to specific dimensions of couple relationships, such as power, gender roles, investment, boundaries, communication, and conflict management.
	How do you think what you saw affected your expectations of your current relationship? Try to draw out both positive and negative aspects of relationship expectations for each partner.
	What other influences have helped shape your relationship expectations? This could refer to relationship of other key adults when growing up (e.g., extended family, close family friends).
Relationship vision	*Can you summarize two or three of the most important points in your relationship vision?* Using probes, help the person to be as specific as possible.
	What aspects of your partner's relationship vision did you particularly like?
	Were there things your partner suggested that you did not include in your relationship vision?

I nearly lost the business, I was so stressed I could not think straight. I just never want to go through that again. That's why I was pretty hesitant about getting into another marriage . . . it was 5 years before I dated anyone.

EDUCATOR: So that was really a hard time and you are very keen to avoid repeating those relationship problems. How do you think getting divorced and all that pain have shaped what you expect of your relationship with Lyn?

GEORGE: It makes me nervous. When I first married Ros we were tight—you know—really good together. Lyn and I are good now, really good, but sometimes I wonder might things with Lyn go the same way as with Ros.

EDUCATOR: OK, so with Ros it started well, but went bad. So what was good at the start?

GEORGE: We had fun together. We both loved the beach and outdoors.

EDUCATOR: So initially it was fun. And then?

GEORGE: We sort of drifted apart, I guess.

EDUCATOR: Drifted apart?

GEORGE: Yeah, I was busy with work, on building sites all day, doing the books at night. Ros was busy with her work and the kids. We never had time for each other. Then the arguing started—I hated the fights.

EDUCATOR: So, there are two things you've mentioned: not having much fun time together, and arguing.

GEORGE: Yeah.

EDUCATOR: Does that mean two things you want in your relationship with Lyn are: (1) to make sure you have time together, to do fun things, so you don't drift apart; and (2) to make sure you can talk about problems without fighting?

GEORGE: Yes, definitely, especially no fighting.

EDUCATOR: So the fighting was so painful, you definitely do not want to do that again. All couples disagree at some stage—it is impossible to agree on everything across a lifetime. So managing disagreements—so they're not destructive—that we can work on. Is that what you're saying you want?

GEORGE: That's it, I just want a marriage without fighting.

SELF-CHANGE

Introducing the Concept of Self-Change

The concept of self-change (or relationship self-regulation, as it is also known) is central to Couple CARE. Self-change plans are used to integrate and apply the ideas covered in each unit. Therefore is it important to ensure that participants understand the concept of self-change and develop skills in implementing self-change plans. I introduce the idea of self-change something like this:

> "The concept of self-change is based on the simple premise that, in order to have a great relationship, people should focus predominantly on what they can influence most effectively, which is their own behavior. If you work at your relationship, then that likely encourages your spouse also to do positive things. There is a positive cycle of each of you showing the other—in lots of little ways—that the relationship matters, that you love each other.
>
> "A key characteristic of unhappy relationships is that partners blame the other person for anything wrong in the relationship. Partner blaming means the only way to improve your relationship is to rely on your spouse making the required changes. This makes you as an individual powerless, and people can easily give up and become unhappy. If you are not doing anything positive, it is likely that your partner will notice that and do less him- or herself. This can lead to a gradual drift to relationship problems.
>
> "Focusing on your behavior and self-change does not mean that you should not say anything about what your spouse does that you might want him or her to change. All of us have habits that might irritate a partner. But most of it is little stuff, and really does not matter. If it does matter to you, then what you can do is to examine how you discuss the changes you would like to see. In later sessions we will look at communication and how to communicate things you want to change. Right now the focus is on what *you* can do to change yourself to be an even better, even more loving, spouse."

In Couple CARE we teach partners a five-step process of self-change that is summarized in Figure 5.3, which is a useful handout to provide to couples. It is important to spend some time on the concept of self-change because the couples need to apply the idea throughout the rest of the program. In essence, this process applies the widely used problem-solving model (Nezu, D'Zurilla,

1. DESCRIBE	**2. FOCUS**
Choose an issue you'd like to work on that involves changing something about your behavior. Describe this aspect clearly and positively (write in the spaces provided).	What do I currently do?
	_____
_____	What are the **pluses** of my current behavior?
_____	
_____	_____
_____	What are the **minuses** of my current behavior?
_____	
_____	_____
	_____

3. GOAL	**4. ACT**
Define as precisely as you can what you want to happen.	What will I do? Where and when will I do it?
_____	_____
_____	_____

5. EVALUATE—After you have implemented your action plan:

What did I actually do?

_____

What positives resulted?

_____

What negatives resulted?

_____

What do I need to do from here?

_____

FIGURE 5.3. Self-change plan.

Zwick, & Nezu, 2004) for self-change within couple relationships. The five steps can be explained with comments something like what follows:

> "DESCRIBE is thinking about how your relationship is going, choosing one thing you'd like to improve, and then describing it clearly. Concentrate on key areas that really make a difference to relationships. The six units of Couple CARE reflect the areas known to be most important in relationships.
>
> "FOCUS means paying the most attention to your own behavior. You have most influence over your own actions, so think about what *you* currently do. Examine the pluses and minuses of how *you* behave to help work out what you can do differently. Focusing on your own behavior does not mean you ignore what your partner does. But start with what *you* do. For example, if your partner is doing something that you would like to change, reflect on *how* you have talked to your partner about that issue.
>
> "GOAL means thinking about what you want in the relationship. Define what outcome you would like. ACT is defining exactly what *you* will do to achieve your goal and then doing it. Set a time limit on when to take your action.
>
> "EVALUATE. Did you do what you said you'd do? What effect did it have on your relationship? Then decide if you need to take further action—for example, if it was helpful, how can you continue to do it? Should you do it a little differently next time?"

There are several ways to help couples understand the concept of self-change. Describing the above steps and illustrating with an example is very useful. Figure 5.4 provides two examples, one for a young couple interested in physical activities, and another for a couple with young children. Note that the final step (EVALUATE) is blank. This step is completed once the person has attempted to implement self-change. In the course of the program, self-change plan implementation from each unit is reviewed during the next unit.

Another option for introducing the concept of self-change is to use the Couple CARE DVD, which has a segment at the end of Unit 1 that introduces the idea of self-change. A scene shows a young man asking his partner to go out for dinner; she declines, saying she is tired; and they become irritable with one another. The young man is then shown reflecting on what happened, and what he could do differently to enhance the relationship. His reflections portray the five steps of the self-change plan, which culminate in him enacting a self-change plan to talk with his partner again, but to talk in a different way.

1. DESCRIBE Choose an issue you'd like to work on that involves changing something about your behavior. Describe this aspect clearly and positively (write in the spaces provided).	**2. FOCUS** What do I currently do? *Go on outings he plans, suggest holidays*
To sustain having fun time together.	What are the **pluses** of my current behavior? *We do have fun now.*
	What are the **minuses** of my current behavior? *I am not suggesting day-to-day fun things, during the week it feels dull.*
3. GOAL Define as precisely as you can what you want to happen. *I can suggest some new stuff for us to try together, that we both might like.*	**4. ACT** What will I do? Where and when will I do it? *Talk to Steve about his ideas, check out the martial arts program at the school next week, find out about yoga classes.*

5. EVALUATE—After you have implemented your action plan:

What did I actually do?

What positives resulted?

What negatives resulted?

What do I need to do from here?

(cont.)

FIGURE 5.4. Self-change plan examples.

1. DESCRIBE	**2. FOCUS**
Choose an issue you'd like to work on that involves changing something about your behavior. Describe this aspect clearly and positively (write in the spaces provided).	What do I currently do?
	Try to chill out when I first get home, read the paper.
The evenings are often stressful when my son Stevie is tired, making that easier.	What are the **pluses** of my current behavior?
	I unwind a little.
	What are the **minuses** of my current behavior?
	Sal gets stressed doing all the care of Stevie, and sometimes she gets mad with me or the kid.

3. GOAL	**4. ACT**
Define as precisely as you can what you want to happen.	What will I do? Where and when will I do it?
Try to take it easy on the drive home, arrive home more relaxed; I can ask Sal ahead of time what she would find most helpful from me.	*Put some soothing music on in the car, talk to Sal on the weekend. Make sure I tell her I want to pick up more slack.*

5. EVALUATE—After you have implemented your action plan:

What did I actually do?

_____

What positives resulted?

_____

What negatives resulted?

_____

What do I need to do from here?

_____

FIGURE 5.4. *(cont.)*

Once you have introduced the concept of self-change it is useful to demonstrate the process of how it can be applied. It can be helpful to get the group as a whole to complete a self-change plan. Some examples of suitable examples for group development of a self-change plan are supporting your partner better, arranging a positive shared activity or date, or being more romantic. Once an issue has been described, get the group members to brainstorm some options for addressing that relationship enhancement goal. Remind the group of the basic rules of brainstorming, that ideas should be freely generated, no idea is too silly or way out, and that no criticism or evaluation of ideas is allowed initially. The educator or a group member should write up the options on a whiteboard or flip chart. Then you can go back and have participants identify the strengths and weaknesses of the various options. I then ask one participant to select an option for what he or she thinks is most likely to be helpful. Asking if others group members would pick a different option highlights the point that there can be a variety of ways of achieving similar goals. In the sessions we will help all participants develop self-change that they believe is likely to be useful in their relationship.

Applying Self-Change

The final exercise in Unit 1 involves having each partner develop a self-change plan. The exercise serves several purposes. First, it provides the opportunity for participants to learn the steps of self-change through application. Second, it allows each participant to experience success in doing something to enhance his or her relationship, and note the positive effects. When implementation of self-change goes well, it often strengthens engagement with, and enthusiasm for, the program. It is not unusual for one partner to have led a somewhat reluctant spouse to attend relationship education; often in my experience it is the woman who initiates attendance of Couple CARE. The active nature of the self-change process often appeals to men who were initially reluctant to attend the program. In completion of the self-change process people often feel they are doing something and "not just talking," and that they are in control of what they get to do. Finally, attempts at self-change planning and implementation allow the educator to assess the level of skill of participants in the self-change process, which can help guide how much assistance particular participants might need during the program.

The self-change planning can begin with an introduction something like this:

> "In keeping with the Couple CARE focus on you, as an individual, taking control over what you want to change, I want to suggest we each

do a self-change plan. I want you to read through what you wrote ear-lier about your relationship vision. Pick one aspect of your relationship that you would like to work on. I am not saying 'look for a problem to fix.' Rather, I am suggesting you try to identify an area you want to strengthen. It might be quality time together; or helping out around the house more; or listening to your spouse talk about a hobby or his or her work. You can choose to work on whatever aspect of your relation-ship you think is important. The idea is to use the self-change plan to identify something specific you will do in the next week to enhance your relationship."

Table 5.6 summarizes some useful guidelines that can assist participants to develop specific self-change plans. These guidelines can be provided as a handout. The educator can suggest people read through them before starting their self-change plans. In a group it can be helpful to give some examples of vague self-change goals, such as those listed as poor examples in Table 5.6, and ask the participants for suggestions of more concrete goals. This helps people to get the idea of what is meant by a behaviorally specific self-change plan.

Some useful questions that can be posed to individuals as you circulate around a group are as follows:

- "What aspect of your relationship vision did you decide to write a self-change plan for?"
- "Can you tell me how you defined the issue?" (Be sure to help each partner to define specific behaviors in specific circumstances.)
- "What are the pluses and minuses of your current behavior?"
- "What is your self-change goal?"
- "What is your action plan?"

Closing the Session

I like to conclude the first session by thanking people for their attendance and participation. It is very useful at the close of the session to ask people to review the content of the unit. I usually ask couples to talk together for a minute or two about what they thought was the most important content covered in the session. We can then ask each couple to briefly summarize a key point. This process of recalling and rehearsing content is an important element in making the learning process active. This review is done to con-clude each session. I also explain the importance of what each partner does between now and the next session. This can be done with something like the following words:

TABLE 5.6. Some Guidelines for Developing Effective Self-Change Plans

Definition	Poor example	Good example
Clear: Be specific and concrete about what happens and when.	We sometimes fight.	After work on busy days, I tend to argue about little things such as whose turn it is to cook.
	We never have time to see each other.	On weekends we each have lots of things we do. We have not gone out as a couple, just the two of us, for 7 weeks. I want to go out together more than that.
Positive: Think about what you *do* want, not what you *don't* want in the relationship. Avoid blaming the other person for things you do not like.	I hate the way we never spend any time together.	I would like to spend more time with my partner.
Specific: Be precise rather than vague about your action plan. Try to focus on behaviors that can be seen.	I want to feel closer to my partner.	I would like to discuss my work and hobbies, which are important to me, with my partner.
Realistic: Select actions you are likely to be able to do.	I will never get angry again.	I will try to be calm, listen to her, and speak quietly when we next talk about this issue.
	I will shower my partner with presents.	Tomorrow I will stop at the store on the way home from work and buy my partner something I know she'll like—a mango.
Time-limited: Define when you will do your actions.	From now on I will cuddle my partner more.	This week, I will cuddle my partner for a few minutes each morning before I get out of bed.

"Next week, and each session after that, we will follow a process similar to this first session. There will be some ideas and skills introduced, and you will work as individuals and as couples to apply the ideas in your relationship. At the end of each session each partner will develop a self-change plan to do something that you think will strengthen your relationship.

"You can do all that, and it will make little difference to helping your relationship. What is really important is to try your self-change plan. Do the one thing this week that you have identified as your self-change goal and see if it makes a positive difference. We find that those people who apply the ideas in their day-to-day lives are the ones who really get the most from this program.

"I hope you have a great week, and I look forward to seeing you all in the next session."

CHALLENGES IN DEVELOPING SELF-CHANGE

Challenges in Exploring Relationship Expectations and Relationship Vision

The exploration of family-of-origin experiences is often highly engaging for couples. There is the risk that this exercise can take up a lot of the time in Unit 1 and prevent covering the rest of the unit content unless the task is well managed. It is important that the educator structures the task so that participants understand the aims of the exercise, which are to gain a broad understanding of one's relationship expectations and their origins, and how these expectations might impact the current relationship. The structure of having people write down key impressions of their parents' relationship relevant to the discussion before talking to their partner helps structure the task. I find suggesting that couples allow themselves about 15 minutes to discuss their relationship expectations helps to manage the time taken. Giving a prompt after 10 minutes that there is 5 minutes to go, and suggesting that each couple ensure both partners have had a chance to speak about their respective expectations is also useful.

In some couples the family-of-origin experiences can raise difficult psychological issues. For example, recollections of abuse sometimes are brought up in the context of this exercise. The educator needs to be circulating among the couples listening to them as they speak to each other. If there are issues being raised by group members that might require more therapeutic intervention, I will suggest the couple speak with me at the end of the session. In that way the couple and the educator can discuss whether the CRE group is appropriate, and whether any additional assistance might be needed.

A challenge in exploring the relationship vision is if spouses identify expectations that are widely discrepant, and that are important to each spouse—for example, discovering one spouse is very keen to have children and the other is not. It can be surprising for the couple (and for educators) to find that despite being in a committed relationship the partners have different views about the relationship, which often have not been previously explored.

If highly discrepant expectations are identified I encourage couples to simply note for now that such discrepancies exist. I normalize such discrepancies by introducing the idea that it is unlikely any couples will agree with their partner on everything about how they want their relationship to function, and note that they will need to work through the program to clarify their expectations and seek out common ground.

Challenges in Developing Self-Change Goals and Plans

There are two common challenges in helping partners develop their first self-change plan. First, some participants can find it hard to be concrete and specific about their goals. In these cases, the educator can guide them, as in the following example.

EDUCATOR: Educator: Roger, what is your self-change goal?

ROGER: I want to be more supportive of Mel. I think she's under a lot of stress with her work.

EDUCATOR: Support from your partner when you feel stressed can be really helpful. How will you try to be supportive?

ROGER: Ahh, um, try to be more tuned into her, you know, notice when she's under pressure.

EDUCATOR: Good, so what could you do in the next few days that would make sure you were tuned into her?

ROGER: Just be sensitive to her moods, I guess.

EDUCATOR: Well, I certainly appreciate my wife doing that for me. I notice she usually asks me about my day when I get home, and I ask her about hers. We just spend a bit of time catching up. I am wondering if you would do something like that, or maybe asking her if you can help in some way. What did you have in mind?

ROGER: Well, I often do ask Mel about her work, though I get distracted by stuff—you know, getting dinner under way, a telephone call, something.

EDUCATOR: So you try to catch up with what's happening for Mel, but sometimes maybe it's not the right time—anyway you get distracted. What do you want to do differently—to improve that?

ROGER: I guess talking over dinner is a good time, I could make sure we chat a bit more then.

EDUCATOR: Excellent, excellent, so let me see if I've got it. Your plan is to ask Mel about her day and how work has been going over dinner. Correct?

ROGER: Yep.

EDUCATOR: OK, well next week in session I will ask how that went and we can see if that change produces the effect you are after.

A second common challenge is ensuring that partners develop self-change goals that can be done in the next week. It is important to do this, as part of the process involves reviewing and assisting people if they struggle to implement effective self-change. Sometimes people develop goals in which something can be done in the next week. For example, stating a desire to take a special holiday together might involve doing some research on possible destinations and discussing that. The important objective in the self-change process is to have each participant make a commitment to do something to enhance the relationship. The session culminates in reviewing what you have covered in the session, and stating that in the following week you will review how people went in implementing their self-change plans. Often I find it useful to go around the group and have each person state briefly their self-change goal for the coming week.

CHAPTER 6

Unit 2

Communication

Unit 2 of Couple CARE focuses on communication. The content of Unit 2 is summarized in Table 6.1. The unit begins with a review of the content of Unit 1 and of the implementation of the self-change plan developed in that unit. The new content begins with the introduction of a model of good communication, which provides couples with an understanding of the key functions of communication in couple relationships. Couples undertake a structured communication exercise in which each partner self-evaluates the strengths and weaknesses of their current communication. This is followed

TABLE 6.1. Overview of Unit 2: Self-Change

Topic and aim	Exercise(s)
Review Unit 1 self-change plan	Review implementation and trouble-shoot as required.
Promote understanding effective couple communication skills	Reflect on the nature of good couple communication; introduce intent–impact model of couple communication.
Communication self-assessment	Couple do communication task, self-evaluate individual communication, receive partner feedback on communication
Emotional bids	Educator introduces idea of emotional bids; individuals self-assess the use of emotional bids in their relationship.
Communication self-change plan	Individuals develop self-change plan for communication; educator reviews plans.

by the introduction of the concept of emotional bids, which are subtle ways of indirectly expressing emotional needs in intimate relationships. Then couples review their use of emotional bids within their relationship. Finally, all participants develop a self-change plan for enhancing their own communication.

The development of couple communication skills undertaken in this unit is a crucial building block for the content of later sessions. In Unit 3 the communication skills covered in the current unit are built upon and applied to express support toward the partner. In Unit 4 these communication skills are extended further and applied as a means of managing differences within a relationship. Effective communication is also important for having couples discuss the sensitive issue of sexuality within their relationship, which is the focus of Unit 5.

REVIEW OF UNIT 1 AND SELF-CHANGE PLAN

In this unit, and all units that follow, the content of the previous unit is reviewed. The reviews are intended to consolidate the learning from the preceding unit. It is useful after welcoming people to the session to ask people to write down one thing they thought was important or useful in the previous session. The educator can then ask people to discuss what they wrote down with their partner, and then report their ideas to the group. When asking people about what they remember most from last week's unit, make sure that you ask at least one male and one female, to ensure that both genders are actively engaged in the process. It also is important to ask each person to be specific about the particular things that they remember by asking questions like, "What was important to you about that theme?" and "Are there specific actions to apply that idea?" It can be useful to ask people about whether they have applied any of the ideas from the previous unit in their own relationship over the past week and, if not, how they might do so.

As explained in Chapter 3, the selection and implementation of self-change is central to the Couple CARE process. When Couple CARE is done in a group setting, the process of review of self-change plans can be done in several ways. It is often useful to ask one or two partners to report back on their self-change plans, and for the leader to review those plans in some detail. This shows the participants the process of review that will be used, and demonstrates how to make the review a positive learning process. After these initial demonstrations you can ask each couple to review their own self-change plans with their spouse. This has the advantage of encouraging spouses to support each other. However, couples who are somewhat distressed in their relationship might struggle to be constructive with each other. Another option is to have pairs of couples work together, as often the presence of other people promotes more positive responses to the spouse. A third option is to pair up same-gender participants, with men mentoring each other, and women mentoring each other. This approach has the advantage of allowing men and women to hear different ideas from someone of their own gender, and promotes members of the group supporting each other. Yet another option is to do the review with the whole group listening and providing support. This last approach maximizes the learning gained by group members from each other, but reviewing everyone's self-change plan can be quite time-consuming, and risks some participants losing concentration.

Across the course of the multiple group sessions that make up a Couple CARE program, it is good to use a mix of different ways to review self-change plan implementation. The variety helps to make things interesting, mixes people around, and draws upon the advantages of the different approaches. In groups with more than one or two distressed couples, I used methods other than having the participants work with their spouse in the first few sessions, or during the session that focuses on conflict management. This reduces the chance of escalating partner negativity in the session. The review of self-change plans going around the entire group tends to work best after several sessions, when the group members have gotten to know each other and participants are familiar with the process of review. This allows the process to be done more quickly, with brief comments from group members.

How to Review Self-Change Plans

Whatever the specific process of reviewing self-change plans, it is important to emphasize that group participants should seek to be constructive, to praise each other's self-change efforts, and to offer any suggestions tentatively. As noted above, the group leader should demonstrate this process. The leader begins the review of the self-change plan by asking someone to spell out exactly what he or she was trying to do in his or her self-change plan (e.g., "Can you tell me exactly what you tried to do?") This can be followed up with an open-ended question asking that individual about how he or she did. It is important to ensure that each person is specific about exactly what he or she did. If the effect of self-change was positive, the educator can build on this success, asking the person how he or she might sustain further positive impacts of such change on the relationship. Asking people to rate the extent to which they were successful in implementing their self-change can be useful. This can be phrased as: "On a scale from 0 to 10 (with 0 being 'did not do anything like I planned' and 10 'completed exactly what I intended'), how well would you rate your carrying out of your self-change plan?" Making such a rating helps people to recognize that the achievement of self-change is not an all-or-nothing phenomenon. Even modest success can produce some benefits. It also is important to review the effects of the self-change on the relationship (e.g., "What effect did doing your self-change plan make?") It can also be helpful to ask the spouse to comment on any positive benefit she or he sees from the self-change. If the effect of self-change was positive, the educator can build on this success, asking the person how he or she might sustain further positive impacts of such change on the relationship. If the change did not have an entirely positive effect, then the educator can help the partner to fine-tune his or her self-change approach.

As an illustration of this review process, consider the following brief transcript in which Gemma is describing her attempts to show greater appreciation for her partner Henri's contribution around the house.

EDUCATOR: Gemma, what exactly was it you set out to do?

GEMMA: I wanted to recognize more what Henri does around the place.

EDUCATOR: Hmm, hmm, great. And how did that go?

GEMMA: Good, good. I made a point of looking around the place on days Henri often does do some of the vacuuming and cleaning. He had tidied up around the second bedroom, and I made a special point of thanking him.

EDUCATOR: It is *great* that you expressed your thanks. And what sort of response did you get from Henri?

GEMMA: Well, it was interesting. Even though Henri knew what I was planning, he still seemed really pleased.

EDUCATOR: Wonderful, we can all do with a "thank you." Knowing that being appreciated means a lot to Henri, Gemma what can you do to make sure you keep doing this?

GEMMA: Try to notice the positive stuff that Henri does and comment on it at least a couple of times.

EDUCATOR: Fantastic. I will check in with you in a week or two, just to see how you're going with that resolution.

Gemma did carry out her self-change plan, but a limitation of what she did was a lack of any specific strategy to maintain expression of appreciation. For some people just making the resolution is enough. Other people might need to practice expression of appreciation a number of times for that behavior to become habitual. The educator signals he will check back with Gemma to see if she carries through on her resolution. It is important to keep reviewing people's self-change attempts, and helping them develop sustained effort to strengthen their relationship with their partner.

Sometimes self-change plans are implemented, but do not have the effects that were intended. It is important to help people see the process of self-change as one of experimentation, of exploring what is most helpful in enhancing their relationship. If this spirit of experimentation is encouraged, then people keep learning important things when they make an effort, regardless of the immediate effect on the relationship. For example, in the following brief transcript, the educator is reviewing Geoff's attempt to organize a date with Janine, which had not worked out as Goeff had hoped.

EDUCATOR: What was your plan, Geoff?

GEOFF: To organize a date. So I made a reservation at this rather nice little Indian place. It's not a style of food that we've eaten very much, but I thought, "Try something different." Neither of us knew what we were ordering. Janine got the vindaloo, which proved to be pretty toxic to her.

EDUCATOR: Toxic?

GEOFF: Yeah, it was much too hot, she didn't enjoy any of the food, and had quite an upset tummy at the end of the night. Not really the romantic dinner effect that I had in mind.

EDUCATOR: It is wonderful that you put in all that effort. When you try new things, sometimes it doesn't work out as you'd hoped. What have you learned from this?

GEOFF: Well, I guess we have pretty conservative tastes in food. But I do like the idea of us going out.

EDUCATOR: I remember you saying earlier that you've been together for some years, and felt you might have got in a rut. It's terrific that you are seeking out things that you really do like. So what happens next?

GEOFF: Italian? (*Laughs.*)

EDUCATOR: Sure, why not? Is that seriously what you want to try?

GEOFF: Yeah, I think so.

Responding to Lack of Self-Change

There are occasions when partners have made little or no progress in implementing their self-change plan. It is very important to carefully review with people lack of action on a self-change plan. It is easy for individuals to feel criticized when reviewing noncompletion of tasks, and this can lead to defensiveness, which is not productive. Hence the review needs to be positively focused and to refine the self-change plan to make it workable.

A useful approach to exploring noncompletion of self-change plans is described in Table 6.2. This approach is based on Shelton and Levy's (1981) model of common sources of failing to complete behavioral assignments. Essentially, Shelton and Levy suggested that there are three common reasons why people fail to do tasks that they state they want to complete. First, individuals may be unclear about exactly what they are to do, or lack the skills to carry out the task. A common example of a lack of skill interfering with successful completion of a task is if participants resolve to be a better listener to their spouse, but lack the communication skills to convey effective listening. The questions suggested in Table 6.2 enable the educator to identify if either lack of understanding or lack of skill applied in the case of an unsuccessful attempt at self-change. The second possibility is that particular thoughts about completing the task may interfere with performance. For example, the person might believe that the self-change goal was not really useful. It is important to probe the person about what he or she *really* thinks about the self-change task. If the person has the requisite knowledge and skills, and believes the task is useful, then it is likely something in the person's environment that is the problem. There might not be a specific prompt that gets the person started. This is often what people mean when they say they "forgot" or "did not get around to it."

The following transcript illustrates the process of how an educator can review noncompletion of a self-change plan. In this case Janine has just reported that she did not "get around to" arranging a planned weekend away.

TABLE 6.2. Some Questions to Explore Noncompletion of Self-Change Plans

Area being explored	Possible questions
Does the person have the knowledge and skills to undertake the task?	*Just to make sure we were clear, tell me what you intended to do in your self-change plan.* (Probe as required to establish exactly what was to be done and when.)
	If you were going to do that, show me how you would start. (For example, have the person ask a question that starts a conversation.)
Do the person's cognitions promote task completion?	*Sometimes people have second thoughts about their self-change plan. What really is your thinking about doing the task?* Probe as to whether the person believes the task is useful, is likely to make a difference to the relationship.
Does the environment promote task completion?	*Was there anything unusual about the past week that made it hard to get the task done? Is there anything extra you can set in place that would make it easier for you to do this?* Probe for exactly where and when the task might be attempted.

EDUCATOR: Janine, what were you trying to do?

JANINE: It was a busy week, and it just did not happen.

EDUCATOR: OK, Janine, so it didn't happen. Just to be sure that I was clear when we were talking, can you tell you exactly what it was that you intended to do during the week?

JANINE: I was going to line up a weekend away for us.

EDUCATOR: OK, and what exactly were you wanting to get done by tonight so you two could have a weekend away?

JANINE: I was looking at a couple of weeks away; I was going to ring up a couple of places up the coast, and see if we could book anything.

EDUCATOR: OK, that seems pretty clear. Now sometimes when people get to the point of actually taking some action they start to wonder if it's really a good idea. Sometimes I develop some really rotten ideas with people, and when it comes time to do it they go "Nah, this is a rotten idea." What do you *really* think about the idea of organizing a weekend away?

JANINE: I liked the idea. We've had very little time away together in the last 12 months or so. But I worry if we have got enough money to be taking weekends away. Our house repayments are pretty high. We're kind of struggling to keep up and maybe a weekend is just beyond us now.

EDUCATOR: Mmm hmm, mmm hmm. So it might just be a bit too much money? So what do you want to do?

JANINE: I think Geoff and I should sit down and review our budget. See what sort of luxuries we really can afford.

EDUCATOR: Excellent, excellent. So you could do a review. If you can afford it, great. If not, maybe there's something else that you might try, which is not quite so expensive.

JANINE: Mmm hmm.

EDUCATOR: So Janine, what will you do in the next week?

JANINE: (*turning to Geoff*) How about we sit down one night this week, go through the budget, and see if we've got $150 or so that we can afford for a weekend away?

EDUCATOR: Geoff?

GEOFF: I think we probably can afford a weekend away, but let's check and see.

EDUCATOR: Janine, it seems to me that just thinking about a weekend away had moved things along. It's got you thinking about how you and Geoff can have fun together in an affordable way. Will you tell us next week what you work out?

JANINE: Yeah, sure.

In the above example, Janine had a thought that interfered with her self-change plan of organizing a weekend away. She had doubts that she and Geoff could really afford the cost. By identifying the blocking thought, the educator helped her to develop a way forward. In other instances the person might really want to carry out the self-change plan, and yet not get around to it. In busy lives, it can be easy for people to let relationship resolutions slip. If this were the case for Janine, it could be useful to discuss what she might do to make her self-change plan happen. For example, she and Geoff could identify a specific day, time, and place to have the planned conversation, or book in time in her diary (if she keeps one) to do the task, or put a note on the fridge to remind them.

In responding to the completion of self-change plans, it is important to praise and support people's change efforts. Even partial attempts should be given encouragement because they reflect effort to enhance the relationship. In the above example the educator praises Janine for having thought about what she intended to do. When self-change plans have not been implemented, it is important to problem-solve, and assist people to set themselves up for future success. The educator undertaking the review process provides a model of how to conduct self-change, as well as assisting the couple to produce positive shifts in the relationship. Each partner learning self-change is central to sustaining long-term couple relationship satisfaction.

Challenges in Helping Couples Learn Self-Change

In research with Couple CARE we find that on average partners in early stage relationships specify and at least partially complete more than 90% of self-change plans (Wilson & Halford, 2008). Partners who have recently had their first child, and who are often extremely busy, complete more than 80% of self-change plans (Halford, Petch, & Creedy, 2010). These very high rates of completion likely reflect the fact that the partners select their own self-change goals. In addition, in the delivery of Couple CARE, we have tried to ensure that the educators provide strong support to partners in attempting self-change.

A mistake some educators make when delivering Couple CARE is to ignore noncompletion of self-change plans. If educators overlook reviewing self-change plans that can inadvertently convey to the couples that the self-change tasks are not all that important. A related mistake is to minimize a lack of completion of self-change plans. For example, some educators when told that the person was "busy in the last week" might respond with "OK, we'll see if you can get it done in the next week." It is important for the educator to be proactive in assisting partners with their self-change efforts. The three-step process defined in Table 6.2 is a really useful approach.

While the rate of noncompletion of self-change plans in Couple CARE usually is low if educators actively support people's self-change efforts, there are at least three situations in which partners might not be able to articulate a specific change they want to make. First, for some couples particular aspects of their relationship might well be strengths and not require any substantive change. When any previous assessment (e.g., RELATE) and what you observe in session suggest that the focus of a particular session is an area of relationship strength, it is important not to push people to make changes they see as unnecessary. Rather, the focus should be on what behavior is currently making this area a relationship strength, and how that important behavior can be sustained. It is noteworthy that this discussion of sustaining strengths is also used when reviewing the RELATE assessment report. The educator needs to praise relationship strengths and help couples to reflect on how to sustain these strengths.

A second reason why some people struggle to define self-change goals is that thinking about specific behaviors is new to them. The self-change plan in Unit 1 is introduced with limited guidance to assist couples in selecting and refining their self-change plans. This is deliberate. It provides an opportunity to gauge how well the partners can do self-change with limited structure or assistance. However, it is important that in Unit 1 the key elements of effective self-change have been introduced, and examples of specific helpful self-change plans shown. If it seems that some people do not understand the concepts, revision might be needed. In subsequent chapters I provide a series of handouts that provide specific suggestions for couples on self-change behaviors they might like to try. The group context also provides opportunities for people to talk together and learn about new relationship-enhancing options. Having people ask their partner for suggestions is another very good source of ideas. The development of self-change is a skill that people develop across the course of the group sessions. In the review of self-change plans at the beginning of Unit 2 the educator is gathering information about the level of assistance each partner might need to develop self-change skills.

A third reason that people often struggle to define a self-change goal is if they have a belief that changing their own behavior is not likely to help the relationship. Sometimes spouse change might be useful, and in such instances the educator might focus on how one partner can express his or her desire for his or her spouse to change in a constructive manner. However, if there is a pervasive belief that all or almost all change to enhance the relationship should come from the spouse, this is unhelpful. As described in Chapter 1, such a belief is almost always associated with relationship distress. If a distressed couple is struggling to make progress within the context of group Couple CARE, I strongly recommend the educator discuss with them whether attending the group is likely to the most helpful approach for them. I explain to couples that if group Couple CARE is to be effective, then each partner needs to be willing to accept some responsibility for enhancing the relationship. If each is waiting for the other to make changes, then a different approach is needed. Halford (2001) sets out the process by which distressed couples might be helped to move toward self-change to enhance their relationship. This usually requires some intensive work by a therapist with the couple, and is best accomplished outside the group context.

WHAT IS GOOD COMMUNICATION?

The focus in this chapter is on the "how to" of running a Couple CARE session to help couples enhance their communication. However, before getting to the specifics of the "how to," I want to briefly review some important research findings on couple communication that shape the approach recommended in this chapter.

Research on Good Communication

Chapter 1 outlined the considerable research on the association between couples' communication and their relationship satisfaction. The literature suggests that the specific behaviors that constitute effective communication vary considerably from one couple to the next. Factors like personal communication style, relationship history, and the culture of each partner influence what behaviors form effective communication in a particular relationship. This means that attempting to teach a particular style of communication to all couples is unlikely to be effective.

As noted in Chapter 2, skill-based relationship education emphasizes communication skill training, and usually is applied universally to couples with the goal of sustaining high relationship satisfaction (Halford, 2004). In many such programs couples are taught specific communication skills on the assumption that all couples will better sustain satisfaction if they learn these skills. For example, some programs recommend that partners use particular formulae for expressing themselves, such as encouraging self-disclosure in the form "I feel X when you do Y." Other programs are less prescriptive, but still focus on particular communication skills. For example, in Markman and colleagues' (2001) description of PREP they advocate couples learning active listening skills, such as paraphrasing, which are intended to prevent potentially destructive negativity.

As noted in Chapter 1, a consistent finding in the communication literature is that high levels of negativity (e.g., criticisms, disagreements) predict deteriorating couple relationship satisfaction (Heyman, 2001). However, reducing negativity does not universally help couples sustain relationship satisfaction (Baucom et al., 2006; Schilling et al., 2003). Communication skill training that reduces negative communication in couples with high initial levels of communication negativity does enhance maintenance of high sustained relationship satisfaction, but it does not have the same beneficial effect in couples with low initial levels of communication negativity (Halford et al., 2001). Since different couples need to make different communication changes to help sustain long-term relationship satisfaction, some couples might need to make little or no change in their communication.

CRE that seeks to reduce already low rates of negative communication may inadvertently promote avoidance of discussion of difficult issues, and such avoidance is likely to lead to deteriorating relationship satisfaction (Heyman, 2001). Some couples at risk for future relationship distress do not show high communication negativity. For instance, Halford, Nicholson, and Sanders (2007) found that low negativity and high withdrawal characterized the communication of couples who had recently formed a stepfamily, a group at high risk for future relationship problems. Stepfamily couples report they often avoid discussing difficult issues as they fear such discussion might escalate into conflict (Afifi & Schrodt, 2003).

In summary, while there is a consistent finding that communication negativity predicts poor relationship satisfaction, research does not show that teaching communication to reduce negativity assists all couple relationships. This analysis of the evidence suggests that communication skill training needs to be tailored to address the strengths and challenges of individual couples. To that end, in Couple CARE the approach is to encourage partners to self-assess their communication effectiveness within their relationship, rather than to promote the use of specific skills to be universally applied. This requires the couple relationship educator to do four things. First, the educator helps couples understand the two key functions of communication, speaking and listening. Second, the educator demonstrates, and helps couples identify, some key communication skills. These skills are different behaviors that can constitute effective speaking and listening. Third, the educator prompts each person to self-evaluate his or her current communication and identify areas of communication strength and challenge. This self-evaluation is framed in terms of the current use of specific communication skills. Finally, the educator helps the partners develop and implement individually selected communication self-change goals.

HELPING COUPLES DEVELOP BETTER COMMUNICATION

In the group-based delivery of Couple CARE it is useful to prompt couples to reflect on the importance and nature of effective communication. The topic of communication might be introduced something like this:

> "A key thing almost all happy couples identify as one of the reasons they are happy is that they communicate well. Phrases like 'we understand each other' and 'we can talk to each other' seem simple and yet capture something vital—that to be truly understood is something really special. In contrast, unhappy couples very often describe poor communication as one of their key problems.
>
> "I would like you to think about a couple you know well, not yourselves but another couple that you think communicates well. It might be parents, other relatives, or close friends. I would like you to talk with your partner—as a couple—about what you notice about how that other couple communicates. Try to describe what you could point out about the couple if we were watching them talking. Take a minute or two to chat about what makes the couple good communicators, and I will ask you what you came up with."

As the couples begin to talk together the educator can circulate among the participants, checking in with each of them to make sure that they have identified a couple they know that communicates well. The educator should help them to be specific about what makes up good communication for that particular couple. For example, if a couple is struggling to be specific, ask them whether the partners listen well to each other, and, if so, how do they express that good listening? As the rate of talking around the group starts to slow up, this is a sign the exercise has had enough time. It can be useful to go around the group asking people what characteristics of good listening they identified, and then write these up on the board.

Another option for introducing the topic of communication is to show the beginning of Unit 2 of the Couple CARE DVD. It shows a series of couples talking about the importance of communication, and what each believes makes up good communication. Once couples are primed to be thinking about good communication, it is time to introduce the intent–impact model of communication.

The Intent–Impact Model of Communication

To assist partners to self-assess their communication the intent–impact model of effective communication provides a useful framework for understanding. The essence of the model is presented schematically in Figure 6.1. In a group the educator could explain the model something like this:

> "Starting at the left of the diagram the speaker forms an intent, which is the feeling or idea the speaker wants to express. The speaker then delivers a message, which is what the speaker actually says, how he or she says the words, and how he or she looks when he or she says these things. Between the speaker and the message is this wavy line, which is called a filter. A filter is anything that changes the message so it does not match what the speaker intended to say. Examples of filters include the speaker's mood, speech habits, and facial expression. The listener also has a filter, shown as the wavy line on the right. The listener's filter is anything that changes the listener's understanding of the message. Examples of listener filters include the listener thinking he or she already knows what the person is going to say and is not listening carefully, the listener being distracted by something else, or the listener's mood. Impact is the listener's final understanding of the message.

FIGURE 6.1. Intent–impact model of effective communication.

"In good communication intent equals impact. That is, the impact of the message on the listener is what the speaker intended. This does not always happen. Sometimes the speaker's intent is not reflected in the message. Have you ever had the experience of hearing your own words and thinking, 'No, that is not really what I meant?' Being tired or stressed can lead us to say things more sharply than we meant to. Listeners can easily misunderstand an unclear message. Even messages that are really clear can be misunderstood if the listener is tired or distracted."

Three key points need to be made about the intent–impact model in order to assist couples. First, it is important for people to speak *and* listen effectively, and each partner needs to find ways to do this that work in their relationship. Second, there is no specific formula that partners have to follow to be effective communicators. Third, filters can interfere with communication. Filters can distort a message so that it becomes different from the intended message. Filters also can interfere with listeners so that the impact of the message is distorted from what an outside observer might conclude from the message.

Key Communication Skills

Figure 6.2 lists four speaking skills and six listening skills, which can serve as a useful handout for the educator to describe the skills. This list of skills is provided to participants to give them a way of describing the communication skills they use. It is important that skills are described and demonstrated by the educator. (The Couple CARE DVD shows a couple having a discussion in which each of these skills is demonstrated and described; showing this segment is another good way to introduce the skills.)

When introducing the key communication skills, it is important to explain that defining these skills is intended to provide a means of describing ways of communicating effectively. People are not expected to use all the skills, or a particular combination of skills, with their partner. Rather, the goal is to have participants self-evaluate the current way that they speak and listen to their partner, and to identify if there might be ways to enhance the effectiveness of that communication.

HELPING COUPLES SELF-ASSESS
THEIR COMMUNICATION

The current exercise is the first of several communication exercises that couples undertake across the course of Couple CARE. In introducing this

Speaker Skills

1. *Describe specifics.* Provide clear and concrete descriptions of behaviors or situations.

2. *Express positives.* Clearly express your thoughts and feelings about the positive aspects of a situation or your partner's behavior, even if things seem mostly negative.

3. *Assert negatives.* Without being aggressive or attacking, say directly what you dislike or want to see change.

4. *Self-disclose feelings.* Share your thoughts and feelings with your partner even if it feels difficult.

Listener Skills

5. *Attend.* Focus your attention on your partner when he or she is speaking. This includes having eye contact, facing your partner, and removing distractions (e.g., put down the newspaper, switch off the television).

6. *Encourage.* This involves saying things like "Oh," "Go on," or "I see" so your partner knows you're interested in what he or she is saying.

7. *Summarize content.* State back to your partner *in your own words* the *key points* of what he or she has just said.

8. *Paraphrase feelings.* Summarize in words the emotion your partner is expressing. Often his or her emotion will not be said in words, but will be reflected in how he or she says things, and how he or she looks.

9. *Ask questions.* Ask open-ended questions that encourage your partner to open his or her up ideas.

10. *Hear your partner out.* Let your partner finish speaking, consider what he or she said, and avoid immediately disagreeing or defending yourself. Put your own opinion on hold until later.

FIGURE 6.2. Key speaker and listener communication skills.

exercise it useful to make three points. First, this communication exercise focuses on understanding and expressing interest in the other person and his or her interests. Having a genuine interest in your partner's world is really important. The happiest spouses know through a series of regular conversations what is happening in their partner's world. If there is a stressful time coming at your spouse's work, you know about it and can be supportive. If there is a special occasion coming up that is important for your partner, you are aware of its importance and might arrange something celebratory. If your spouse has a real passion (e.g., for a sports team, for an artistic activity), then you can plan other activities not to clash with key events related to this passion.

Second, this exercise will be built upon to help partners communicate support for each other effectively (covered in Unit 3) and manage differences (covered in Unit 4). Reviewing one's communication is important as a building block for these other areas. However, the first step is to focus on expressing interest. The third point to be made when introducing the communication exercise is to pique participants' interest in discovering more about their partner by highlighting how it relates to sustaining passion in a relationship. This point might be made something like this:

> "Passion. Almost everyone feels passion early in a relationship. It is that wonderful walk-into-walls, can't-think-of-anything-but-your-partner, overwhelmed-by-your-hormones, type feeling. It's a wonderful feeling. If you still have it in your relationship now, savor it. Many couples find passion fades, even disappears.
>
> "But passion can be sustained. Passion is, according to a famous social psychologist Baumeister, the thrill of novelty, of the new. Passion happens in new relationships because we are constantly learning new things about the other person. We learn about them the first time we stay up late just talking, the first time we kiss, make love, stay together for a weekend.
>
> "Routine, the same activities, year after year, can be comfortable. Routine is necessary to get to work, to take care of family, to pay the bills. But to sustain passion we need to learn new things about each other. One way to do that is by really listening to each other. Across years we build more understanding of each other, we rejoice in the new strengths we discover. We come to understand—and often accept—the inevitable human failings.
>
> "Each of you is in a committed relationship. You know the other person well. But in the next 3 to 4 minutes I want you to try to learn something new, something different about your partner. I want you to really try to better understand one piece of your partner's world."

The self-assessment of communication exercise consists of four steps. First, each partner is asked to select a topic to discuss with his or her spouse. The topic selected should be something that the speaker is interested in, but that the spouse knows relatively little about. For example, it could be discussing a hobby or sport of interest to the speaker, a work issue, or an extended family-related issue. The topic should not be something that has been a source of conflict between the partners. The goal in this communication exercise is for effective communication of interests; management of conflict is covered in Unit 4.

The second step is for each partner to define a communication goal for the discussion. This involves each person defining particular behaviors he or she will do. The checklist of skills can be consulted to help people define specific goals. This step of goal setting is intended to encourage the partners to focus on their own behavior and to be intentional in trying to be a better communicator.

The third step is to have the conversation. Each partner takes turns speaking for about 5 minutes on his or her chosen topic. The task of the speaker is to convey what is of interest to him or her about the topic. The role of the spouse is to listen carefully, to convey interest, and to learn more about the topic. Once the couple has spoken for 3–4 minutes on the selected topic, they then swap the speaker and listener roles and have the second conversation. The final step is for partners to individually self-evaluate their communication during the conversations using the form that appears as Figure 6.3.

Partner Feedback on Communication

Feedback from a spouse about communication can be very helpful to people in developing more effective communication. However, it is important that the feedback that is provided is constructive, is provided in such a manner that it is easy for the person to understand, and is presented positively. Therefore, in Couple CARE the concept of what is useful feedback is introduced at this point in the program. The general principles of how to provide constructive feedback are used in subsequent units.

Figure 6.4 sets out some useful guidelines for providing effective feedback. This can be used as a handout to introduce the idea of feedback. Three key points to be made about effective feedback are as follows:

1. Most people appreciate positive feedback for what they do well, and it is very important in developing effective communication to identify what is helpful and to keep doing that.
2. Criticism tends to elicit defensiveness and not to be helpful feedback. The comment "You never look at me when I talk to you" often elicits

On your own . . . Place a check mark in the appropriate box to describe how *you* think it went during the discussion using this key. (Don't feel that you have to have used all the 10 skills.)

0	No use of this skill
1	Some use of this skill
2	OK, but could be better
3	Good use of this skill
N/A	Skill not applicable

	Skill	0	1	2	3	N/A
Speaker skills	Describe specifics					
	Express positives					
	Assert negatives					
	Self-disclose feelings					
Listener skills	Attend					
	Encourage					
	Summarize content					
	Paraphrase feelings					
	Ask questions					
	Hear my partner out					

My communication strengths: _____

_____

_____

Communication goals I want to work on: _____

_____

_____

FIGURE 6.3. Communication self-evaluation form.

From *Marriage and Relationship Education* by W. Kim Halford. Copyright 2011 by The Guilford Press. Permission to photocopy this figure is granted to purchasers of this book for personal use only (see copyright page for details). Purchasers may download a larger version of this figure from the book's page on The Guilford Press website.

Less helpful	More helpful
"I think that all went very well." (*What exactly did the person do that was good?*)	"I thought you did a really good job of telling me your ideas about the problems; you were clear and to the point."
"You were very vague." (*What are you suggesting to the speaker?*)	"It would have helped me if you had been specific about what you wanted to say to your sister."
"You did a great job of listening to me." (*What exactly was done that conveyed to you that you were being listened to?*)	"You looked at me, asked me questions, and heard me out. That made me feel you were really listening."
"I thought you were rude; you did not seem at all interested in listening to me." (*What could the person do to show he or she was really listening?*)	"If you looked at me more, and asked a question or two, I would feel like you were really focused on me."

FIGURE 6.4. Less helpful and more helpful forms of feedback.

From *Marriage and Relationship Education* by W. Kim Halford. Copyright 2011 by The Guilford Press. Permission to photocopy this figure is granted to purchasers of this book for personal use only (see copyright page for details). Purchasers may download a larger version of this figure from the book's page on The Guilford Press website.

a defensive response, such as a disagreement ("Yes I do") or a justification ("Well, it's hard when you go on and on and on").

3. In contrast, most people are responsive to positive suggestions on how they can improve their communication, provided that the feedback is provided as a suggestion.

Feedback formulated as an instruction like "You have to start looking at me when I talk to you" tends to be less well received than the suggestion "It might help to convey you are really listening if you looked at me more when I am talking."

In providing feedback each partner writes down two specific things he or she believes their spouse did well when communicating with them, and one suggestion to enhance the communication. The feedback should be framed positively and as a suggestion. Partners then give each other the feedback and discuss that feedback, culminating in each person reflecting on his or her self-evaluation of their communication and modifying that evaluation as required based on the partner feedback.

Reviewing the Communication Exercise

The educator plays a very important role in helping the partners to clarify their communication self-evaluation and assisting them to identify specific changes they might want to make. The leader should circulate among the couples asking open-ended questions like the following, which help partners explore and clarify their communication self-evaluation.

- "What topic did you discuss when you were the listener?"
- "What were your communication goals for the communication task?"
- "What did you rate as your key strengths and weaknesses as a communicator?"
- "What feedback did your partner give you about your communication self-evaluation?"

It is highly desirable that the educator hears at least some of the couple's communication to check the accuracy of each partner's appraisal of communication. The educator can then shape up accurate self-evaluation as required. For example, consider the following exchange after just a minute or so of a couple's discussion. The educator helps the male partner develop accurate self-evaluation of his listening.

PAUL: (*laughing*) So, is it the men in tights? The strange leaping about?

SOPHIE: I really love the ballet, Paul, I always have.

PAUL: OK, OK, you really like ballet. That's great, but I don't.

SOPHIE: I know that Paul, you are clear that you don't want to go.

PAUL: Well it's really expensive. Even if we both liked going we cannot really afford it.

SOPHIE: I know, I am not trying to say we should go.

EDUCATOR: I want to pause you for a moment. Paul, what is the topic you are discussing?

PAUL: Sophie is talking about her and ballet.

EDUCATOR: Really? (*turning to Sophie*) I don't know *anything* about ballet, but my wife really loves it. So maybe Paul and *I* can learn something really important from this conversation. (*turning to Paul*) So, Paul, what did you like about how you were listening to Sophie?

PAUL: Like? Ahh . . .

EDUCATOR: Have a look at the handout in front of you on self-evaluation of communication. What listening skills do you think you were using?

PAUL: Umm . . . asking questions?

EDUCATOR: Well I only caught the last few sentences of the conversation. I did hear you ask some questions. You asked if Sophie liked men in tights, or "strange leaping around" I think you said.

PAUL: Well, I was joking around.

EDUCATOR: OK. Did Sophie laugh?

PAUL: No, she looked kind of annoyed.

EDUCATOR: So while your intent was to be lighthearted, it did not help the conversation?

PAUL: No, no.

EDUCATOR: I am wondering if there is a real, open question that might help Sophie to explain to us about her fascination with ballet. Any thoughts?

PAUL: Not sure what you mean . . .

EDUCATOR: Paul, how about I show you what I mean? Sophie, would you be willing to tell me a little about your love of ballet? (*Sophie nods.*) OK, I really know nothing, so help me to get it. What does ballet mean to you?

SOPHIE: I did ballet as a girl. I always loved the physical challenge of it. How it took lots of practice to do even the most basic move. When I watch a really good ballerina, I am awestruck how she can make such incredible moves look so easy, and be so expressive.

EDUCATOR: So part of it is the sheer athleticism, the ability to do incredible physical moves, and part of it is applying that to expression?

SOPHIE: Yes, exactly. You know, I see Paul awestruck by football players doing a little sidestep. I watch a ballerina leap a meter in the air, move to horizontal with a swirl of her arms and seem to float in just the right place for her partner to catch and hold her there. She does all this to express ecstasy or joy. It's beautiful. Yet Paul calls this "strange leaping about."

EDUCATOR: So, Paul, what is Sophie telling us?

PAUL: That she sees dancers like athletes?

EDUCATOR: Great, that does seem to be part of it, athletes that can express themselves in special, fascinating ways. Is there a question Paul you might ask now to move things along further?

PAUL: Um, maybe what got her interested? (*Educator signals with a flat palm toward Sophie that Paul should ask the question.*) Soph, how did you get so interested in ballet?

SOPHIE: Well, I spent 2 to 3 hours per day 6 days per week for 9 years practicing ballet. I started at just 5. I injured my knee and had to give it up, but even now I still miss it.

EDUCATOR: Part of you wants still to be dancing, expressing yourself in that very physical way?

SOPHIE: Yes, when I danced well I felt alive—more alive than at just about any other time. There was no conscious thought, just the flow of movements, feelings.

EDUCATOR: That sounds very special. Paul, what is Sophie telling you?

PAUL: That she felt "in the zone" dancing?

SOPHIE: Yes, yes. And when I see the ballet, only on TV now—but even on TV—I get some of that feeling.

EDUCATOR: Sophie, thank you. You are helping us start to understand the sheer physical beauty of ballet that so moves you. Perhaps this is a conversation you two might like to continue at home. For now let's focus on what you just did Paul. What did you do when listening to Sophie?

PAUL: I asked her a question.

EDUCATOR: Yes, you did. And it was a great question. "What got you interested in ballet?" really got things going. Then what did you do?

PAUL: I asked another question about if that was like being in the zone.

EDUCATOR: I guess that is a question in one way. But really you were paraphrasing her feelings. Putting in your own words what she felt. Paraphrasing is really hard to do well; you have to be really listening. Do you remember what Sophie said after that?

PAUL: Ah, then she said something about watching ballet on TV.

EDUCATOR: She did, she kept talking—explaining more. And before that she said "yes, yes," meaning—I think—that you got it, you really got it. So, Paul, what are the couple of strengths of yours we have identified?

PAUL: Paraphrasing, um . . .

EDUCATOR: And asking questions. Great. Sophie, let's turn to your communication. What strengths did you notice in your speaking?

If a partner is really struggling to identify ways of enhancing his or her communication, then it can be useful to demonstrate some positive communication skills. As in the interaction with Paul and Sophie this can involve picking up the conversation with the spouse and illustrating how a conversation can be deepened and extended with effective communication. The goal at the end of the self-evaluation of communication is that both partners can accurately describe some specific strengths of their current communication, and identify at least one specific way in which they could further strengthen their communication. In the process the partners are encouraged to show real interest in each other. Often they discover important new aspects of each other. This can have profound effects. One woman who had been married for 28 years described it as "falling in love all over again."

EMOTIONAL BIDS

Emotional bids are indirect requests for attention or approval in a relationship. Figure 6.5 lists some examples of statements that might be emotional bids. It can be useful to talk about the function of emotional bids. You might explain it this way:

> "Couples often use emotional bids in their relationship. Such bids serve to indirectly express a need for closeness, and by expressing this need indirectly it reduces the chance of overt rejection. Consider Example 1 in the handout [Figure 6.5]. Imagine you are sitting on the lounge with your partner and he or she says that to you. If your partner wants a cuddle, why would they not just say so? What do you think?"

Often couples will be able to talk about the desire to avoid rejection. If not, I would talk specifically about the idea of anxiety about being rejected, and how almost everybody worries about that at some level. Emotional bids allow an attempt to get closeness without carrying the same risk of overt rejection as a direct request. It is normal and quite healthy to have emotional bids in relationships.

Another way to introduce this concept to couples is to show them the Couple CARE DVD segment that introduces the idea in Unit 2. The segment shows a couple sitting apart on a sofa. The woman comments that it is cold in the room. A voiceover commentary notes that this comment might mean it really is cold, but it also might mean she would like a cuddle from her partner.

While emotional bids can reduce the risk of rejection, their subtlety means sometimes the speaker's intended message does not have the impact

Emotional bid	Possible implicit message
1. "It's a bit cold in here, isn't it?"	"Can we cuddle and be close?"
2. "I am off to bed for an early night, how about you?"	"Will you come with me and make love?"
3. "Do you really like this new outfit?"	"Do you still find me attractive? Do I really look alright to you?"
4. "I see that new movie Jean was telling us about is on this afternoon."	"Would you like to spend the afternoon with me at the movie?"
5. "Are you working late again tonight?"	"Would you spend the evening with me, I would really like you to."
6. "The kids missed you while you were away."	"I missed you while you were away."
7. "Joey arranged to go away camping with Jeanette last weekend to that new place in the hinterland. Jeanette said it was very pretty."	"I'd love it if you arranged a weekend away for us somewhere special. It doesn't have to be anywhere expensive."

FIGURE 6.5. Examples of emotional bids in close relationships.

on the listener that is intended. In Couple CARE we invite both partners to write down some examples of emotional bids they use in their relationship using the handout presented as Figure 6.6. They then discuss the advantages and disadvantages of their current use of emotional bids with their spouse. The goal is to have partners reflect on whether there might be emotional needs they have in the relationship that could be communicated more effectively.

It is useful to invite the couples to present to the group examples of emotional bids from their relationship that they are prepared to share. This illustrates the wide use of emotional bids. Also discuss what couples identified as the advantages and disadvantages of emotional bids in their relationship; such discussion can help to broaden the learning. Two concluding points are often worth making. First, emotional bids are a normal and healthy part of intimate relationships. Second, in good relationships partners watch out for,

On your own, write down two examples of emotional bids you have made toward your partner.

Two examples of emotional bids I have used in my relationship:

1. _____

   _____

   _____

   _____

2. _____

   _____

   _____

   _____

As a couple, discuss the pluses of using emotional bids in your relationship. How do emotional bids work with you two? Also discuss the minuses of emotional bids. What possible misunderstandings or problems can emotional bids generate?

The pluses of emotional bids: _____

_____

_____

_____

_____

The minuses of emotional bids: _____

_____

_____

_____

_____

FIGURE 6.6. Reflecting on emotional bids in your relationship.

and try to respond positively to, the emotional bids of their spouse. In fact, in some cultures (e.g., the Chinese culture), directly stating one's needs can be seen as bad manners and it is expected that people will be able to understand the needs of others. In relationships with partners from different cultures or backgrounds, not understanding emotional bids can pose a significant challenge.

COMMUNICATION SELF-CHANGE PLAN

Each partner is invited to develop a self-change plan based on the content covered in Unit 2 on communication. The structure of the plan has the same five steps that were used for the self-change plan in Unit 1. This same structure is applied at the end of each unit throughout Couple CARE. Two examples of communication self-change plans are provided in Figure 6.7. The common strength of each example is that the person is trying to be a better listener to her partner. It can be useful to have couples compare the two examples, identify what is different, and determine what might be the more helpful self-change plan. (Note: The examples have the same self-evaluation, but the second one provides more specific goals for change. A limitation of the second example is that the person is trying to make four changes at once. It is generally better to do just one or two things at a time.)

After this exercise all participants draft a communication self-change plan using the form in Figure 6.8. Ask at least some of the participants to read out the self-change plan they have developed. If partners offer self-change goals that are vague, the educator helps to clarify and make concrete the specific behaviors that are to be implemented.

FINISHING THE SESSION

After completion of the development of the self-change plan, it is useful to review the session content. Ask the participants to speak with their partners about what they thought was the most important content covered in the session. Asking the couples to summarize one key point to the group helps reinforce the learning, and also gives feedback to the educator about what couples are learning. It also is useful to ask the couples if there are questions or concerns raised by the content of the unit.

At around Session 2 I also routinely ask couples whether the program to this point is heading in the right direction for them. Do they feel that the

(text resumes on page 167)

1. DESCRIBE	**2. FOCUS**
Choose an aspect of your communication you'd like to work on. Describe this aspect clearly and positively (write in the spaces provided).	What do I currently do?
	Try to chill out and listen, but then get pushy for him to get to the point.
To be more positive when I listen to Steve and not be so impatient.	What are the **pluses** of my current behavior?
	I ease back a little more than I used to.
	What are the **minuses** of my current behavior?
	Steve gets stressed and feels bad.
3. GOAL	**4. ACT**
Define as precisely as you can what you want to happen.	What will I do? Where and when will I do it?
To be less impatient.	*Try to stay relaxed, let him finish even if he is rambling.*

5. EVALUATE—After you have implemented your action plan:

What did I actually do?

What positives resulted?

What negatives resulted?

What do I need to do from here?

(cont.)

FIGURE 6.7. Communication self-change plan examples.

1. DESCRIBE

Choose an aspect of your communication you'd like to work on. Describe this aspect clearly and positively (write in the spaces provided).

To be more positive when I listen to Steve

and not be so impatient.

_____

_____

_____

_____

_____

2. FOCUS

What do I currently do?

Try to chill out and listen, but then get

pushy for him to get to the point.

What are the **pluses** of my current behavior?

I ease back a little more than I used to.

_____

What are the **minuses** of my current behavior?

Steve gets stressed and feels bad.

_____

3. GOAL

Define as precisely as you can what you want to happen.

Really give him my time and undivided

attention, show him he is important to

_me._

4. ACT

What will I do? Where and when will I do it?

Take it slow, ask questions, talk slowly, let

Steve finish what he is saying.

_____

5. EVALUATE—After you have implemented your action plan:

What did I actually do?

_____

What positives resulted?

_____

What negatives resulted?

_____

What do I need to do from here?

_____

FIGURE 6.7. *(cont.)*

1. DESCRIBE	**2. FOCUS**
Choose an aspect of your communication you'd like to work on. Describe this aspect clearly and positively (write in the spaces provided).	What do I currently do?
	What are the **pluses** of my current behavior?
	What are the **minuses** of my current behavior?
3. GOAL	4. **ACT**
Define as precisely as you can what you want to happen.	What will I do? Where and when will I do it?

5. EVALUATE—After you have implemented your action plan:

What did I actually do?

What positives resulted?

What negatives resulted?

What do I need to do from here?

FIGURE 6.8. Communication self-change plan.

content covered so far, and how we are working together, is achieving what they hoped from participating in Couple CARE? Listening carefully to the feedback and adjusting the group process as required can make a big difference in how well the whole process of Couple CARE goes.

CHALLENGES IN HELPING COUPLES DEVELOP THEIR COMMUNICATION

There are five common challenges in developing participants' communication that warrant discussion of how they can be managed. First, in some couples one partner is a substantially better communicator than the other. Such an imbalance can make the less skilled communicator feel uncomfortable or incompetent, and the more skilled communicator frustrated. In such instances it is often helpful to tell the couple that some people find learning intimate communication to be more challenging than others, and that is perfectly understandable. Not everybody can be a great communicator, and that is not essential to having a good relationship. The most important thing is to work at improving communication as best one can. The fact that one is trying seems to do as much good for a relationship as achieving any particular standard.

It also is worth noting that in most couples the partners bring different strengths to a relationship. One partner might be more effective at expressing feelings, the other partner better at remaining calm in a crisis, or having certain useful practical skills—like earning or managing money, or doing home maintenance. An important advantage of being in a couple relationship is that partners can, to some extent, specialize in what they do best.

A second common challenge is when participants mistake hearing for listening. Sometimes participants can be looking away, not responding to what their partner is saying, perhaps even attending to something else, and yet state, "I am listening, I can hear him [or her]." Hearing is the physical process of recognizing sound. Listening is an active process of thinking about what the person is saying, really trying to understand, and communicating that attempt to listen in an active way. Looking at the speaker, having an open body posture (not arms crossed), nodding, using encouragers like "uh-huh" and "yeah," asking questions, and summarizing or paraphrasing are different ways in which active listening is communicated. It can be useful to get people struggling with the idea of active listening to talk about something they are interested in to the educator. The educator begins hearing but not listening and then changes to active listening. The participants are asked to describe the change in the educator's behavior. Participants can then try using active listening with their own spouse.

A third challenge is the wordy speaker. Some people describe things in a long, circumstantial manner, which can make it difficult for the listener to extract the key message. Some people tell a story as they experienced it, rather than extracting the key points they really wanted to communicate. Shaping people up to be more concise and to focus on the key elements of the intended message is important. This makes it much easier for a listener to get the speaker's intended message. Consider the following example.

> JUDY: I wanted to tell you about the other day when I went to the mall with Norma—you remember Norma, she's married to Rich and they live out on the west side. Well I just pulled into her place when Rich came out to say hello. He's put on a lot of weight, and looks quite pale. I wonder if he's had some sort of illness? Anyway . . . where was I?
>
> SAM: Going to the mall with Norma?
>
> JUDY: Right, so anyway Norma comes to the car and starts telling Rich where we are going. It's strange how some wives seem to feel obliged to tell their husband exactly where they are going and what they are going to do. It's almost like they're asking permission. Not that I'm saying Rich demands Norma tells him . . .
>
> SAM: Where is all this going, Judy?
>
> EDUCATOR: Sam, it seems you are feeling kind of lost here.
>
> SAM: Yeah, I really am. I've got no idea of the point of this story.
>
> EDUCATOR: Judy, you tell a story rich with detail. But maybe all the detail is making it hard for Sam to get your key points. Are you able to say in one sentence one key point you want to express to Sam?
>
> JUDY: "Well, I was trying to illustrate some of the tensions, problems I see for Norma and Rich. You know Norma was telling me that she and Rich don't sleep in the same room anymore . . . "
>
> EDUCATOR: Judy, I am not sure if I have it. Are you saying you think Norma's marriage is in trouble?
>
> JUDY: Yes, I am sure it is, and I am really worried about her—and Rich.

Sometimes it takes a while to get people to spell out a key point succinctly. But the key issue in the above transcript is that the need to be clear and to the point often needs to be shaped up. Sometimes the best way to do that is to listen to the whole story and then summarize the key point(s), and have the person repeat the story but focusing on the key points. It also can be useful to try to get wordy speakers to begin with the end in mind. That is, to start by stating the point, and then building up detail as needed. For example, Judy could begin with her final statement of "I think Norma and Rich's marriage is in trouble, and I am really worried about them."

A fourth common challenge in teaching communication is participants who use little self-disclosure. Self-disclosure is making statements about one's own feelings, thoughts, or behavior. Self-disclosure usually involves a degree of risk in opening oneself up. Self-disclosure helps develop intimacy in close relationships. It is important when working with couples to prompt them to speak about feelings, and to get them to discuss the effects when they do talk openly about feelings.

Finally, some participants report that when they try to communicate differently, it does not feel "natural." I point out to people that feeling slightly uncomfortable is a good thing, it occurs when people are pushing themselves to try something different. Whenever we try something new it does not feel natural. Feeling natural happens when something has been practiced so much that it requires little conscious effort; it has become a habit. Almost no one feels "natural" when they first drive a car, swing a golf club, play a musical instrument, or deliver a public talk. With practice people learn the habits required to feel natural. Importantly, as people practice, they develop habits that do the important things required, and also learn their own unique way to do these critical elements. As people practice new communication skills they become habits, and people tend to find their own voice to use the skill in their own way.

CHAPTER 7

Unit 3

Intimacy and Caring

Unit 3 of Couple CARE is focused on promoting couple intimacy and caring. The content is summarized in Table 7.1. As with the structure of the previous unit, Unit 3 begins with a review of the content of the previous session, and discussion of how partners did with their communication self-change plans. Unit 3's intimacy and caring content has three components: developing effective mutual support between the partners, enhancing expression of caring, and reviewing and optimizing the balance of individual and couple activities. The social support content begins by introducing information on different forms of partner support. The couple then does an exercise that

TABLE 7.1. Overview of Unit 1: Intimacy and Caring

Topic and aim	Exercise(s)
Review Unit 2 communication self-change	Review each person's self-change plan; troubleshoot and provide extra skill training as required.
Understanding and self-assessment of social support	Introduce concepts of emotional and problem-focused support; have couple self-evaluate communication of support.
Caring behaviors	Introduce the importance of showing caring; partner feedback on showing caring; develop new ideas for showing caring.
Individual and couple activities	Introduce the importance of shared and individual activities, importance of novelty; self-evaluation of the balance of individual and couple activities.
Self-change plan	Individual develops self-change plans; educator assists.

involves having two discussions in which each partner has a turn at being supportive of the other; they each then self-evaluate their communication of support. As noted previously, this exercise builds upon the communication skills introduced in Unit 2.

To express caring content, both partners review the behaviors that express caring in their relationship, and both partners receive feedback from their spouse on their expression of caring. The partners then identify additional ways in which they can express caring. The partners also review their current balance of individual, couple, and other positive activities, and the range of activities that they engage in. As in previous units, partners are invited to develop at least one self-change plan to enhance their relationship.

The previous unit on communication mentioned that there is an association between discovering new things about your partner and sustaining relationship passion. In introducing the current unit it can be helpful to link the content of this unit to sustaining relationship passion. This might be done with the following words:

"Welcome back, everybody. The session today focuses on intimacy and caring, which are central to sustaining passion. We are going to touch on three areas, each of which is linked to passionate relationships. First we will talk about social support, how we help our spouse through difficult times. When people conjure up images of love, they often think about romance, happy times. Important as such times are, passion is also forged in the flames of adversity. Across a lifetime all couples will experience tough times together. Parents will likely age and die; the demands of caring for young children can be exhausting; at times you are each likely to experience some work stress, a significant illness, and other life demands. A couple that stands together, and supports each other in the tough times, finds a closeness that is built on the shared experiences unique to that couple."

In discussing this issue of mutual support I sometimes self-disclose about how my wife and I have supported each other when our respective parents were aging. Educators who appropriately use self-disclosure can help make the meaning of sharing the struggles of life understandable to couples.

"A second focus in today's session is on expressing caring—the little ways we show care, love, and respect. Finally we will look at how you spend your time, the balance of individual and couple activities. Having fun together in new ways and expressing caring both help to sustain passion, and we will explore together how that works. But first, I want to review the communication self-change you planned in last week's session."

REVIEWING COMMUNICATION SELF-CHANGE

Ensuring that both partners are enhancing their communication is important because effective communication underpins content addressed later in the program. Some useful questions for reviewing with partners their understanding of the content of Unit 2 are as follows:

- "What stands out in your mind as the most important part of last week's unit?"
- "Have you applied any of what we discussed last week in your relationship?"
- "How might you apply ideas from our exploration of communication to your relationship?"

As noted previously, you can pose these questions in various formats. You might ask individuals to write down an answer and chat with their spouse about it, and then report back to the group. You could have two or more men speak together and two or more women speak together, which can draw out gender differences in what is emphasized. You could pose the question to the group as a whole. In my experience, varying the format of the review of previous sessions adds variety to the group process: different things are learned from each format of review.

The review of the communication self-change plan can also follow a variety of formats. Given that this is only the second group review of self-change plans, it is usually helpful for the educator to review at least one or two self-change plans in front of the whole group, so they develop an understanding of the process. Useful questions to pose include the following:

- "Can you tell me exactly what you tried to do to improve your communication?"
- "How did you go with last week's self-change plan?"
- "On a scale from 0 to 10 (with 0 being 'did not do anything like I planned' and 10 'completed exactly what I intended'), how well would you rate your carrying through of your self-change plan?"

If someone has not completed his or her self-change plan, go through the three-step review of uncompleted self-change plans described in the previous chapter. That is, check to make sure the person was clear on what he or she was trying to do. Ask him or her to report honestly on his or her own thoughts about the usefulness of the selected self-change plan, and explore environmental influences on completing the plan. Use this process to problem-solve how the person could successfully implement a communication self-change plan in the next week.

For people who successfully completed their self-change plan it is helpful to explore this success. Questions like the following can be used:

- "What was the difficult part, if anything, in carrying out your communication self-change plan?"
- "What effect did changing your communication have on the conversation with your partner?"
- "What have you learned from this in terms of what you want to do in the future?"

In group sessions it can be helpful to have people write down answers to these questions, and the educator can circulate among the couples, discussing their answers with them. Having couples report back to the group on what they tried to change and their successes is also useful to do. After the discussion based on these questions it is helpful to have the couple continue the discussion that was part of the self-change plan and for the educator to provide feedback on the accuracy of each partner's self-evaluation of their communication. Often this sampling of communication shows that one or both partners needs further coaching to effectively develop their communication. This process is illustrated in the following example.

EDUCATOR: Mick, how did you do with last week's communication self-change?

MICK: Pretty good, I think.

EDUCATOR: Great, can you tell me exactly what you set out to do?

MICK: I wanted to listen to Georgia better.

EDUCATOR: Mmm-hmm, and what were you going to do to try to listen better?

MICK: Aaah, you know just focus on her, what she is saying, not jump in too soon with my ideas.

EDUCATOR: Right, I think you expressed it as letting her finish talking—not interrupting and also asking questions of Georgia. Is that what you mean?

MICK: Yep, that was it.

EDUCATOR: So, did you have a conversation in which you tried to do these things?

MICK: Yeah, we talked about Georgia's passion for jewelry making; she's done it as a hobby for years. I tried to really listen to her as she talked about it.

EDUCATOR: On the usual 0 to 10 scale we use, how do you think you did?

MICK: Well, umm, I thought I was doing OK, but somehow I got the feeling Georgia was not convinced. I probably give myself an 8, but I don't know, Georgia seemed irritated toward the end and asked if I was listening.

EDUCATOR: So, Mick, you tried to let her finish, ask questions, and not jump in—and you thought you were doing those things, but you felt maybe the conversation still was not working all that well?

MICK: Yeah. Toward the end Georgia said, "Are you listening?" and we were nearly out of time so I just said, "That's enough then" and we stopped. (*Laughs.*)

At this point the educator has a reasonably clear statement of the goals in the self-change plan and Mick's self-evaluation of his implementation of the plan. However, it is not clear if Mick actually did what he intended or not. The educator has two potential sources of information to assess this: the report of Mick's partner Georgia, and directly observing Mick's communication. In the following transcript the educator uses both these sources of information to assess Mick's communication.

EDUCATOR: Georgia, you've heard Mick on what he was trying to do and how he felt it went. Do you remember the conversation?

GEORGIA: Yeah, yeah, I do.

EDUCATOR: So can you tell us one thing you thought Mick did well in that conversation?

GEORGIA: Well, he did try to listen more, at least at the start. He asked a few things about what I like about jewelry making. But then I was talking about the creative bits in the design process, and he seemed to drift off.

EDUCATOR: Great feedback. So Mick is doing a good job listening to you, drawing you on some key things about your love of jewelry making. Then you say he sort of drifted off. What was he doing that gave you the impression he had drifted away from what you were saying?

GEORGIA: He went quiet, he was sort of ah-ha-ing and nodding but stopped asking questions or really showing interest.

EDUCATOR: So when he's active, asking questions, you feel he's there with you. But the nods and stuff—you think maybe he's just going through the motions, [that he is] not really all that interested?

GEORGIA: Yeah, exactly.

EDUCATOR: OK, that is really useful information. Mick, you're trying to be a better listener by letting Georgia finish and asking questions. Both you and Georgia seem to feel you did that well at the start of the conversation, but Georgia feels it sort of fell away. I suggest we get you to continue the conversation about jewelry making right now—maybe by asking Georgia about the design process she just mentioned. Then we all can discuss how it goes. Would that be OK?

MICK: Now? (*Educator nods.*) OK. Aaah . . . (*Pause.*)

EDUCATOR: Mick, why don't you ask Georgia to tell you about the process of designing jewelry, and really try to listen and ask questions.

MICK: Georgia, what is it you like about designing jewelry?

GEORGIA: Well the good stuff is thinking about a theme, you know like a concept—say the curves of the sail of a boat and how you could reflect that curve in earrings or say in a set of earrings and a necklace.

MICK: Right. Aaah . . . so, why sails?

GEORGIA: Sails is just an example, it might be a color, or mood, or some combination of inspirations, you know?

MICK: Mmm-hmm.

At this point Mick seems stuck, unsure how to develop the conversation. So the educator prompts self-evaluation by Mick. Such a self-evaluation tests whether the person is realistic in his or her appraisal of his or her communication, and the educator can offer suggestions for something different for him or her to try. In the continuing transcript the self-evaluation suggests that Mick is struggling. The educator then models how to proceed and next passes the conversation back to Mick.

EDUCATOR: Let me interrupt for a moment. Mick, what is one good thing you have done in talking with Georgia?

MICK: Well, I did ask her a question at the start, but I just don't know anything about jewelry making.

EDUCATOR: You're feeling stuck?

MICK: Yeah, I mean I am not sure what else there is to say.

EDUCATOR: Well we are in the same dilemma—I know nothing about jewelry making either. But I am curious about a couple of things Georgia said. Georgia, can I ask you a couple of questions? (*Georgia nods.*) Like I said to Mick, I really have no idea about this. I am hoping you can help me to understand the creative process a bit more. You mentioned the example of the sails: can you tell me about what happens that leads up to you having an idea, like the sails, as a theme for your creativity?

GEORGIA: It is hard to describe. I have a piece of paper in front of me, and I start sort of doodling. I might be thinking of someone I know who I want to make a gift for, and I think about them and their interests. I imagine them standing in front of me and their skin colors and the clothes they wear, their shape, and start to make associations. Half ideas about size, shape, color, themes start to form and I sort of—I don't know . . .

EDUCATOR: It sounds like sort of brainstorming within yourself, you are thinking about aspects of the person, shapes, colors, themes. The ideas seem kind of half formed, if I have understood, is that right?

GEORGIA: Yeah, it's not that you just have a design pop into your head. It's more like, you know, I think something dramatic is needed, it should be large, perhaps red drop earrings with a big curve. Then I start sort of doodling the curve.

EDUCATOR: I can see your fingers twitching, you really do get energized by the creativity, don't you?

GEORGIA: I love the randomness of it, you start thinking big and red but maybe it's the curve that becomes the defining theme, that gives the drama.

EDUCATOR: Let me just turn back to Mick for a moment. Mick, Georgia is telling us some fascinating stuff about how her head works when she is in creative mode. What did I do that got her started talking on this?

MICK: Well, first you said you knew nothing, I can do that. (*Laughs.*) You also pushed her to describe the creative process.

EDUCATOR: Have you got any questions that would help to get a better handle on the creative process Georgia so enjoys?

MICK: Georgia, when . . . what is it that you like so much about this?

EDUCATOR: Great question, Mick. Go ahead, Georgia.

GEORGIA: It's the whole thing, the initial focus, starting with nothing and developing a concept, playing with it, having it take shape, then actually building the piece. If it's good then you turn it around, put it on, look at it.

MICK: Mmm. So you make something beautiful right from nothing.

EDUCATOR: Mick, that is a really nice response, you are tracking what Georgia is telling you and showing her you really want to understand this passion of hers. Georgia, your response to Mick's comment?

GEORGIA: Yes, yes, Mick. There is just a part idea to start and then it becomes real.

A couple of important points are illustrated in the transcript of the session with Georgia and Mick. First, the educator needs to be active, prompting the partners to self-evaluate their behavior, modeling crucial skills, and providing encouragement for positive change. Second, often the educator is modeling curiosity and interest in the partner. Helping each person to appreciate the interesting things his or her spouse has to say, and encouraging each partner to really understand his or her spouse helps build the basis for positive communication. Often an interaction like the preceding one would then lead to development of another self-change plan. For example, Mick could be asked after the positive conversation what he learned about being a better listener and invited to develop a self-change plan to apply those skills in another conversation.

In a group setting, it can be useful to do a review process like that illustrated by the case of Georgia and Mick in front of the group—if the couple is willing to do this. It allows all the couples to see examples of effective communication, and how the communication process can be improved. The goal at this point is to have all participants identify a specific way in which they can enhance their communication with their partner.

DEVELOPING MUTUAL PARTNER SUPPORT

The development of mutual partner support involves two steps. First, the couples are introduced to a model of the types of partner support, and asked to consider the types of support that are most helpful in different circumstances. Second, the partners have two conversations, with each taking turns to be supportive of the other when discussing a stressful topic. They each then self-evaluate their communication of support, which involves identifying the strengths and weaknesses in how they communicated support to each other.

Introducing a Model of Types of Spouse Support

There are two broad forms of support partners offer each other. The first is *emotion-focused support,* which is listening, showing understanding, and helping your partner to talk about a problem. The second is *problem-focused support,* which is helping your partner to find solutions to a problem, and offering practical help to manage the problem.

In a group setting it can be useful to illustrate the different support needs of people by having the couples consider some hypothetical situations in which they might need spouse support. For example, I have asked each person to write down one really helpful thing their spouse could do to support them in the following situations: (1) one of your parents becomes seriously ill and you do not know if he or she will recover; (2) you have friends coming over for dinner later today and the house is a mess; (3) you recently had surgery to remove a benign (not cancerous) growth on your chest; (4) there is a big project happening over the next 2 weeks at work and you have a lot of extra work during that time. I have people read out their answers and then use the answers they provide to illustrate the types of support and how people vary in their desired support.

There is a key point to make about effective spouse support. People often seek different types of support from their spouse, and different situations require different sorts of support. It is important to be able to provide the sort of support that is wanted by the spouse and likely to be helpful. For example, suppose a partner is struggling with work demands and feels overwhelmed by his or her supervisor's work expectations. Emotional support would seek to show understanding of that experience; problem-solving support would try to identify actions to solve the problem, and might include specific actions to help manage the situation (e.g., picking up more of the household tasks for a time to reduce the overall burden). Each of these options is potentially useful, but offering unwanted types of support can be unhelpful.

On average, men tend to prefer and offer more problem-solving support, while women tend to prefer and offer more emotion-focused support. When talking with a couple I often ask the woman, "Have you ever had the experience of wanting to talk about something with your partner, and you really want to be listened to, but you feel he just keeps telling you what to do?" Many women report that this happens to them, and they find it frustrating. Many men report that they feel helpless if they cannot do something practical to help with a problem, and often see just listening as not doing enough to be supportive.

The common disjunction of the type of support needed and offered by men and women was graphically illustrated for me some years ago when I spoke with a group of women who had experienced breast cancer and their partners. Many of the men reported feeling powerless after the diagnosis because they could not do anything to make the cancer go away. They also said that if they spoke to their wife about the cancer she often became teary, and then they felt bad for "having upset her." Many men reported they then tried to "cheer their partner up" by changing the topic or suggesting an outing or activity. In commenting on the same discussions many of the women reported experiencing their partner as avoiding talking about her feelings. Once the men learned that their wives found that just listening was often very helpful, the couples coped with the stresses of diagnosis and treatment much more effectively (Scott et al., 2004).

Evaluating Communication of Spouse Support

This exercise of self-evaluation of the communication of social support builds upon the self-assessment of communication done in Unit 2. Figure 7.1 is a handout participants can use to self-evaluate their communication of support. As is evident from that figure, the same speaker and listener skills that were the focus of the self-evaluation in Unit 2 are included in this exercise. In addition, skills in emotion-focused and problem-solving support are added to the list of communication skills for self-evaluation. Two skills are added to express emotion-focused social support. *Help partner express feelings* is introduced to emphasize the importance of helping people to do that. Usually people do this through active listening, although appropriate self-disclosure of one's own feelings also prompts expression of feelings in the partner. *Encourage, reassure, and give affection* are forms of positive emotional support that can be helpful when someone is feeling bad. Problem-focused support is helping the other person to think through what needs to be done, and offering practical assistance that might help. We also add the final skill of asking what support is desired. This essentially means asking the partner, "Do you want me just to listen or do you want to try to think about what to do about this?" This question can be really useful to people who are unsure what sort of support their partner desires.

The structure of the current exercise is similar to that undertaken in Unit 2. The couple has two brief discussions, each partner self-evaluates his or her communication, and each also receives feedback from his or her spouse. However, in the current exercise the couple discusses topics in which one person seeks the support of the other. Each partner selects a topic that reflects an issue that is either (1) something he or she would like to change about him- or herself (e.g., get fit, stop smoking, manage stress better, improve a relationship with a work colleague, family member, or friend); or (2) something he or she is concerned about (e.g., their future career, the health of an aging

On your own . . . place a check mark in the appropriate box to rate your support skills.

0	No use of this skill
1	Some use of this skill
2	Adequate but there is room for improvement
3	Good use of this skill
N/A	Skill not applicable

	Skill	0	1	2	3	N/A
Speaker skills	Describe specifics					
	Express positives					
	Assert negatives					
	Self-disclose feelings					
Listener skills	Attend					
	Encourage					
	Summarize content					
	Paraphrase feelings					
	Ask questions					
	Hear my partner out					
Emotion-focused support	Help partner express feelings					
	Encourage, reassure, give affection					
Problem-focused support	Help define the problem					
	Suggest specific plan of action					
	Offer specific assistance					
Other support	Ask type of support wanted					

My strengths in communicating support: _____

_____

Things I need to work on in communicating support: _____

_____

_____

FIGURE 7.1. Support skill self-evaluation form.

From *Marriage and Relationship Education* by W. Kim Halford. Copyright 2011 by The Guilford Press. Permission to photocopy this figure is granted to purchasers of this book for personal use only (see copyright page for details). Purchasers may download a larger version of this figure from the book's page on The Guilford Press website.

parent). The topics should not be related to the couple's own relationship, and should not be subjects that the couple has had conflict about previously. How to manage differences is covered in Unit 4; the focus in the current unit is on talking in supportive ways with your spouse about issues other than the couple relationship.

The couples undertake this exercise while the educator circulates among the group members. It is best if the couples limit their discussion to just 3–4 minutes, so they can remember the process of what is happening for their self-evaluation. After a couple completes one discussion, the support partner self-evaluates their communication during that discussion. The person attempting to be supportive then receives feedback from his or her spouse. It is important to remind partners to start their feedback by identifying two positive things about their spouse's communication of support, and then to offer one suggestion for improvement. The educator should circulate among the couples, listening to the feedback and coaching people as required.

Sometimes the issue that the partner discusses is relatively easy for the spouse to be supportive about. But other times the issue can be quite difficult, and ensuring the educational goal of enhancing communication of support requires attention to the feelings of each partner. The following example illustrates a couple who were talking about the wife being harassed by a coworker, which was an emotionally laden topic for both partners. This became evident when the educator asked the woman to provide feedback on what her husband could do differently to express support.

SALLY: Well, see there is this sleazy guy at work who keeps trying to hit on me. I really dislike him, but when I tell the boss he just won't take it seriously. Andrew tells me to slap the guy or punch him in the nose—but I can't do that.

EDUCATOR: OK, so this is a tough problem you were discussing. This guy is harassing you at work, sounds like you tried to get the boss to tell him to back off, but you feel you're not getting any support. You tell Andrew about the problem, and you feel he tells you to do stuff that just is not a good idea. We've got two issues here, the harassment problem itself and the discussion about the problem. Let's stick with talking about the discussion process to start with. Any thoughts on what Andrew could have done that would have been really helpful?

SALLY: This guy he keeps telling me how much he wants me, you know, and I am frightened by him. I just want Andrew to understand, it is awful the way this guy behaves—he's so creepy—it makes me hate going to work.

EDUCATOR: Sal, that sounds awful, you are really dreading turning up at the office because this male coworker makes your life miserable.

SALLY: Yeah. (*Her eyes well up.*) I feel so angry that the boss won't do anything. And Andy just tells me to hit this guy. I mean, how is this going to go down if I start punching people at work? And the guy is over 6 feet tall.

EDUCATOR: So it's really important to you that Andrew understands the tough jam you're in. Andrew, I am guessing this is a tough thing for you to hear about. Sally, your partner, the woman you love, is getting sexually harassed by a man at her work.

ANDREW: I want to hit him. Tell him to back off.

EDUCATOR: I think I would feel the same way if this was happening to my wife. But Sal is asking for something a bit different. She wants you to really understand what she feels and what is going on. Then more than likely Sally will work out what she wants to do. It's hard for you—and me, any man—to be sure we really get this about being harassed. Do you want to know what it really means to Sal?

ANDREW: Of course. OK, I need to understand. What do I do?

EDUCATOR: Great question Andrew. Sally, what can Andrew do or say when he's talking to you that would make it easier for you to talk and feel understood?

SALLY: Just listen. Stop telling me what to do.

EDUCATOR: That is very specific, and really helpful. Andrew, do you think you can do that—listen, maybe ask questions, but no advice, at least for now?

At this point the educator had the couple restart the discussion. Andrew listened to Sally speak and then asked a great question: "Sally, what effect is all this stuff having on you?" Then the educator complimented Andrew on the question and the couple continued. The goal at the end of the process is for each partner to have a clear, behaviorally specific description of their strengths in communicating support and some areas they could work on. This can form the basis of a possible self-change plan for communicating support.

As the couples are having their support discussions and reviewing their communication of support, the educator circulates among the couples, assisting as required. Some useful questions that you can pose to prompt reflection include the following:

- "What sort of support do you think you provide most often?"
- "What goals do you have in relation to the support you provide to your partner at the moment?"

As partners reflect on their communication of support, these questions are useful:

- "What topic did you discuss when you were the support person?"
- "What were your communication goals for the support task?"
- "What did you rate as your key strengths and weaknesses as a communicator of support?"
- "What feedback did your partner give you on your communication of support?"
- "What aspects of your communication of support would you like to work on?"

SHOWING CARING

Introducing the Importance of Showing Caring

One way to introduce the importance of caring to a group of couples is with words like the following:

> "All partners need to show they care about their spouse. Caring is the small actions undertaken on a day-to-day basis that express love. There are many ways to show caring, such as saying 'I love you,' giving a hug, offering a warm greeting at the end of the day, making a telephone call to check on how that important meeting went, giving a back rub, remembering that birthday and getting something special, preparing a special meal, or complimenting a particular shirt."

An observation I often share with couples is how often we inadvertently can fail to show caring toward our spouse, when we would be unlikely to overlook that toward other people. For example, if friends invite you over for a drink or a meal, it would be usual to thank them. Some people might even take a small gift, perhaps wine to have with dinner, or some flowers for the table. Yet often spouses cook for each other and there is no thank you, and no sign of appreciation. Similarly, greeting a friend is often done with a big smile, a statement of how good it is to see him or her, perhaps a handshake or a hug. In contrast, many people do not expend the same enthusiasm or warmth when seeing their partner at the end of the day. Failure to express caring can become a habit that makes the relationship dull and mundane.

There are three observations about how to express caring in an effective manner that are useful to draw to couples' attention. Introducing these observations to a group of couples can be done with something like the following words[1]:

> "There are three really important guidelines for showing caring toward your spouse that help make relationships strong. First, there are different expressions of caring that are effective for different people. The challenge for all of us is to find the ways of expressing caring that are really meaningful to you and your partner. Second, you need to keep finding new ways of showing caring. Bringing your partner flowers on Friday night is nice, but if you do that every week the effect starts to wear off. We need to be creative in finding new meaningful ways of expressing how we feel about our partner. Third, sometimes we need to show caring when things are not going well in a relationship. Any couple will, across a lifetime together, have stressful times. There might be long work hours, or young children keeping us awake. There might be an argument, or there might be a big issue that is not resolved. At times like this when we are busy, stressed, or even angry with our partner, then showing caring can drop away. At such times, a little caring can help return things to a more even keel. So, I invite you to review how you currently express caring in your relationship, and to explore ideas about how you might show caring more effectively."

In a group setting it also can be useful to have people brainstorm different ideas about how they could show caring toward their partner. If these are written up, people can develop a range of ideas that they might want to try in their own relationship. I also sometimes have group members pick their top two or three behaviors, which they would most like to be done for them in their relationship. Having people indicate their preferences, and recording the votes for various caring behaviors, can highlight the different preferences people have.

It also can be useful to have people discuss where they might get ideas for being more creative in showing caring toward their partner. I often begin such a conversation by making the observation that many people discuss how to be better at their jobs with colleagues or friends, or seek out ideas from books or training. (Typically it is the people who are good at their jobs who

---

[1] Another option for introducing the concept of caring is to show the beginning of the caring section of Unit 3 of the Couple CARE DVD. This section shows numerous vignettes of people explaining how they show caring toward their partner. This can prime people to the importance of showing caring, and the diversity of ways caring can be expressed.

work to become even better.) In the same way people can seek out ideas about how to be more creative in expressing caring. I find that it can be instructive in group settings to have the men and women form separate groups to generate ideas about caring behaviors, and then compare the lists they generate.

Figure 7.2 is a useful handout in which partners identify caring things their spouse does for them, and nominate possible new caring behaviors they could do for their partner. I have partners complete the forms, swap them with each other, and then discuss what each has written down. This can be very useful in guiding more effective expression of caring. It can be helpful to ask people to report on their favorites of their partner's caring behaviors to the group. I make a point of asking people what it is about that behavior that they really like, and what effect feeling cared for has on them.

Figure 7.3 is a handout that lists some ideas for caring behaviors, which is another starting point for each individual to enhance his or her repertoire of caring behaviors. Developing a self-change plan to enhance caring is something I encourage almost all partners to try. Even if people show high levels of caring toward each other, making a little extra effort to do something new can often create really positive feelings that enhance the couple's engagement and enjoyment of the whole Couple CARE program.

As the educator circulates among the group members some useful questions to pose to couples include the following:

- "What did you learn when you reviewed how you express caring in your relationship?"
- "What caring acts does your partner do that you most value?"
- "What caring acts do you do that your partner most values?"
- " What aspect of your caring might you focus on in a self-change plan?"

INDIVIDUAL AND COUPLE ACTIVITIES

There are three goals in having couples review their balance of individual, couple, and other activities. It is useful to outline these goals for the couples as an introduction to the process of reviewing activities. The first goal is to help couples develop a broader range of positive shared activities, and to develop skills in continuing to identify new shared activities. Developing new shared activities provides the couple with variety, and the sharing of a variety of novel experiences is an important element of enhancing couple intimacy and passion (Baumeister & Bratslavsky, 1999). A second goals is to help the partners to reflect on whether they might be over or underemphasizing shared activities. Couples who lack adequate shared activities often

Caring things my partner does for me	Self-rating of how positive (from 1 to 10)	Possible *new* caring behaviors I could do for my partner	Partner rating of how positive (from 1 to 10)
1		1	
2		2	
3		3	
4		4	
5		5	
6		6	
7		7	
8		8	
9		9	
10		10	

FIGURE 7.2. Caring behaviors checklist.

Getting a household repair done
Preparing an entire meal
Helping with the dinner
Taking care of the car
Doing some shopping for things we need
Doing the laundry

Balancing the check book
Paying a bill
Doing some needed gardening
Doing the dishes
Cleaning or straightening up a bit
Mending my partner's clothes

Doing an errand
Taking out the garbage
Feeding or taking care of the pets
Telling my partner something confidential
Starting a conversation with my partner
Asking my partner how he or she feels

Mowing the lawn
Setting the alarm clock
Having an enjoyable conversation
Making some extra money
Summarizing my partner's point of view so
    she or he knows I am listening

Doing something my partner asked
Helping to dress the children
Giving my partner a nice greeting when we
    meet after being apart
Giving my partner a massage or rubdown
Talking to my partner when he or she asks
    for some attention

Forgiving my partner for something
Asking for my partner's opinion
Smiling at my partner or laughing with him
    or her
Initiating sex
Renting a video
Being nice to my partner's friends

Trying to cheer my partner up
Touching my partner affectionately
Looking nice (dress, shaving, etc.)
Hugging or kissing my partner
Making his or her favorite food
Cuddling

Paying my partner a compliment
Being nice to my partner even though he
    or she was mean to me
Praising my partner
Responding to sexual advances
Bringing my partner a present

Doing something sexual he or she really
    likes
Talking together about finances to help us
    stick to the budget
Going out to dinner, a movie, or a bar
Playing sports together
Playing games together
Suggesting something fun for us to do

Showing that sex was enjoyable
Shopping for something together
Talking about his or her friends or relatives
Talking together about making a purchase
Spending time together having fun
Planning or helping with a social event
Doing something together in the evening

FIGURE 7.3. Ideas for caring behaviors.

feel distant and disengaged from each other. In contrast, couples who have little time apart might feel there is a lack of outside stimulation in their lives. Moreover, couples who do not nurture relationships other than with their spouse can become overly reliant on the spouse for support and recreation. Isolation from other relationships is associated with increased couple relationship problems (Holman, 2001). The third goal is to have each partner reflect on individual activities and activities with other friends that he or she might want to develop.

A useful place to start in having couples examine their balance of individual and couple activities is to consider a couple activity timeline. I draw a long horizontal line on a whiteboard to symbolize a couple's life together. The left-hand point of the line represents when they first meet and start going out. The right-hand side of the line designates reaching a healthy old age together. I ask the couples to draw a similar line on a piece of paper, and to mark in the year and age of each partner when they met. They then should write in some of the couple activities they did most frequently when they first met. Then I ask each couple to write in the activities they currently do most often as a couple (just the two of them). I ask couples to volunteer some of their activities when they first met. I then focus on couples that have been together for longer, and ask them about their current activities. It is useful to talk about what has influenced the changes they report. For example, many couples report going out a lot at night when they first met—on dates. Often this declines as people move in together, they start to do activities related to setting up their home, and perhaps have children.

It is good to ask people to describe how various life changes might modify their activities together. (Couples are invited to guess if they have not experienced the changes.) We discuss having children, first very young children and then primary- and high-school-age children. We discuss the effects of aging parents, of changing work responsibilities, and of changing levels of disposable income. The key point to be drawn from this discussion is that for relationships to survive, they have to evolve over time. What people do together when they first get together is not what they will be doing 30 years later. In good relationships partners recognize that change is ongoing, and seek to ensure that there are new things being tried, and a good balance of independent, couple, and shared activities is maintained. The next exercise helps the couples apply these ideas to their own relationship.

You can use Figure 7.4 as a handout for partners (individually) to write down regular activities each partner has done in the last 2 months. As is evident in the form, activities are classified into three categories: (1) activities done independently of their partner, either on their own or with other friends or family; (2) activities done as a couple; and (3) activities done as a couple with other friends or family. After writing down their recent activities each

Individual activities without your partner:

_____

_____

_____

_____

_____

_____

Couple activities (just the two of you):

_____

_____

_____

_____

_____

_____

_____

Shared activities with your partner and others:

_____

_____

_____

_____

_____

_____

What did you discover from doing this exercise? Which boxes did you fill up the most?
Which ones were the emptiest? Please answer the following questions.

(cont.)

FIGURE 7.4. My current regular activities over the last 2 months.

On your own, check the boxes that apply to you. (You might check one or two boxes in each group.)

☐ I would like more *independent* activities.

☐ I would like fewer *independent* activities.

☐ I would like some new *independent* activities.

☐ I am happy with my *independent* activities as they are, no changes are needed.

☐ I would like more *couple* activities with my partner.

☐ I would like fewer *couple* activities with my partner.

☐ I would like some new *couple* activities with my partner.

☐ I am happy with our *couple* activities, no changes are needed.

☐ I would like more *shared* activities with my partner and others.

☐ I would like fewer *shared* activities with my partner and others.

☐ I would like some new *shared* activities with my partner and others.

☐ I am happy with my *shared* activities, no changes are needed.

FIGURE 7.4. *(cont.)*

person rates whether he or she wants more or less of independent, couple, and shared activities than they have experienced in the past couple of months. They also indicate if they would like to try some new activities in any of the three categories.

It can be helpful to highlight that expectations about the balance of individual, couple, and couple plus family or friends activities vary considerably between couples. Family-of-origin experiences influence expectations. For example, if your parents made a point of having dates as a couple, that is likely to influence your expectations. Culture also influences expectations. For example, in many Western cultures, individual time and couple time are highly valued. In contrast, in many Asian cultures, couples expect to spend a lot of time with extended family, and individual time and couple time are seen as less important. There is no correct balance of individual, couple, and couple plus others time, but it is important for the partners to develop a mutually acceptable balance.

The final phase of this task is to have the partners speak together about their individual reflections on the current pattern of activities they undertake. The couple can be asked to report back to the group on what they jointly decide about their current balance of activities. It can be useful to then have the couples discuss the following question: "Based on the checklists you completed and your discussion, what aspects of your shared or individual activities would you most like to work on?" Figure 7.5 provides a list of possible individual, couple, and shared activities that people might like to add to their current activities. This handout can be a useful resource to people if they decide change in patterns of activity is something they want to work on.

DEVELOPING AN INTIMACY AND CARING SELF-CHANGE PLAN

Three different aspects of intimacy and caring are covered in this unit: social support, expression of caring, and balancing shared and individual activities. As in all previous units, the current unit culminates in each partner developing at least one self-change plan intended to enhance their relationship. It is useful to remind participants of the three aspects covered, and ask them to summarize to their partner their self-evaluation in each area. Once this is done, each partner is asked to complete a written self-change plan. As in previous units, the educator can circulate and assist people to develop self-change plans that are specific and achievable. As the self-change plan follows the same format each week, it is a good idea to produce a sizable number of copies of that form and make them available in each session. Ask people to report to the group on (1) what they thought was a key idea covered in the current session, and (2) their selected self-change plans is useful to do, if there is time.

CHALLENGES IN PROMOTING INTIMACY AND CARING

There are five common challenges in making this unit work well that are useful to consider. First, some people (most often men) struggle with providing emotional support. Such people tend to fall back to offering advice and giving practical support. One useful strategy is to remind people of the two different modes of offering support (emotional and practical) and suggest they use a modality check when offering support. A modality check is asking the person what sort of support he or she seeks. (For example, you might say: "Do you want me just to listen or should we work to try to come up with a solution?") It also can be helpful to cue the spouse to request the sort of support he or she desires. (For example, the spouse might say, "I really need you to just hear me about this, we don't have to solve the problem.")

(text resumes on page 195)

Ideas for Couple Activities

Going bicycle riding before Sunday breakfast

Visiting friends

Camping

Having a shower or bath together

Visiting a museum or art gallery together

Playing Scrabble together

Starting an aquarium

Playing tennis

Going to a sporting event (basketball, football, baseball, etc.)

Jogging

Making wine together

Doing relaxation exercises or meditating together

Gardening together

Doing the bills together

Going to a bar and talking

Treating yourselves to a big breakfast of pancakes, eggs, bacon, orange juice, toast

Going sailing

Playing music together (guitar, piano, etc.)

Visiting a national park with a waterfall

Going to see a band

Playing golf (or miniature golf) together

Going to the race track

Going to the botanical gardens

Buying a new CD together

Stargazing: lying on your back and learning to recognize all the constellations and bright stars

Going secondhand shopping

Making home-made pizzas and throwing lots of stuff on them

Browsing in a bookstore together

Turning down the sound on the TV and making up funny scripts

Meeting for lunch or coffee during the day

Having a BBQ in the park together

Doing jobs together—wasting an hour or two driving around, going into different shops to get things

Playing pool

Daydreaming about a fantastic holiday you know you can't afford

Renting a rowboat or canoe for the afternoon

Writing letters to friends

Going on a picnic

Playing charades

Reading a play aloud

Reading the weekend papers together

Taking dancing lessons

Playing Frisbee

Going to a festival/ markets

Making a collage

Going to a concert

Going to the beach

Going skating

Going window shopping together

Buying fish and chips

Just sitting around with the lights low and talking

Watching TV together

Playing cards

Cooking an exciting meal together

Working for a political candidate

Painting the house

Calling up an old mutual friend on the phone long-distance

Climbing a mountain

Backpacking

Planning a family reunion

Gossiping

Going roller-blading

Riding bikes together

Going for a drive

Visiting a brand-new interesting place for a day

(cont.)

FIGURE 7.5. Ideas for activities.

Flying a kite
Doing exercises (yoga, dance, aerobics, etc.)
Joining a new group or club together
Looking at slides, photos, or home movies
Eating pizza (at home or at a restaurant)
Washing the car
Inviting someone new over for dinner or drinks
Going out to eat
Playing in the rain or leaves
Reading in bed together
Working on crafts together (tie-dying, pottery, candle-making, etc.)
Talking about day-to-day happenings
Exploring new places, places you'd never usually go (junkyard, new bars, new areas of town, etc.)
Making or planning home improvements
Going swimming in the nude
Playing with pets
Spending a romantic evening alone (dinner, candlelight, music)
Reading poetry out loud
Reading science fiction or mysteries out loud in bed at night
Going to a party
Going to the library; browsing through the books and records together
Going swimming
Going dancing (ballroom, folk dancing, square dancing)
Cooking something you've never cooked before

Buying new home decorations
Going for a walk in the forest
Doing a jigsaw or crossword puzzle together
Looking around in secondhand or antique shops
Going horseback riding
Watching late movies on TV and cuddling during the commercials
Going to church
Going to a movie together
Baking bread together
Listening to music
Fishing
Making love
Watercolouring or fingerpainting
Hanging out in a new coffee shop talking and trying out new coffees
Getting up to see the sunrise
Going to the opera or ballet
Eating breakfast out
Going to a play
Going to an auction
Taking a picnic lunch to a nearby park and going hiking together or with friends
Inviting old friends over for Sunday lunch
Arranging and taking pictures
Going on a shopping spree
Giving a party
Eating and talking together
Sunbathing
Going to a motel for the night

Ideas for Individual Activities

Creative Activities

Doing artwork
Knitting, needlework, or sewing
Cooking something special or new
Redecorating
Doing woodwork or carpentry
Doing artwork
Knitting, needlework, or sewing
Cooking something special or new

Doing pottery, ceramics
Taking a course in a creative skill (e.g., art, photography, cooking, or pottery)
Restoring furniture or antiques
Repairing things
Doing pottery, ceramics
Taking a course in a creative skill (e.g., art, photography, cooking, or pottery)

(cont.)

FIGURE 7.5. *(cont.)*

Redecorating
Doing woodwork or carpentry
Working with machines, engines, or electrical equipment
Thinking up or arranging songs or music
Playing a musical instrument
Acting or taking acting lessons
Reading books, articles, magazines related to your creative interests

Restoring furniture or antiques
Repairing things
Photography
Writing
Singing or dancing
Learning to play a musical instrument
Participating in an organization related to your creative interests

Entertainment Activities

Watching TV
Listening to music
Seeing a film
Going to an art gallery, exhibition, or museum
Going to a sports event

Listening to the radio
Going to a play or drama
Going to concerts, opera, ballet
Going to see bands play
Going to the races (auto, boat, horse, etc.)

Educational Activities

Reading books, plays, or poems
Going to lecture courses or other classes that interest you
Learning to do something new (e.g., acquiring a new skill)

Reading academic literature on a subject that interests you
Learning a foreign language
Going to the library

Physical Activities

Playing tennis or squash
Going boating or sailing
Going hiking, mountain climbing, or camping
Playing basketball or netball
Going jogging, running, or bicycle riding
Going to the gym or doing weight-lifting

Playing golf
Going fishing
Going swimming, diving, or surfing
Going bowling, skating, or playing pool
Going horseback riding
Driving a 4WD, sports car, or motorcycle for the sheer fun of it

Other Activities

Having an active involvement in politics, community, or social action groups
Playing chess or checkers
Collecting things (e.g., stamps, coins, or wine)
Gardening
Visiting interesting outdoor places (e.g., zoo, parks, riverside, harbor)
Having or planning a holiday (on your own)
Going to a sauna or doing health-related activities

Being involved in religious or church activities
Speaking a foreign language
Buying something for yourself
Gathering natural objects (flowers, rocks, or driftwood)
Caring for or being with animals or pets
Being in the country or mountains
Having massages or back rubs
Doing yoga or meditation

FIGURE 7.5. *(cont.)*

Some people feel a strong urge to suggest solutions when discussing a problem, and find it hard to provide emotion-focused support. For such people it can be useful to listen to them and draw out how they feel if they do not offer advice. An example of this process follows.

BEN: I feel so useless when we are talking about Tian's mom." [Tian's mother, a widow living in Vietnam, is frail, and is struggling living alone.] She gets so upset every time she speaks to her mom. I try to cheer her up, suggest we do things.

EDUCATOR: How does Tian react when you do that?

BEN: She gets mad at me! Tells me I don't understand. I'm trying, but what can I do?

EDUCATOR: So you're doing your best to support Tian, but it does not seem to work?

BEN: No, and I want to help—but her mom isn't allowed to come here, and we can't get there with the kids and everything.

EDUCATOR: So, Ben, the more you look for a solution, the more frustrated you feel?

BEN: Yeah, there seems no way forward.

EDUCATOR: Some things just don't have a solution and the best we can do is just be there and listen. When my mother was dying from dementia there was no cure. She got worse and worse. Toward the end, every time I visited her I was devastated. She didn't know me, couldn't talk. She stared at me in this really weird way. My wife used to let me talk about those visits, sometimes I would talk for a minute, sometimes for hours. Her listening didn't change what was happening to my mom. But being listened to helped me bear it. I am wondering if you might be able to provide emotional support to Tian like my partner did for me.

In this transcript I used a self-disclosure to assist Ben to understand the value of emotional support. Then I prompted Ben to try providing emotional support for Tian, and coached Ben in active listening so he could develop his skills.

A second challenge in developing intimacy and caring is when people find direct expression of caring uncomfortable. In some families and cultures, direct expression of affection is done infrequently, which can lead people to feel uncomfortable with such expression. Practice is very effective. Practice can be graduated by identifying ways of expressing feelings that are more comfortable, and gradually building toward saying more uncomfortable things. For example, I had a man who felt very uncomfortable saying "I love you" practice saying "I respect you, you are a good wife." When he got more comfortable with that he found it easier to say "I love you."

It also is useful to make the point that caring can be expressed in many ways. Even if someone never says "I love you," he or she might be able to show love in many other ways. For example, for Chinese people extended family is very important, and expressing caring for one's partner can be shown by being respectful and helpful to one's in-laws (Ting-Toomey & Takai, 2006).

Some people find any expression of caring or intimacy difficult, and this can limit their own and their partner's sense of satisfaction in their relationship. Coming from a family of origin where little affection was expressed is associated with people reporting difficulty in expressing positive feelings in their own adult relationships. For people who were victims of abuse, closeness can be very uncomfortable. If an educator has reason to believe that these sorts of experiences might be affecting a partner, then the educator might want to have a private discussion with the person—perhaps at the end of a session, perhaps in a telephone call—to explore whether referral for individual or couple therapy might be helpful. If a RELATE assessment has been done that provides the educator with information about family-of-origin experiences including abuse, knowing about such experiences enables the educator to sensitively and privately explore the impact of such experiences on the individual.

A third challenge is that in some couples partners report quite distinct interests in activities, with few shared interests. Usually people start relationships with someone who shares at least some of their interests. However, interests can drift apart over time. For example, I have worked with a number of couples in which one partner continued doing the same activities as when the couple first met, but the other person had changed his or her interests. In such cases the challenge for the couple is to develop new interests that are enjoyed by both partners. Sometimes that might mean one or both partners making a sacrifice to give up current activities to provide time for shared activities. For example, Trevor was a keen golfer. When he and Nancy first met she played golf from time to time with Trevor, but since they had children she has lost interest and feels she does not have the time to play. Trevor still plays a regular round of golf with friends most Saturdays. This made it difficult for Nancy and Trevor to have time together. After much discussion Trevor decided he needed to find another sporting activity that he enjoyed, but that took up less time on the weekends, so he and Nancy could have time together.

The concept of sacrifice is important for couples. To sustain a relationship there are times when each of us needs to make a sacrifice. It might be refusing a promotion at work that requires relocation to a new city that does not fit family needs well, it might be cutting back on time with friends, it might be giving up golf—at least for the time being. Sustaining relationship satisfaction means thinking about your life and choices from a couple perspective, and sometimes making individual sacrifices to make the couple relationship work.

A fourth challenge many couples find when reviewing their pattern of time use together is that they feel they have little discretionary time. A persistent state of being busy, with work, family responsibilities, and social commitments can leave a couple with little time to devote to themselves as a couple. There are two related issues here. One is that there are certain times in couples' lives when getting time together might be challenging: when there are small children in the house is one example, a health crisis is another. If this occurs over a relatively constrained period of time then the couple might accept this as how things are for now. For example, if a child is sick for a week, that might require the couple to focus on their child's needs and forgo any time as a couple. However, if they have a child with a chronic illness or disability, then the couple needs to negotiate how they manage both care of their child and having some time as a couple. (It is worth noting that many couples with severely disabled or chronically ill children separate, probably at least partly because getting such a balance can be hard to achieve [Floyd & Zmich, 1991]. Yet, failing to work toward getting a balance makes things much worse for everybody.)

It is useful to make the distinction between acute and chronic patterns of low couple time, and to ask the couple to diagnose their current situation. If the couple has a chronic lack of shared time, then they might want to review what has led to that problem. For example, Janice and Graham described how each was working two jobs to try to save for a deposit on a home. They were determined to buy a house in the next few months as the government was offering some time-limited financial support to first home buyers. The couple had not had a date going out together as a couple for nearly a year, and they were finding that they were increasingly irritable with each other. Coming to the CRE program had been prompted by them having what each saw as their first real argument. Talking this issue through, they decided that trying to get their home deposit was really important to them. At the same time, they knew it would take at least another 6 months to get the required deposit saved, and that little or no time together for another 6 months was a high price to pay. It could even drive them further apart. Janice and Graham resolved to rearrange their work schedules so that they would have one night at home together each week, during which they would take turns cooking each other a special meal.

The last example also raises the fifth challenge in developing intimacy and caring. Sometimes when exploring a seemingly straightforward issue, like spending time together, deeper and more complex problems are uncovered. In the case of the couple above, it was the priority they attached to financial security and having their own home relative to having quality time together. There are at least two potentially useful responses to such deep issues. One is to refer back to the relationship vision the couple developed in Unit 1. What were the core values couples stated that were critical to them, and are they living their lives in accordance with those core values? A second response is to note that management of differences is the focus of Unit 4, which follows the current unit. Issues that seem a source of significant dissent can be reviewed as part of that unit.

CHAPTER 8

Unit 4
Managing Differences

Unit 4 of Couple CARE is focused on managing differences. The content is summarized in Table 8.1. The unit begins with a review of the content of the previous session. Then there is a review of the partners' implementation of their self-change plans from the previous unit, which focused on promoting intimacy and caring. Next is an introduction to the importance of managing differences effectively, noting that partner differences can be relationship assets. Couples are asked to identify areas that currently are a source of disagreement and the patterns of interaction they use when discussing

TABLE 8.1. Overview of Unit 4: Managing Differences

Topic and aim	Exercise(s)
Review of intimacy and caring self-change plan	Review implementation and troubleshoot as required.
Importance and current patterns of managing differences	Introduce patterns of managing differences; couples self-assess current patterns of managing differences.
Conflict management guidelines and ground rules	Review and practice of conflict management guidelines; review and couple self-selection of conflict management ground rules.
Conflict management communication skills	Couple self-assessment of communication skills when managing conflict.
Recovering from conflict	Role of thoughts in recovering from conflict, discussion of recovering from conflict.
Self-change plan	Review of key ideas in unit and development of managing difference self-change plan.

these areas of difference. Couples are asked to identify some ground rules they want to use in their relationship to manage conflict effectively. Then the couple discusses a difficult topic and self-evaluates their communication when discussing this topic. Couples learn about how to help their relationship recover should destructive conflict occur. Finally, each partner formulates a self-change plan to enhance his or her management of differences within their relationship.

Couples rate learning to manage conflict as one of the most valuable aspects of skill-based CRE (Stanley et al., 2001; Wilson & Halford, 2008). Helping couples to manage conflict better is one of the more challenging aspects of the program for educators to deliver. Couples need to be able to discuss their differences without experiencing destructive conflict; the educator needs to create the context that allows couples to do that. The educator should be ready to intervene quickly if a couple is experiencing escalating negativity and to guide them back to more constructive methods of communication. In a group context this requires a sufficient number of educators for the number of couples (I suggest at least one educator for each four couples), so that the educators can closely monitor how each couple is progressing.

REVIEWING INTIMACY AND CARING SELF-CHANGE

The review of the content of the previous session follows a similar procedure to that of previous units. Some useful questions to pose of partners are as follows:

- "What stands out in your mind as the most important part of last week's unit?"
- "Was there anything in addition to your self-change plan that you did in the past week based on what was covered last week?"

The review of the intimacy and caring self-change plan follows the same procedure as the review of self-change implementation in previous units.

- "Can you tell me exactly what you tried to do?"
- "How did you do with last week's self-change plan?"
- "On a scale from 0 to 10 (with 0 being 'did not do anything like I planned' and 10 'completed exactly what I intended'), how well did you do your self-change plan?"

If the person did as he or she planned, then the following questions are useful:

- "What benefit, if any, was there for your relationship or your partner from you doing this?"
- "What else do you plan to do to follow up on this?"

The focus in the intimacy and caring unit is enhancing the expression of positive feelings. In the review of the self-change plan, it is useful to highlight the emotional impact of any changes implemented. When reviewing intimacy and caring self-change plans, I ask questions along the following lines:

- "How did you feel when you did this for your partner?"
- "How did your partner react to what you did?"

If the educator can draw out positive feelings about giving and receiving expressions of caring and intimacy, this strengthens the chance that the couple will do more of these types of behaviors in the future.

Occasionally people report that they feel it is contrived ("artificial") to do extra caring behaviors using the structure of self-change plans. This can be expressed as "It feels unnatural/phony/artificial to plan to do this" or "I think these things should just happen, you should not need to plan." This sort of concern about "faking" versus "being natural" can be raised in any of the units, but most often is raised in implementing ideas from Unit 3. It is important to explore with these people what they experience when they think about, and then implement, their self-change plans. A common issue is their negative thoughts about this being "unnatural." For example, people might report that they think, "I feel I am faking being nice," "It feels phony," or "If I am feeling tired, and not particularly loving, why should I need to fake it?" When addressing such issues, the following observations are often useful to make:

"A lot of human behavior is automatic, in the sense that we do not have to consciously think through what we are doing. When you drive a car, play tennis, type at a keyboard, chat with friends, or pour yourself a drink, you do not have to think or plan what you are doing. The behavior just seems to happen 'naturally.' But, do you remember when you first learned to drive a car? Do you remember not being sure what pedal was which, or how far to turn the steering wheel to go around a corner? Similarly, learning to play tennis, or to type, almost certainly felt 'unnatural' initially. When you were a little kid, even talking and pouring a drink were not natural; you had to learn these things. Learning required you to really think about what you were doing. As you learn new things, and gradually master them, then they become automatic and feel natural.

"In Couple CARE we ask you to review what you do now in your relationship, and identify what you want to change. When you try new things they feel unfamiliar and maybe artificial. I remember when my wife, Barbara, and I first got married. It felt really strange when I introduced her to friends as my wife. I felt like I was being a fake, just playing the role of being a married man. Within a short space of time it felt very normal and natural. Now 30 years later it feels part of who I am. I feel very proud to introduce Barbara as my wife to people. In the same way you select relationship habits you want to become natural, part of how you are as a couple. Initially these feel a little strange, but new habits will feel natural with practice."

THE VALUE AND CURRENT PATTERNS OF MANAGEMENT OF DIFFERENCES

Introducing the Importance of Managing Differences

In introducing the topic of managing differences, there are two important points to make. First, differences between partners are inevitable: no two people are likely to agree on everything across a whole lifetime together. Successful relationships do not prevent or avoid differences, they manage the differences constructively. Second, the differences between partners can be of great value to relationships. For example, I often mention that in my own relationship I tend to make decisions quickly, whereas my partner is more reflective. When making large decisions, like buying a home or a car, the two of us balance each other. My partner as the slower decision maker ensures that sufficient time is taken to consider the decision, while I as the more decisive (some might say "impulsive") partner ensure we do not agonize for too long and miss opportunities.

It is useful to ask each couple to discuss some differences between the two of them that enhance their relationship. Examples of the sort of answers often generated include partners having complementary interests that enhance getting required tasks done (e.g., one person likes to cook, the other likes gardening); complementary role preferences (e.g., one partner is keen to pursue his or her career and enhance family income while the other prefers a home-and-family focus); and complementary skills (e.g., one person is good with budgeting and the other with decorating and making their home attractive). In the group it can be instructive to have couples describe to each other the way in which their differences enhance their relationship.

A key point of this initial focus is to highlight the point that there are always differences between partners, and that this has advantages. At the same time, differences can be a challenge to manage. Destructive conflict can arise if differences are not managed well. The focus of Unit 4 is to help couples review and then enhance their management of differences.

Assessing Current Patterns of Managing Differences

Figure 8.1 lists some common areas of disagreement between partners. I ask each partner to rate how often they disagree about these topics, and then discuss their ratings with their spouses. This helps couples identify the areas of disagreement that might need resolution.

Figure 8.2 describes four common patterns of conflict management, and asks the couple to rate how often they use these different patterns. When working with groups of couples I usually give Figure 8.2 as a handout and introduce these different patterns. Here are some general observations to share with couples to help them make sense of these patterns:

> "There are four common patterns of conflict management I want to discuss with you. The approach–withdraw pattern is when one person approaches by raising the topic he or she wants to talk about. Sometimes, this can be in the form of a criticism, other times it can be a request for change. The other person withdraws. The withdrawal can take various forms. The withdrawer might ignore the initial comment, look away, change the topic, or turn on the television. Withdrawal often leaves the approacher feeling really frustrated. Have you ever had the experience of really wanting to talk about something that is bugging you, but your partner just seems to be unreachable?
>
> "This pattern is usually uncomfortable for the withdrawer as well. Withdrawers often experience the situation as being like a rabbit in a spotlight, dazzled, trapped, frozen, and not able to escape. The more the approacher pushes, the more pressured the withdrawer feels and the more the withdrawer pulls away. And what happens then? The approacher pushes even harder. This is not a helpful approach to managing conflict.
>
> "The avoid pattern is—as the name suggests—when both partners do not raise an issue of difference. Avoidance has one major advantage— at least in the short term—you avoid uncomfortable discussions or arguments. The problem with avoidance is that issues never get dealt with. Suppose money is a hot topic for a couple, as it is for many couples. Avoidance of talking about money typically means the couple does not develop an agreed-upon budget, might not be clear on who is supposed to pay bills, and has no plan on how the income coming into the house

Most couples have disagreements. **On your own**, check the answer that best describes how often you disagree about each area listed. Write in any other topics about which you disagree.

	Always agree	Almost always agree	Occasionally disagree	Frequently disagree	Almost always disagree	Always disagree
1. Handling family finances						
2. Matters of recreation						
3. Religious matters						
4. Demonstrations of affection						
5. Friends						
6. Sex relations						
7. Conventionality (correct or proper behavior)						
8. Philosophy of life						
9. Ways of dealing with parents or in-laws						
10. Aims, goals, and things believed important						
11. Amount of time spent together						
12. Making major decisions						
13. Household tasks						
14. Leisure time interests and activities						
15. Career decisions						
16. Other (please specify): _____						
17. Other (please specify): _____						

FIGURE 8.1. Areas of disagreement.

Approach–withdraw

When a problem arises, one of us tries to talk about the problem (the approacher). Often the approacher will complain or criticize. The other person talks little, may not listen, leaves the room, or just refuses to discuss the issue (the withdrawer).

Does this pattern apply to you two?

☐ Almost all of the time
☐ Most of the time
☐ Sometimes
☐ Rarely
☐ Never

In approach–withdraw the demander often feels frustrated and not listened to. The withdrawer often feels attacked and may feel that talking achieves little. In approach–withdraw it is difficult to understand each other.

Escalate

When we talk about a relationship problem, we tend to blame, attack, and criticize each other. We tend not to listen to each other, and things can get heated.

Does this pattern apply to you two?

☐ Almost all of the time
☐ Most of the time
☐ Sometimes
☐ Rarely
☐ Never

When couples escalate, nasty fights can result. Often problems remain unsolved, and partners frequently have hurt feelings.

Avoid

When a difficult problem arises in the relationship, we do not get around to talking.

Does this pattern apply to you two?

☐ Almost all of the time
☐ Most of the time
☐ Sometimes
☐ Rarely
☐ Never

Avoidance often means conflict is not obvious, but partners can become irritated and distant from each other. The problems are rarely solved. Avoidance often occurs in response to particularly difficult issues.

Effective conflict management

When a problem arises in the relationship we both talk about the problem, and hear each other out. We listen before suggesting possible solutions and compromises.

Does this pattern apply to you two?

☐ Almost all of the time
☐ Most of the time
☐ Sometimes
☐ Rarely
☐ Never

In effective conflict management, both partners are active in the discussion. Both use effective listener and speaker skills. They usually feel that they can talk about and solve problems.

FIGURE 8.3. Common patterns of couple conflict management.

From *Marriage and Relationship Education* by W. Kim Halford. Copyright 2011 by The Guilford Press. Permission to photocopy this figure is granted to purchasers of this book for personal use only (see copyright page for details). Purchasers may download a larger version of this figure from the book's page on The Guilford Press website.

is divided up. Eventually the pile of unpaid bills, or the credit card going over the limit, or running out of money between paychecks, forces the couple to address the money problem. At this point the couple is under great pressure from the pileup of debts, and talking calmly to solve the problems often gives way to arguing. 'How could you let your credit card get to the limit?' 'Well, how come you never pay the bills?' There are lots of issues that a couple must discuss, and avoidance just does not work in the long term.

"Escalation is the most obvious of problems in managing conflict. You argue, maybe it is relatively mild; a little sarcasm is swapped for a criticism or two. Sometimes it might get more heated, which could involve some serious criticism, maybe a really mean insult or some name calling in the heat of the moment. At worst, really nasty fights can occur, where partners trade insults and accusations; maybe it even escalates to physical aggression—pushing, slapping, shoving, or even worse. Any sort of escalation tends to leave both partners feeling hurt, and possibly angry. These types of fights can feed on themselves, like a fire getting out of control, and seriously damage a relationship.

"These different negative patterns—of approach–withdraw, avoid, and escalate—can all occur in the one couple. Sometimes a bad fight involving escalation leads to avoidance of talking about a sensitive issue. Frustration at the approach–withdraw pattern can escalate to a nasty fight.

"Effective conflict management involves both partners having the chance to speak, both partners listening to each other, and both being respectful of the other person's point of view. In effective conflict management, partners talk things through so that each understands the other's point of view before they try to work out solutions. Effective conflict management is a skill—it can be learned just like any other skill. The aim of the current unit is to review how you currently manage conflict and to offer some suggestions about how you can use effective conflict management."

In making this introduction it is useful to be interactive. I tend to act out each pattern with examples, even overplay it for humorous effect, and ask partners if they ever have experienced that pattern of conflict management.

Partners talk to one another and rate how often they use each of the four patterns of conflict management on the form in Figure 8.2. The couples then discuss spouse-to-spouse the strengths and the challenges of their current approaches to conflict management. The goal is to have them consider whether changing their patterns of conflict management might be helpful. It is also useful to mention that the couples will soon be asked to have a discussion about an area of disagreement, and to identify what pattern of conflict management they used during that discussion.

As couples discuss these conflict management patterns, I circulate among them and help them to clarify their ideas. It can be useful to have the group explore the issues raised during these discussions. A couple of points typically emerge. First, couples typically experience a mix of patterns. Often I ask couples to do a show of hands about who has never experienced the approach–withdraw pattern, who has never experienced the avoidance pattern, and who has never experienced the escalate pattern. Many couples have experienced each of these patterns at some point.

A second point that often emerges relates to the approach–withdraw pattern. It is often the woman who approaches and the man who withdraws. Often I ask couples with a show of hands whether they ever use the approach–withdraw pattern, and for those that do, whether it is the man who does the approaching. This usually highlights the prevalence of the woman approach–man withdraw pattern. Some psychologists suggest that this is an inherent difference between women and men. The well-known relationship psychologist John Gottman has argued that men are intrinsically more likely to withdraw and avoid conflict (Gottman, 1993). At the same time, it has been found that men approach and women withdraw when the men are asking the women to change something (Christensen & Heavey, 1990). So, at least partially, the approach role relates to the person who approaches wanting change.

I often follow up the point on the woman approach–man withdraw pattern with a comment addressed to the men. This point is an important reminder of the impact of ineffective conflict management.

> "Men, women often approach us about concerns they have in the relationship. At least some of what they complain about we need to do something about. For example, in couples in which both partners work full time, women typically do about 70–80% of the household chores. Many relationships start with a fairer split of responsibilities, but adopt this uneven pattern over time—particularly after having children. It's worth knowing that women initiate about 70% of divorces in this country. Avoidance can prevent an argument right now, but if you want a happy relationship, listen to your partner. If she has a fair point then you need to change.
>
> "If you can't cook, learn. If you don't clean, make a start. If you don't grocery shop, go along with your wife and learn. Doing your fair share is important, and that is an easy problem to solve."

A follow-up point for women is worth making:

"Women, men can help by listening and responding to your legitimate concerns. You can make it easier for your men to listen and respond to your concerns. Research shows it is common for women to start their expression of concerns by being quite negative and critical of their partner. If you start a discussion with your man that begins with a complaint, often that leads the man to feel overwhelmed and to withdraw. When you have a concern to raise, start up slowly. Be gentle, be polite. Avoid comments like, 'Why is this place still such a mess, do I have to do it all?' Take it slow, and start with something like 'There is something that has been worrying me that I would like to talk with you about.' A gentle start-up makes it more likely that your man will hear what you have to say."

CONFLICT MANAGEMENT GUIDELINES AND GROUND RULES

There are some guidelines and ground rules for managing conflict that couples often find helpful. "Guidelines" refer to suggestions of what couples can do while discussing conflict that make it easier to manage conflict effectively. "Ground rules" are a set of ideas that couples can agree on before discussing areas of differences, which structure discussions and make it easier to maintain effective conflict management. This section of the unit introduces these ideas; couples apply these ideas to their relationship in the sections that follow.

Conflict Management Guidelines

Figure 8.3 sets out some conflict management guidelines, which can serve as a useful handout to review with couples. The first point reminds the partners to begin a discussion about a conflict topic gently and slowly. A gentle invitation to discuss an area of concern tends to result in a more constructive discussion than beginning with an angry criticism. It can be helpful to look back to the topics of potential disagreement listed in Figure 8.1 and ask people what words they might use to (1) begin with a criticism, or (2) to have a gentle start-up to a discussion of one of these topics. Often I will illustrate the point first, and then ask group members to provide examples of criticisms and gentle start-ups for other topics. For example, after asking people to look at the handout on areas of disagreement (Figure 8.1), the discussion in one group started as follows.

1. Start up slowly.

2. Use your communication skills to understand each other.
   - Hear each other out.
   - Provide specific/concrete descriptions of problem behavior.
   - Attend to and encourage each other.
   - Take turns speaking and listening.
   - Ask for feedback when in the speaker role.

3. Use the floor technique, if required.
   - One person has the floor and is the speaker.
   - The other person can only listen, no speaking.
   - Once the speaker is done he or she yields the floor to the other person.

4. Only try to solve the problem once you both understand each other's point of view.

5. When you try to solve the problem:
   - Suggest specific positive solutions.
   - Ask for your partner's suggestions.
   - Listen carefully to your partner's suggestions; do not automatically reject.

FIGURE 8.3. Conflict management guidelines.

From *Marriage and Relationship Education* by W. Kim Halford. Copyright 2011 by The Guilford Press. Permission to photocopy this figure is granted to purchasers of this book for personal use only (see copyright page for details). Purchasers may download a larger version of this figure from the book's page on The Guilford Press website.

EDUCATOR: So, suppose I want to discuss family finances—maybe because we just got a whopping credit card bill. I could begin with: "What is all this?" (*Points to a piece of paper in his hand.*) "How did the credit card get to the limit? Like what's this, $320 on your cell phone, and you put it on the credit card? How could you possibly spend $320 in a month on your phone?" Gayle, how would that work if Geoff started a discussion that way?

GAYLE: I think you must have been to our house! (*Laughs.*) Well, I think the first one would get my back up a lot. After that, I am looking at the credit card account for stuff Geoff has put there, probably his fees for the last round of golf.

EDUCATOR: Right, I think we can all recognize the starting-with-a-criticism trap. *Or* I could begin with: 'Honey, I would like to talk with you about our money. Is this a good time?' What difference might it make to the discussion using these two start-ups?

GAYLE: I would be better if it was raised that way.

GEOFF: Maybe, but if money is a big problem then maybe no matter how you raise it there is going to be an argument.

EDUCATOR: So, Gayle is saying that particular words might get things off badly. But Geoff has raised the important issue that maybe there are touchy subjects that might lead to a fight anyway. *Always* being calm and reasonable, never having an argument, is probably beyond any couple. But finding the right words to start discussion of a sensitive topic—maybe something we have argued about before—might help. For example, if my partner and I have had words before about money maybe I should comment on that. "Honey I am a little wary of raising the topic of money since we have had a few disagreements on money. But I am kind of concerned about our level of debt, and I think we need to talk about it. I want to hear your thoughts and see if we can work out what we want to do." What do you think, Geoff?

GEOFF: Actually I like that—label the problem.

EDUCATOR: Let's try with another area. Geoff, is there a topic you and Gayle disagree about that you're willing to discuss?

GEOFF: Household tasks. Gayle is not as tidy around the place as I am . . .

GAYLE: What do you mean, not as tidy?

EDUCATOR: Geoff, you have identified a topic, but it sounded like a criticism of Gayle. And even though she is smiling, I am not sure she is all that happy with being described as untidy. How might you describe the topic trying to give a gentle start-up?

GEOFF: Gee, um, Gayle, we seem to have different, ah, views about how the house should be kept.

EDUCATOR: Good, Geoff, and maybe you want to ask Gayle to tell you about how she sees this issue?

GEOFF: Right, so can we talk about this. I would like to hear your views about how we share the chores around the place.

EDUCATOR: Good, you're giving an invitation for Gayle to tell her side of the story. And it's really important that each of you listens to the other's point of view, particularly important if it's a sensitive topic about which you have disagreed before. Terri, is there a topic you and Martin disagree about on the list?

The second point in Figure 8.3 reminds couples to use the communication skills they were introduced to in Unit 2, and which they applied to pro-

viding mutual support in Unit 3. Point 3 in Figure 8.3 refers to the speaker–
listener technique. This is a structure many couples find helpful to ensure that
each person is able to speak about his or her point of view, and be listened to
effectively. Essentially the idea is one partner is given "the floor," meaning it
is their turn to speak. I have a small square of carpet that I take to group sessions and I hand it to one partner to symbolize the idea of him or her having
the floor. The person with the floor is the speaker, the other person listens.
That means they should use listening skills (attend, encourage, ask questions,
summarize, paraphrase, and hear the partner out), but not speak. They also
should not disagree. The idea is that the speaker is listened to, and has the
chance to fully express his or her thoughts and feelings. Once the speaker
feels understood by the partner, then they swap roles. I usually ask a couple
to discuss an issue and coach them in use of the floor technique. I then get
all couples to try it, so that they are familiar with this strategy. (Couples can
use a piece of paper to symbolize the floor.) It can be very helpful for couples
struggling with an escalating conflict pattern to use the floor technique to
ensure that they listen to each other. The transcript below illustrates introducing the floor technique.

> EDUCATOR: Eric, Jana, this is the "floor" and we are going to use this to
> help you two talk through this issue of where to live. In a moment
> I am going to give one of you the floor. When you have the floor it
> is your chance to speak. Your job as the speaker is to explain your
> thinking about what you want in a place to live. If you don't have
> the floor, you're the listener. The listener's job is to listen, let the
> person finish what he or she has to say. The listener is not to dis-
> agree or talk about his or her own ideas. The listener has to focus
> on what the person with the floor is saying, and summarize what
> the speaker is saying. Got that? OK, who is going to have the floor
> first? (*Jana extends her hand.*) OK, Jana, you have the floor. Eric,
> your job is to really listen to Jana, maybe ask her some questions to
> make sure you get it. OK? Jana, please tell Eric about your thoughts
> on where you want to live.
>
> JANA: I really want us to have a nice place we can call home, you know
> with a garden, and a place for us to sit with friends, some space . . .
>
> ERIC: Uh-huh . . .
>
> JANA: I just feel that an apartment, you know, stuck up in a high-rise in
> the inner city, it's not somewhere friends, family will want to visit.
>
> ERIC: But a house in the suburbs is such high maintenance, we'll spend
> all our time gardening, painting, that's . . .

EDUCATOR: Eric, I want to stop you for a moment. Remember, your job right now is to listen to Jana. In a few minutes you will get the floor. Then it's really important for you to explain your ideas. But for now, what has Jana just said to you?

ERIC: That she wants to live in a house.

EDUCATOR: Good, and why does she want to live in house?

ERIC: Because of the space, the garden and stuff.

EDUCATOR: Is there anything you want to ask her about what she has said?

ERIC: Ah . . . (*pause*)

EDUCATOR: I am wondering what is important to her about this. How about asking her what she really likes about the idea of a house?

ERIC: Jana, what is it about the house thing that so grabs you?

JANA: It's the chance for us to build a place that really feels like ours. With all the moving around till now, I've never felt we put down roots, made somewhere our place. Now I want that, you know? I want somewhere that your folks can come over and have a meal, which my mother can stay at for weekends. I want to grow herbs in the backyard, and have a seat under a tree, and to be able to sit out and have a glass of wine in *our* place.

ERIC: Hmm.

EDUCATOR: Eric, can you summarize what Jana just said.

ERIC: Well, she has this picture of our families visiting, of somewhere that sort of feels like home to her.

EDUCATOR: Great job, good summary! Jana, do you think Eric has understood what you were saying?

JANA: Yes. And it's really important to me, this building a home.

ERIC: Doesn't our apartment feel like home?

JANA: With the two of us there, yeah, but there's no room for Mom or your folks. And I want to garden, I like getting my hands into the soil and watching stuff grow.

ERIC: Yeah, OK. You love a garden, I see you at your mom's place.

EDUCATOR: Jana, if you think Eric has got your key message, how about yielding the floor to him? (*Jana yields the floor to Eric.*) OK. Now, Jana, it's your turn to listen. Go ahead, Eric.

ERIC: I am worried that a house will take up all our time on weekends, you know, gardening, looking after the place. And we won't have time to do things we really enjoy.

JANA: But we can plan a low-maintenance garden, you know lots of native plants and stuff.

EDUCATOR: Jana, are you listening or speaking right now?

JANA: I should be listening?

EDUCATOR: Mmm-hmm. So let's get back to what Eric said. Can you summarize to Eric what he just said?

JANA: Eric, you suggested that it might tie us up with chores on weekends.

ERIC: Yeah, I mean we both work hard during the week, and I want to be able to chill out, see friends, go to the movies, do what we do now.

JANA: So you're worried that if we go into a house we become tied down with gardening and stuff and never get time for fun?

ERIC: I am. I see lots of guys at work who seem to have nothing to talk about except renovations and gardening. I don't want to get stuck in that suburban rut.

JANA: So you see a house as eating away at your interests, preventing you doing stuff you want to do?

EDUCATOR: Fantastic, Jana, good summary. It's interesting that as you two are talking we are hearing how important it is to Eric that he have time to maintain his range of interests, and Jana is saying how much she values the idea of a home, which for her means a garden and space.

The aim in the above process was to have the couple understand the speaker and listener roles, and how to apply the floor technique to provide structure to a discussion. As illustrated in the transcript, the educator is active, prompting the partners to stick to their assigned listener and speaker roles, and reinforcing their positive efforts. This transcript is from a group session with couples. At the end of the above interaction I then asked Eric and Jana to continue their conversation together and asked the other couples in the group to discuss an area of difference using the floor technique.

A common mistake is for couples to stop conversations about important topics prematurely, thinking they have understood each other when there are still unexplored and important issues. In the case of Jana and Eric, I came back to them a few minutes later and they reported they had finished talking about where to live. I asked Eric what he meant by his earlier comment about "getting stuck in the suburban rut."

> ERIC: I just do not want to live my life coming and going to work, working around the house on weekends. There should be more to life than that.
>
> EDUCATOR: Jana, I am thinking it is potentially important for you to understand what Eric is driving at here. Can you ask him about what he means, and I will come back and ask you what you find out.

Returning to Jana several minutes later I asked her what she had learned from Eric, and she told me the following.

> JANA: Eric's parents split up when he was in his late teens. He just told me that when his dad told him that he was leaving the family, his dad said, "I can't take this grind of living in suburbia, work all week, and then work on the house all weekend." Eric says he's really worried by the idea of getting into that same rut his father could not stand.
>
> EDUCATOR: So, Eric wants to avoid what his father felt trapped by?
>
> JANA: Yeah. He sees living in the inner city, with the access to theater and restaurants, and so forth as part of . . . he called it "the good life."

Jana and Eric continued their conversation at some length at home after this session, exploring what each of them felt made up a "good life" together. The transcript illustrates how, when partners really start to listen to each other, important issues can emerge. In many couples important issues remain hidden and unexplored because the couple never gets beyond the initial disagreement—as in Eric and Jana's case when they focused only on their disagreement about whether to buy a house or not. The educator often can help couples to open up hidden issues by prompting partners' curiosity about each other, and encouraging each person to keep asking questions. The educator can also look for key phrases that seem to have emotional meaning, like Eric's comment about "getting stuck in the suburban rut," and show how to open up discussion on these issues.

The fourth point in Figure 8.3 is the need to understand each other before solutions are offered. This is a crucial point for couples who repeatedly get stuck in the same argument. The idea can be introduced with words like the following:

"A common mistake many couples make when managing a difference is to try to solve the problem. Strange as it might seem, trying to solve the problem right from the start does not work for difficult problems, or for problems where you and your partner disagree strongly. For example, suppose you are trying to pick where you will spend your next vacation, and you and your partner have disagreed about vacation destinations in the past. Starting the conversation with 'I think we should go to X' is likely to lead your partner to say "I want to go to Y, I hate X." You have a dead end. In contrast, suppose you start with, 'We've disagreed about vacations before. Let's try to find something we will both enjoy. What would you really like on our next vacation?' This opening might help you to understand your partner's needs and then the two of you might come up with ideas that suit both of you.

"In other words, it is really important that each partner listens effectively to the other, and ensures that he or she truly understands the spouse's perspective before trying to identify solutions. In summary, if you really want to fix a difficult problem, don't try to solve it. Instead, focus on listening to your spouse and make sure you find out how he or she sees things. Seek first to understand, then to be understood. Once understanding is achieved, then good solutions can be generated."

Conflict Management Ground Rules

Figure 8.4 sets out some potential ground rules that couples might use to enhance their conflict management. Here are some comments that can be useful for introducing the idea of ground rules using Figure 8.4 as a handout:

"Ground rules for managing conflict try to address three issues: (1) Where and when are we most likely to manage our differences effectively? (2) What structure, if any, might help us to talk constructively? (3) If we start to escalate, how do we prevent destructive conflict? Let us consider the where and when question. Psychology researchers have had couples keep a diary of where, when, and under what circumstances they had conflict (Halford et al., 1992). Couples most often fight when they are tired or stressed, and when they are distracted—by the television, by tired children, and the like. So the first three guidelines are possible ways to set up discussion when you are calm and focused.

"The second group of possible guidelines (numbered 4 to 7) suggests structure for your discussion. Structure includes agreeing how to talk, such as using the speaker–listener technique, having an agreed-on agenda, or using a problem-solving worksheet. The final two sugges-

Ground rules are agreed-upon ways of managing conflict. **Below is a list of possible ground rules for handling conflict.**

As a couple, discuss and check-mark which ground rules you think would help you two manage conflict. There are some suggestions, and there also is room to write your own ground rules.

1. Freedom to raise issues any time Either of us can bring up an issue at any time. (As distinct from trying to find a good time and place to raise issues.)	☐ Yes	☐ No
2. Right to reschedule A partner can say, "This is not a good time." This partner should set up a time to talk soon. (You need to decide what "soon" means. Some people like to set a 24-hour limit; others leave it for a little longer.)	☐ Yes Time limit: ————	☐ No
3. Regular relationship meetings We will hold regular couple meetings when we are relaxed and alert.	☐ Yes	☐ No
4. Under stress, focus on the immediate issue Under stress, we deal with the immediate issue on the spot, then talk about the larger relationship issue later at our couple meeting or at a time we set.	☐ Yes	☐ No
5. Use of problem-solving sheet Sometimes we can use a written problem-solving sheet to help stay focused on the topic under discussion. (Note: A sample problem-solving sheet is available for you to look at.)	☐ Yes	☐ No
6. Clear agenda We can agree sometimes to discuss just *one* issue at a relationship meeting.	☐ Yes	☐ No
7. Understand, then solve When discussing a problem we first try to listen to each other about the nature of the problem. Suggestions to solve the problem will come only after we understand each other's point of view.	☐ Yes	☐ No
8. Use of stop If we start to become angry or upset either one of us can call a brief "stop." This means taking a few minutes off, like a mini-"time-out." The stop gives a few minutes to reflect, and to try to talk more calmly.	☐ Yes	☐ No
9. Use of time-out If we start to become angry or upset either one of us can call a "time-out." The partner who calls the "time-out" will schedule a time soon to talk more, when he or she is feeling calmer.	☐ Yes	☐ No
10. Your ground rule (1): _____ _____	☐ Yes	☐ No
11. Your ground rule (2): _____ _____	☐ Yes	☐ No

FIGURE 8.4. Ground rules for good conflict management.

tions (numbered 8 and 9) are if things start to get negative, so you can bring the conversation back to being helpful."

Three of the possible ground rules for managing conflict are worth describing in some detail. The first is ground rule 4, that under stress you focus on the immediate issue. Often issues for couples can arise when there is time pressure. For example, suppose both partners are trying to leave home for work in the morning, and there has been a misunderstanding about who is to drop their child off to day care. It is easy for couples in this situation to start debating how equitable the division of child care and other responsibilities are in their relationship. But there is not really the time to address that complex issue. What needs to be done is to solve the immediate issue: Who will drop their child off to day care? Discussion about a fair division of child care responsibilities needs to happen, but it is just not feasible at that exact time. A good resolution is something like this: "I'll do the drop-off this morning. When we have more time, maybe tonight, I would like us to discuss the general issue of who should do what."

It is worth mentioning that many couples avoid discussing their hot topics. By "hot topics," I mean those issues that are most likely to lead to unhelpful conflict. Unfortunately, such avoidance means that the topics are often only dealt with under stress. For example, child care responsibilities are discussed in the morning when the drop-off to day care is about to happen, sharing of household chores is only discussed when it is late and there is no food in the house because no one shopped, finances are only discussed when there are four unpaid bills and not enough money in the account to pay them, and so forth. Holding regular relationship meetings, and discussing hot topics when you are both relaxed, helps prevent having to deal with hot topics under stress.

A second ground rule worthy of discussion is the use of a structured problem-solving approach. Figure 8.5 shows the structure of problem solving in a worksheet that couples can use. I show couples this worksheet and explain what is involved in each of the steps. In a group context it is useful to identify a common problem for couples and have the group do a problem-solving exercise. For example, you could have couples discuss which partners might do what level of paid work after the birth of a first child. The group can be asked to brainstorm up a range of options, and then to identify the possible advantages and disadvantages of each option.

The formal structure of problem solving is something that couples typically apply only when they are dealing with a difficult or particularly important decision, such as considering a new job or making a major purchase. This level of structure in problem solving is unlikely to be necessary for minor decisions, like whether to go out for dinner. However, some couples

This problem-solving sheet is used when you have a difficult problem to solve. First, define the problem. Write down each partner's point of view and a "joint" point of view. It may take some discussion to come up with a "joint" point of view. Then generate some possible solutions to the problem. Next, think about the pros (positives) and cons (negatives) for each possible solution. Finally, choose the solution that best suits you as a couple.

1. Define the issue (define clearly, specifically, positively):

Partner 1's point of view: _____

_____

_____

Partner 2's point of view: _____

_____

_____

Joint point of view: _____

_____

_____

2. Generate options	3. Evaluate options	
	Advantages	Disadvantages
a.		
b.		
c.		

4. Select solution: _____

FIGURE 8.5. Couple problem-solving sheet.

find the structure helpful if talking about an issue that has led to conflict in the past.

Consistent with the focus on self-change throughout the Couple CARE program, each couple discusses the ideas and then selects those ground rules that they believe might be useful for them. As illustrated in Figure 8.4, couples also are encouraged to develop their own ideas if they have good suggestions. The educator circulates among the couples to clarify what is meant by each of the ground rules, and facilitate the partners' discussion of what ground rules they choose to apply in their relationship. It is useful to have the couples report to the group a ground rule that they liked and what appealed to them about that ground rule. This group discussion often leads to other suggestions of combining or generating new ground rules. The educator can point out to the couples that implementing selected ground rules is a possible focus for a self-change plan for this unit.

CONFLICT MANAGEMENT COMMUNICATION SKILLS

Couples are asked to identify an area of disagreement in their relationship, and to hold a conversation of 3–4 minutes on that topic. It is best to select a topic that has been a source of disagreement and is of moderate difficulty to discuss. I advise couples not to select their hottest topic for discussion, as it is difficult for them to try new ways of managing conflict if they begin with a very difficult issue. If couples have difficulty identifying a topic, they can refer to the areas of disagreement in Figure 8.1.

Figure 8.6 sets out a conflict management self-assessment form. The identified communication skills build upon those already introduced in Unit 2, adding some skills of particular relevance to managing conflict. The first additional conflict skill is listening before offering solutions. The second is listening and speaking about equally. The form also adds some of the couple ground rules that couples might choose to use. Couples use the form to do a self-evaluation of their communication after the conflict discussion, using a process similar to that used in previous communication skill development exercises.

It is important to focus couples on the goal of developing more effective means of conflict management. It can be useful to have all participants write down a specific goal they have for the discussion about how they want to talk with their partner. It also is important to warn couples that some people find it hard to stop talking about a topic of disagreement. Many people get caught up in what they are saying. It is an important skill for people to be able to break off a discussion about differences and return to the topic at a better time. This task provides the chance to practice that skill. This last point can be expressed something like this:

On your own . . . Place a check mark in the box that best describes how *you* think it went during the discussion. (Remember, you won't necessarily use all these skills.)

0	No use of this skill
1	Some use of this skill
2	Adequate but there is room for improvement
3	Good use of this skill
N/A	Skill not applicable

	Skill	0	1	2	3	N/A
Conflict skills	Listen before offering solutions					
	Listening and speaking about equally					
Speaker Skills	Describe specifics					
	Express positives					
	Assert negatives					
	Self-disclose feelings					
Listener skills	Attend					
	Encourage					
	Summarize content					
	Paraphrase feelings					
	Ask questions					
	Hear your partner out					
Couple ground rules	Use written problem-solving sheet					
	Stay with an agenda of one issue					
	Use the floor technique					
	I called a time-out					
	I called a brief stop					
	Other ground rule (write in):					

My strengths in managing conflict are: _____

_____

_____

Things I want to work on in managing conflict are: _____

_____

_____

FIGURE 8.6. Conflict skills self-evaluation form.

"There are times when it is not helpful to continue a discussion. Visitors are about to arrive, you are due at work, the discussion is getting really heated. Being able to stop, even when an issue is really important to you, is a very useful skill to develop. So I am going to ask you to stop talking when I signal time is up. Some people can find it frustrating—hard even—to stop. But I want you to focus on the idea that we are not necessarily going to solve the problem right here and now. That is not the point. Rather we are helping you develop skills to talk about problems together. These are skills you can use in your life together. And being able to stop talking when it is better to do so is an important skill that you need to practice."

Asking one person to act as a timekeeper, and to say when 4 minutes are up, is a useful way to limit the discussion. The educator moves among the couples, assisting them with their communication during a conflict discussion, as with the communication skill exercises done in earlier units. As noted previously, intervene if a couple is escalating in negativity. This requires the educator to keep moving among the couples and monitoring how each couple is proceeding.

The educator should try to hear at least a short sample of each couple's conflict discussion. The educator can then compare the self-evaluation made by each partner with the discussion, and help shape up a realistic self-evaluation. If some couples have struggled in earlier sessions to develop specific, realistic communication self-evaluation, then it is a good idea to go to those couples first to assist them.

After the discussion each partner completes the self-evaluation form in Figure 8.6. Next, each partner should write down some feedback to give to his or her spouse about his or her communication during the discussion. As in previous partner feedback, the educator asks each person to identify two positive things that his or her spouse did during the discussion, and state them first. Then the partners offer their spouses one suggestion for change. Based on their own self-evaluation and the feedback from the spouse, each person should have identified some areas of strength in their current communication during conflict and one area they could improve upon.

In the group setting it is useful to have couples report back to the larger group on their strengths and areas for change. I often ask people: "Did anyone get a good suggestion for change from their spouse? What was it? What is helpful about that suggestion?" An alternative to group discussion is to have each person discuss his or her strengths and weaknesses with one other group member. The aim is to have everyone receive reinforcement of some of their strengths as a communicator, and to have specific ideas for something to work on to enhance their communication.

RECOVERING AFTER A CONFLICT

To this point in the unit, the intention with the exercises has been to make conflict management effective, and to reduce the chance of destructive conflict. Effective conflict management is likely to reduce the severity of negativity during conflict, which makes recovery easier. However, even people with very good conflict management skills can experience destructive conflict if they are stressed. Being able to recover after a negative interaction is important for all couples.

There are two parts to this exercise. First, each partner reflects on, and writes down, the thoughts and feelings that occur to them after conflict with their partner. Second, the couple discusses how they currently recover after an argument or disagreement. These ideas can be introduced referring to Figure 8.7, which shows some negative, unhelpful thoughts and some positive, helpful thoughts that someone might have after conflict with his or her partner. Words like the following can help explain the ideas:

> "If you ever have an argument with each other—and across a lifetime together it is almost certain you will—then how you react after the argument is really important. Most of us have a series of thoughts, like statements we make quietly in our heads to ourselves, after something upsetting. Sometimes these self-statements are negative; they keep us focused on stoking our anger and upset. Look at the thoughts listed in the left-hand column of the handout [Figure 8.7]. Notice how each of these thoughts focuses on what the spouse did wrong, how unfair he or she was, or how powerless the thinker is to change things."

The educator can say the negative thoughts out loud as if having those thoughts, and ask the partners to talk about what effect having such thoughts might have on how they feel. You also can ask: "How might having these thoughts affect what you say or do?" Asking people to imagine they have just had an argument with their spouse and to say these thoughts to themselves can illustrate the effect of negative thoughts on feelings. It is useful to review the positive thoughts in the right-hand column, and highlight how they focus on identifying the helpful and unhelpful things the thinker did during the conversation. The focus is on what individuals can change about their own feelings and behavior: on thinking calming thoughts, telling yourself to relax, and thinking about what you can do to repair things with your spouse.

In helping couples to recover more successfully after a conflict it can be useful to have them discuss positive things they have done in the past to

Negative thoughts	Positive thoughts
"How could she/he do this to me?"	"What was the issue we were trying to resolve?"
"(Partner) is being stupid/unfair/cruel."	"What was I thinking that led me to feel so upset/angry?"
"(Partner) should not talk to me like that."	"What did I say or do that was helpful to talking this through?"
"Why is (partner) not seeing he or she is wrong?"	"What did I do that was unhelpful during the discussion?"
"I hate it when this happens."	"Take slow, deep breaths, calm myself down."
"It's pointless, we'll never work this out."	"What can I say or do differently when we talk about this again?"

FIGURE 8.7. Negative and positive thinking after conflict.

recover after conflict, and then to consider what they might do differently. In a group setting it can be instructive to have couples tell the group the most helpful things they have done in the past to recover after arguments. Two points that often are useful to draw out from such a discussion are as follows. First, often people need a little time to process negative feelings, so giving each other some space after a disagreement can be useful. This does not mean storming out of the house, slamming the door and shouting, "I may not be back." It does mean leaving the person alone, perhaps suggesting, "Look, we are both upset, how about we each take a little time to calm down, and then let's talk about things later." Second, saying sorry and perhaps even saying that you love the person is very useful. That does not mean you are saying the other person has no responsibility for what happened. It does mean that you are expressing regret that you made a contribution that might have upset the other person. Importantly, you are communicating that, despite the upset, the relationship remains important.

DEVELOPING A MANAGING DIFFERENCES
SELF-CHANGE PLAN

The unit on managing differences raises a number of ideas that partners might want to focus on in a self-change plan. By this point in the program, partners are usually familiar with the structure of the self-change plan and often are quite competent in formulating plans in behaviorally specific terms. The educator can now assist partners to build upon previous learning, and to develop their skills in selecting self-change goals that are most likely to bring benefits to the relationship. I often review with the partners all the ideas covered in the unit, and ask them to talk about which ideas particularly appeal to them. These can be incorporated into their self-change plan.

CHALLENGES IN HELPING COUPLES
MANAGE DIFFERENCES

There are four major challenges in helping couples manage differences. The first is the struggle that some people have to recognize the need to listen when managing differences. It is important to help people to develop their listening skills, and to highlight for them how that can assist in reconciling after conflict. The process is illustrated below.

> EDUCATOR: Patrick, what thoughts do you have about a self-change plan for managing differences?
>
> PATRICK: I did not explain myself clearly when we talked about where Callum [their 4-year-old son] might go to school. I am keen for him to go to my old school, but Tammy [Patrick's wife] does not like the whole private school thing. We need to make a decision soon if he is to get in.
>
> EDUCATOR: That sounds like a good choice, an important aspect of managing an important topic. What do you have in mind that you will do to be a better speaker?
>
> PATRICK: Well, I want to set out what I see as the big pluses of the school for Callum.
>
> EDUCATOR: Right, so you want to explain the key points you see in favor of your old school. And if you do that, what effect do you think that might have on how you and Tammy talk about this issue?
>
> PATRICK: Tammy will understand my point of view, and . . . well, I still don't think she will agree. So I feel we likely will still be stuck.

EDUCATOR: Patrick, you have focused on making sure you explain your message clearly to Tammy, but now you are saying that even if you do that, it might not actually help resolve the problem. Any thoughts on what else you might do that would actually solve the problem?

PATRICK: I think the only way it's going to get settled is if I give in.

EDUCATOR: Really? So no matter what you say, you feel Tammy has no likelihood of changing her view?

PATRICK: Yeah, I mean she just seems so set against Callum going to Redlands, for reasons I just don't get.

EDUCATOR: Interesting. I am thinking that maybe you want to do something to help you understand Tammy's views better as well as making sure she gets yours.

PATRICK: Like what?

EDUCATOR: Well, think about the listening skills we covered, what could you work on to get a better understanding of Tammy's view?

PATRICK: Look, I do switch off sometimes when we talk; I just feel we've been around and around this. Maybe I need to ask her some questions.

EDUCATOR: That's a really good focus. So you have two aims, first, to listen and ask lots of questions, and really attend to the answers. Second, when you speak to be clear on the advantages you see for your old school. Have I got it right?

PATRICK: Mmm-hmm. I can do that, listen and then speak.

A common theme running through this example, and many partners' communication, is that they need prompting to listen. Patrick is like many other people who imagine that if they can just find the right words, then their spouse will change his or her mind. But of course the spouse is also likely to be convinced that he or she has the right solution. Unless each person listens to the other, things do not change. A useful maxim for people is: "If you wish to be understood, seek first to understand." In this example, despite his resolution, Patrick did not listen to Tammy. I broke in and praised him for his clarity of speaking but asked him if he had done any listening. He acknowledged that he had not, so I had the couple use a piece of paper as the floor and gave it to Tammy. Even then, Patrick kept disagreeing with Tammy's comments. I broke in for a second time and modeled for Patrick how to listen actively to Tammy. One issue that Tammy mentioned was her concern that Callum would meet only a narrow, elite cross-section of the community if he went to a private secondary school. This issue had not previously been broached and Patrick got interested in that issue. This particular example illustrates an important issue: sometimes the educator needs to use a variety of strategies to help people develop their listening skills, particularly when they are discussing something that is important to them.

A second challenge, which also was evident in Patrick and Tammy's discussion, was the common mistake that people make of beginning a discussion about differences by suggesting a solution. This inhibits a full discussion of each person's view. Tammy began the discussion by saying, "I think Callum should go to our local high school. It's a good school and the money we save in school fees can give him lots of opportunities." The educator pointed out that she had started with the solution before either partner had described what they thought were the important issues in selecting a school. The educator asked Tammy to start again, but this time to talk about some of the things she wanted to see in a school for her son.

A third challenge is when couples escalate to arguing. If couples have an unpleasant exchange, they often feel embarrassed, and some couples might drop out of the CRE program if that occurs. There are four important things an educator can do to prevent destructive conflict in the session about managing differences. The first is to create the setting so that the chance of escalation is reduced. This means that the educator needs throughout the process of the group to be pleasant and polite to all participants, and to make it clear that civility is expected of all participants toward each other. Second, the task of discussing a conflict topic needs thorough preparation. This includes making sure people have a clear understanding of the various conflict management strategies covered in the unit, structuring the discussion task so that people are trying to be constructive and focusing on positive strategies they are trying to employ, and ensuring people are discussing moderately hot rather than very hot topics. Third, the educator needs to monitor couples carefully during the discussion exercise and move over to couples quickly if things start to escalate. This is only possible if the number of couples per educator is not too high.

Finally, if a couple has escalated into negativity, it is important to be able to manage this effectively. In this process it is necessary for the educator to assertively manage the situation to stop further escalation, and to be empathic with the upset felt by both partners. The following is an example of the process.

DOREEN: (*angry, raised voice*) Tony, that's rubbish. You never clean up.

TONY: (*derisively*) Hah, you mean you never notice.

EDUCATOR: I want to stop you there, folks. Doreen you seem angry, and Tony you don't look very comfortable either.

DOREEN: Well, Tony frustrates the hell out of me. He just won't do anything around the house. And I am sick of doing everything!

EDUCATOR: (*turning to Tony*) It seems things are not going well in the discussion.

TONY: No, Doreen is working herself up.

EDUCATOR: OK, look, all three of us need to understand what is happening here. Tony, I want to ask for your help. I want you just to listen for a few minutes while I speak to Doreen. I want you to remain quiet and really listen. Once Doreen has had a chance to explain her point of view, I will ask you to say in your own words how she sees things. You don't need to agree with what Doreen is about to say, but I do want you to try to understand her. OK? Will you do that?

TONY: OK.

EDUCATOR: Doreen the floor is yours. Please tell me how you were feeling in the discussion with Tony.

DOREEN: I get so frustrated. I feel we go over this time and time again. We both work long hours. We both earn money. But I finish up doing everything around the house.

EDUCATOR: OK, so you see Tony as not doing his fair share, and you keep raising that but it does not seem to get anywhere. Is that it?

DOREEN: Yeah, we have the discussion. And like just now Tony denies, he says, 'What about how I cooked dinner Thursday night?'. Yeah, he did but I cooked Monday, Tuesday, Wednesday, Friday, and whatever. I did the shopping, I washed the floors.

EDUCATOR: And when you point out what you see as the unfairness, what happens?

DOREEN: He argues the point with me. He comes up with an odd chore done here or there.

EDUCATOR: So it sounds like you two get into a debate about who did what and when, and your big point—that you feel the bulk of chores unfairly falls to you—never gets resolved.

DOREEN: Exactly.

EDUCATOR: And you're frustrated and angry that a similar conversation keeps happening?

DOREEN: Absolutely, I am really fed up with this.

At this point the educator notices Doreen's anger is abating a little. He checks that he has really understood and then asks Tony to summarize

Doreen's viewpoint. Then the educator talks to Tony about his experience of the discussion. In this instance both partners agreed that the discussion was a recurrent problem. The usual pattern was that Doreen would start the conversation with a complaint, Tony would become defensive and argue back, the discussion would escalate with a focus on each person debating their contribution, and usually Tony would withdraw. The educator talked to them about ways to overcome this pattern of approach and withdraw, and suggested they try the floor technique.

This example illustrates the importance of the structure of listening empathically to one partner at a time. I usually start with whomever seems the most upset, as it is often more challenging for him or her to listen to the partner. Through the exploration of the discussion I try to identify the process of what is going on, how the person feels, and something of his or her views on the topic at hand. Being empathically listened to usually helps people to manage their negative feelings, and you can then steer the couple toward different possible ways of approaching the conversation.

The fourth and final challenge I want to mention in helping couples manage differences is when individual vulnerabilities in one or both partners make a particular topic elicit intense negative emotions. When I find a topic is eliciting very strong negative feelings that do not respond to the process described above, then I start to look for what makes this such a crucial issue for the person.

I have found it is often useful to self-disclose to illustrate the idea of how prior learning experiences might induce a vulnerability. For example, when I was about 13 years of age my father—who had been a quite successful salesman—got fired and went through an extended period (2 years) of unemployment. Before losing his job our family had been middle class and quite well off. Two years later, things were pretty tough financially. In desperation, Dad took out a second mortgage on the house, bought a small corner store, and worked in it 12 hours per day, 6 days per week for many years. For years when my wife and I talked about money I would get bristly, sort of defensive. I think my experience growing up made me a bit anxious about money; I felt that even if things seem to be going well, it can go wrong quite quickly.

Building on my self-disclosure, I ask the partners to reflect on their earlier experiences of couple relationships, which were discussed in the first unit. It is helpful to think about their parents' relationship in their family of origin, and how they handled the hot issue. (Was it a problem for them? How did they manage it?) I encourage people to reflect on the other experiences that they have had that might make a particular issue like the division of chores, or money, or sex, a sensitive topic. Sometimes this exploration helps the partners to understand and empathize with each other. Other times this might raise issues that need to be managed outside the group. For example, I have had partners report that they had previously been abused, and that this history of abuse is affecting them. The RELATE assessment does include questions that address these kinds of issues. Asking couples initially to complete RELATE, or a similar assessment like FOCCUS or PREPARE, often allows educators to discuss the appropriateness of the group form of CRE before couples commence. However, even when such an assessment has been done, sometimes individual vulnerability only becomes evident in the process of the group.

In essence, the pervasive challenge in helping couples manage differences is to create a safe environment in which each person feels comfortable to express him- or herself. Some couple therapists reading this might question the wisdom of exploring difficult issues in a group context. However, doing CRE is different from couple therapy. Most of the time the couples undertaking CRE can discuss differences without escalating to destructive conflict. Nonetheless, relationship educators do need to monitor how effectively couples undertaking CRE are managing conflict, and be ready to assist couples that lapse into destructive conflict.

CHAPTER 9

Unit 5
Sexuality

Unit 5 of Couple CARE is focused on sexuality. The content is summarized in Table 9.1. The unit begins with the usual review of the content covered in the previous unit and of the self-change plan. The review of the managing differences self-change plan should be done thoroughly so that couples have confidence in their capacity to manage conflict; effective conflict management is essential to the long-term maintenance of relationship satisfaction. Furthermore, if couples have struggled to manage conflict effectively in the recent past, they often do not respond well to the content on sexuality. Con-

TABLE 9.1. Overview of Unit 5: Sexuality

Topic and aim	Exercise(s)
Review of managing differences self-change plan	Review implementation and troubleshoot as required.
Preparing couples to discuss their sexuality	Introduce guidelines for the exploration of couple sexuality.
Early learning and beliefs about sexuality	Explore early learning experiences about sexuality, couples discuss early learning experiences; explore beliefs about sexuality, couples discuss sexual beliefs.
Couple discussion of sexuality	Couples discuss sexual preferences, managing differences in sexual desire, influences on sexuality, identification of sexual relationship strengths and challenges.
Self-change plan	Review key ideas in unit and development of sexuality self-change plan.

sequently, it is good to allow up to 1 full hour of the 2-hour group session for reviewing the managing differences self-change plan.

The content on sexuality begins with individuals reflecting on their learning about sex through childhood and early adulthood, and how this has shaped their current expectations and beliefs. Then the couple discusses these learning experiences and the strengths and challenges they might present for their relationship. The second activity involves reflecting on some commonly held beliefs about sexuality. Next the partners are asked to discuss a range of issues with their spouse, such as how often they have sex, who typically initiates sex, and the way in which they have sex. The intent is to assist couples to be able to discuss their sex lives and identify strengths and challenges in their current patterns of sexual interaction. Occasionally, some couples participating in Couple CARE have not had sex together (e.g., some engaged couples decide to postpone sex until after they marry). For these couples, the focus is on encouraging them to discuss how they would like their sexual relationship to be. Based on these discussions, each partner identifies some strengths of their current sex life and an area to work on. Next the couples identify things that might impact their sex lives, either positively or negatively, and consider how they could increase the positive and decrease the negative effects of those influences. Finally, both partners develop a self-change plan to enhance their sex life with their spouse.

For many couples sexuality is a very private aspect of their relationship. Thus, some couples find explicit discussion of their sexuality with an educator uncomfortable. Other couples value the chance to discuss and enhance aspects of their sex life. Educators need to be explicit in their discussion of sex to help such couples achieve their goals. Given the diversity of comfort levels couples have for explicit discussion of sexuality, this unit provides a lot of choice to each couple in how much they disclose to the educator. Even when delivering Couple CARE to groups of couples it is possible to provide each couple with choice—this chapter includes description of how to provide that choice.

REVIEWING THE CONFLICT MANAGEMENT
SELF-CHANGE PLAN

The review of the conflict management self-change plan follows the same structure as that of reviews of self-change plans in previous units. The educator begins by asking each partner about the ideas he or she liked from the previous unit, and how each partner has used those ideas. Then the educator asks both partners individually to report specifically on what they were seeking to do in the self-change plan, and how they went in carrying through on the plan. Often by this point in the group program couples know each other well enough to be comfortable reviewing their self-change plans in front of the group. Participants are also now familiar with the self-change plan review and most can do this process quite efficiently.

If the self-change plan involved changing communication when discussing conflict topics—for most couples, this is the focus of their self-change plans—then it is useful to have a sample of the couple's communication to review with them. A helpful option is to have the couple continue the conversation from where they left off previously while the educator listens. The exercise works best if the educator keeps the sample to be reviewed brief (no more than 1½–2 minutes). The review process typically proceeds with an initial statement of self-evaluation by a partner, then listening to a sample of couple conversation, and finally reviewing the self-evaluation in the light of that conversation.

> EDUCATOR: Tony, can you tell me what you saw as a couple of strengths in the way you talked with Michelle?
>
> TONY: Well I really tried to attend, you know, looking at her and focusing.
>
> EDUCATOR: Good. And . . . another strength?
>
> TONY: I asked questions, open questions this time." [In earlier work, the educator had highlighted the value of open questions that invite your partner to express his or her ideas, as distinct from closed questions that tend to ask your partner to endorse the question asker's ideas.]
>
> EDUCATOR: Terrific, I am glad you took these ideas on board. What about things to change?
>
> TONY: I was pretty happy with how it went; I am sort of struggling here to think of anything.
>
> EDUCATOR: OK. It would be helpful for me to listen to you talking so we can see if there are any other ideas about what you might change. Maybe between the three of us we can come up with a new idea. What was the topic again?
>
> TONY: When and for how long Michelle's mother might stay with us after the baby is born.
>
> EDUCATOR: Good. Well, can you pick up the conversation where you left off? Is that OK, Michelle?
>
> MICHELLE: Sure. Tony, I need a hand in those first few weeks from

Mom. Everybody keeps telling me it's really tough after the birth with little sleep, and she really wants to be with me.

TONY: But don't you think it would be good to have a few weeks to ourselves, you know, for us to get to know our son and how we cope?

MICHELLE: No. No, I don't think that would be better. I have to give birth, I have to breastfeed, and I think I will need someone to help.

TONY: But can't that be me that helps?

EDUCATOR: Let me stop you there for a moment. Tony, what is something good you are doing?

TONY: Well, I am asking questions.

EDUCATOR: You are, that's true. And you really were focused and listening. What sort of questions were you asking?

TONY: Open ones, I think.

EDUCATOR: Remember open questions are like essay questions, "What do you think about . . . ", "What would you like to happen?", "What makes this the best way to go in your mind?". Which of your questions do you think was open?

TONY: Well, what about the one about wouldn't it be a good idea to have a few weeks to ourselves?

EDUCATOR: Can Michelle answer that with a yes or no?

TONY: I guess she did, she said "no." But I still think it might not be a bad idea.

EDUCATOR: And *maybe* that is right. But you were really saying, "This is what I think we should do, don't you agree?", which is not really what you set out to do—to find out Michelle's ideas. What about a question like: "Michelle, what is important to you about having your mom there in those first few weeks?" That might tell you what she thinks is important. Remember the solution comes after you feel you understand each other. Would you ask her that question?

TONY: Michelle, what is so important to you about having your mom around in those first few weeks?

The educator continued working with the couple. What emerged was that Michelle had several friends who had found adjusting to motherhood very difficult, and one friend who had suffered severe postnatal depression. Michelle lacked confidence in her capacity to manage the initial stresses of motherhood. As Tony came to understand that concern, and then to show

Michelle he understood her concern, the couple made progress about deciding how to manage that concern. Equally importantly, Tony learned that asking open questions did serve to add new information that helped resolve what had been a source of significant, ongoing conflict. The transcript illustrates the importance of having a sample of couple communication by which the educator can evaluate the realism of both partners' self-evaluation of their conflict management.

When this review process is done in front of the group, it can facilitate very powerful learning for the other couples. It is very important to retain the engagement of the other couples when working predominantly with one couple. The educator can call on participants for suggestions about how someone could listen or speak more effectively. When eliciting such suggestions, it is important not to allow the group to get distracted by participants' views about how the couple should solve the issue. If someone is trying to solve another couple's problems, remind him or her that the goal is to enhance the couple's ability to solve their own issues. Avoid questions that might inadvertently lead to a focus on solving the couple's issue for them, such as "What did you think was going on here?" Instead, pose questions that specifically request feedback on how the couple is managing their differences. For example, the educator can ask:

- "What did you think was a good thing that was done to listen?"
- "Do you have a suggestion of what else could be done to listen more effectively?"
- "What was good about how X was speaking?"
- "Do you a suggestion of one thing X could try to speak more effectively?"

HELPING COUPLES TO EXPLORE SEXUAL ISSUES

The issue of respect for privacy about sexual issues needs to be addressed in CRE. This is of particular importance when relationship education is being done in groups. To assist couples to make the most of their discussion with their spouses, the educator can introduce the guidelines presented in Figure 9.1 to couples before asking them to undertake the exercises in the unit on sexuality. The table can be a useful handout, or the key points can be summarized verbally, or presented in a slide. These guidelines make explicit the message that partners have a choice about what they disclose to their spouse and to the educator. I recommend that the educator reads through these points and provides the opportunity for couples to ask questions or comment.

1. Many people feel a bit uncomfortable when taking about sex. If you find such discussion difficult, it can be useful to tell this to your partner.

2. Only disclose as much in your writing and speaking as you feel comfortable with.

3. Sometimes it helps to tell your partner things about your past experience of sex so that he or she can understand your current feelings.

4. Some people find it hard to hear about their partner's prior sexual experiences. It often is unhelpful to give lots of detail about prior sexual experiences.

5. Respect your spouse's privacy: do not read what he or she has written or push him or her to speak about things if he or she feels uncomfortable.

6. There might be topics you want to discuss with your spouse, but not with me as an educator. That is OK. In the rest of the session when you are speaking as a couple I will only come over if you raise your hand and ask me to.

7. Please spread yourselves out and use the room available. Do not listen in on each other's conversations.

8. I will not ask people to report the content of their conversation with their spouse to the group, unless they want to do that.

FIGURE 9.1. Guidelines when discussing sex with your partner.

EARLY LEARNING AND BELIEFS ABOUT SEXUALITY

Early Learning about Sexuality

At the start of Unit 1 of Couple CARE, partners reflect on prior learning experiences about couple relationships and their relationship expectations. Unit 5 follows a similar process, but this time the focus is specifically on prior learning and expectations about sexuality. Figure 9.2 provides a useful handout for couples. Each partner is asked to write down some thoughts about these questions. The couples then discuss the ideas they have written down together.

The aim in reviewing early learning about sex is to identify how these early experiences shape both helpful and unhelpful beliefs about sexuality. If couples are comfortable discussing these areas with the educator, it can be useful to ask each partner the following questions:

On your own, write down your thoughts about the following areas.

Childhood

What did your parents and any brothers or sisters communicate to you about sex? Did they talk about sex much? Did they talk about sex positively or negatively?

_____
_____
_____
_____
_____
_____
_____
_____
_____

"I learned about sex from my older sisters—it was something naughty and exotic—my sisters called it "the deed." I thought sex was probably good but you didn't talk about it. I still find it a bit hard to talk about sex with my partner, even though he is very open about it. It's something I'm working on."—Lee, 34, married 3 years to Rob, 28

"My parents were hippies, always wandering around naked. It was pretty embarrassing. So I just didn't like to talk with them about sex."—Shane, 28

Adolescence

What was your parents' attitude toward you and sex in your teenage years? Were they strict? Easygoing? Punishing?

_____
_____
_____
_____
_____
_____
_____
_____
_____
_____
_____
_____

"My dad didn't want to talk to me about sex. He just gave me a bunch of men's magazines when I was 14. I thought that sex was an all-night festival of the flesh. But that's not how it was, not at all the first time. I felt like a dismal failure as a man. Later on I talked to my friend. I worked out I wasn't the only one who felt that way."—Rob, 28, married 3 years to Lee, 34

"My mom was very open, cool about sex. I was the only one at school who really understood about condoms. But my dad, if a boy so much as looked at me, dad would jump on him. I never brought boys home, it would have been a nightmare."—Angela, 44

(cont.)

FIGURE 9.2. Reflections on early learning experiences.

What about friends? Did you see yourself as more or less sexually active than your friends? What was the craziest thing anyone ever tried to tell you about sex?

_____
_____
_____
_____
_____
_____
_____
_____

"I had a girlfriend who told me you wouldn't get pregnant if you did it standing up. But she was always in the back of some guy's car, so I couldn't see how she could stand up."—Natalie, 19

"At school the other guys were always boasting about what they did on the weekend. You know, claiming to have had lots of sex and all that. Looking back I am sure they were full of it, but at the time I felt I was the only guy missing out."—Glenn, 39

Other Experiences

How have other experiences influenced your attitudes to sex? How have you decided what is OK/not OK for you?

_____
_____
_____
_____
_____
_____

"Paolo is sensitive to my likes and dislikes. He is OK and does not take it personally if I don't feel like sex. Being with him has made me a more demanding lover. I never used to start sex before, now I do. And I ask what he likes. Which made me a better lover too. At least I hope so!"—Natasha, 34, partner to Paolo, 32, for 4 years

Today

What attitudes do you have now that help your sex life with your partner?

_____
_____
_____

What attitudes (if any) do you have now that do not help your sex life with your partner?

_____
_____
_____

As a couple, talk to each other about any of the aspects of what you have written down that you wish to share with your partner. Focus in particular on the positive things you bring to your sexual relationship.

FIGURE 9.2. *(cont.)*

- "What do you see as the key messages about sexuality you received when growing up?"
- "How do you think this benefits your sexual relationship now?"
- "Are there any negative effects from that early learning?"

It also can be useful to pose the following questions to the couple:

- "When you two discussed your early learning experiences, what did you see as the similarities and differences in those early learning experiences?"
- "What effects do you think these early learning experiences have on your sex life together?"

Exploring Sexual Beliefs

Figure 9.3 lists sexual beliefs that can influence how people respond sexually to their partners. The intent in this exercise is to help partners explicate their beliefs about sexuality and to discuss these with their spouses. The goal is to identify beliefs that might need gentle challenging and that might lead to self-change to enhance the couple's sex life. The way the exercise is introduced is crucial to how effective it is as a learning exercise. This is intended not as a test of people's sexual knowledge but rather as a means of exploring people's sexual beliefs, and helping them to consider what beliefs are helpful or unhelpful. Explaining this idea can be done using something like the following words:

> "All of us have ideas about how sex should be, and what our partner desires—or does not desire. The handout I am about to give you lists common sexual beliefs. There are beliefs that can help you to have a good sex life, and other beliefs that can get in the way of having a good sex life. I want you to read through the list of beliefs and indicate whether you think that belief is true or false. This is not a test and there is no right or wrong answer. The handout is to promote discussion. You can place a mark beside any beliefs that you might like to discuss. We can talk about some of these in the group, or I can talk with you about them as a couple."

The educator should allow a few minutes for the couples to get started on their discussions. The educator can then circulate among the couples asking for their responses to the sexual beliefs, and chatting through the issues

(text resumes on page 242)

On your own, read through the following sexual beliefs. Indicate whether you think the belief is true or not by writing a T for "true" or an F for "false" beside each belief

Belief	True or false?
1. True sexual enjoyment means having an orgasm.	
2. If you are really in love sex will be really good almost all the time.	
3. My body should be perfect in order to have a good sex life.	
4. Only intercourse is real sex.	
5. Sometimes you can enjoy sex without achieving orgasm.	
6. Male impotence is always a sign of serious problems.	
7. Men come too fast and women too slowly.	
8. Men need sex more often than women.	
9. If your relationship is good, you should both feel like sex at the same time.	
10. You do not have to be physically fit to enjoy sex.	
11. Almost all couples have times when only one partner feels like sex.	
12. Most women experience discomfort or even pain sometimes during sex.	
13. If your partner ever masturbates, something is wrong with your sex life.	
14. After the birth of a baby, a couple's sex life pretty much stops for a year.	
15. By the time people are 50–60 years of age they lose interest in sex.	

FIGURE 9.3. Common sexual beliefs.

Orgasms and Sex

Sex does not have to be just about reaching orgasm. Sex is about lots of things. Sex can be relaxing and sensual without having an orgasm. Sex can be about giving pleasure to your partner. Sex can be expressing how you feel.

For most women orgasm does not occur every time they have sex. In fact, only one-third of women say they reach climax from intercourse "most of the time." Another third of women say they reach orgasm "some of the time," and a third say they "rarely or never" reach orgasm during intercourse.

Most men do reach orgasm most of the time with intercourse. But it is common for men not to reach orgasm from time to time.

If you never or hardly ever have orgasm, you might want to try to change this. There is no correct or normal way to be. If you are satisfied with your current sex life and how often you achieve orgasm, then that is fine. If you are not satisfied, there are things you can try to enhance your sexual enjoyment. You relationship educator can give you advice.

How Good Does Sex Have to Be?

In all relationships sex varies. More than likely sometimes sex will be great, sometimes just OK, and much of the time sex will be pretty good. Sex tends to be better more of the time in relationships where the couple:

- Do their best to stay fit and healthy.
- Spend time on being romantic and having special couple time.
- Make time for sex to be leisurely.
- The relationship as a whole is working well.

Even when all these things are present, couples will still get tired from time to time, or feel stressed or not in the mood. The important things are to have realistic expectations, and then to assess whether sex in your relationship is usually good enough.

Physical Appearance and Sex

Most models look rotten in the morning. The glamour seen in magazines and movies is mainly good lighting and makeup. No one has perfect looks.

A good sex life usually means we need to accept how we look. If you hate your body or how it looks, it can be hard to have a good sex life. At the same time people who are physically healthy and stay in shape tend to have better sex lives. Making an effort to look healthy for yourself and your partner is a good thing.

(cont.)

FIGURE 9.4. Some useful information for discussing common sexual beliefs.

If you feel uncomfortable with how you look naked, talk this over with your relationship educator.

Intercourse and Other Aspects of Sex

Happy couples tend to have a wide variety of sexual and sensual things they do together. Sometimes a cuddle, massage, or petting can be fun and can express sensual and sexual feelings without intercourse.

There are times when options other than intercourse can be good. Some couples like oral sex or mutual masturbation for variety.

Sometimes intercourse is not a good option. For example, some couples dislike intercourse when the woman has her period. For a time after childbirth, sex may be uncomfortable for the woman. At such times other forms of sex, such as mutual touching, can be good.

On the other hand, some people feel they need great variety to have really experienced sex. It is important that the sexual behaviors couples use are acceptable to both partners. For example, if one partner does not like oral sex, that does not stop the couple from having a great sex life.

Matching Desired Frequency of Sex

Everyone varies in how sexy they feel. Everyone has days when he or she is too tired, or just does not feel that way. So it is impossible for one partner to always desire sex at the same time as the other partner.

It is important that the couple find ways of signaling to each other when they do feel like sex. And it is important to respect when your partner does not feel like sex.

If one partner does not feel like sex at a particular time, masturbation can provide release. Most people do masturbate from time to time.

Sexual Problems Like Pain or Impotence

Impotence is the inability to get or keep an erection during sex. Many men are impotent from time to time. Sometimes impotence is caused by a clear medical problem. Other times psychological factors can cause impotence. For example, stress and too much to drink can cause impotence. If impotence is causing problems in your relationship, talk to a doctor. Many impotence problems can now be treated.

Discomfort during intercourse can occur in women from time to time. The most common type of discomfort is rubbing at the entrance to the vagina caused by vaginal dryness, which can be managed with better attention to foreplay or use of lubricants. However, persistent discomfort or severe pain should not be ignored. This can have a variety of causes such as a vaginal infection or a more serious medical condition. If you do have persistent discomfort or pain, see your doctor.

(cont.)

FIGURE 9.4. *(cont.)*

Differences in Men's and Women's Sexual Response

Individuals vary greatly in how quickly they become aroused, and by what. It is common for men to achieve orgasm during intercourse more quickly than women, but this varies from time to time and from couple to couple. Try to make sure that sex occurs when both partners are interested. Foreplay needs to be arousing for both partners. This requires letting each other know what is pleasurable. If there are differences in how quickly each of you reaches orgasm, and if this is a problem in your relationship, talk to your relationship educator.

Differences in Men's and Women's Sexual Desire

Interest in sex varies between people, and for each person from one time to another. On average across all men and women, men tend to desire intercourse more often than women. Developing ways to negotiate having sex at a frequency and in ways that are acceptable to each partner makes for a good relationship.

FIGURE 9.4. *(cont.)*

with them. After the couples have had a while to talk, I distribute Figure 9.4 as a handout. In the group context I often run through the beliefs included in Figure 9.3, highlighting the issues underlying the statements. The information provided in Figure 9.4 is a useful resource for presenting facts on these issues. Once some information has been provided, I ask the couples to discuss their responses to the beliefs with their partner. Often this provokes further discussion with the educator, either one on one or in the group setting.

In most groups the ideas presented in Figures 9.3 and 9.4 are sufficiently general that couples are comfortable discussing them in the group. I try to draw people out on their responses to the ideas put forward. A key point to make is that all of the statements in Figure 9.3 are partially but not completely true. For example, I will often discuss statement 14 that "After the birth of a baby, a couple's sex life pretty much stops for a year." Some useful points to cover are as follows:

"It is true that most couples report a decline in frequency of sex across pregnancy and after the birth. It is false that couples tend not to have sex at all in the year after the birth.

"Most couples decrease how often they have sex when the woman is pregnant, and often do not have intercourse at all in the last month or two of pregnancy. After the birth intercourse is quite uncomfortable— even painful—for the woman if attempted in the first few weeks after birth. Pain can be particularly severe if the woman had trauma to her vagina or perineum (the skin between the vagina and the anus) during birth. Most couples first attempt intercourse about 6–8 weeks after the birth, though some couples might pet or engage in other sexual behavior before that. When couples resume having intercourse, the woman often finds it uncomfortable for a while. Some couples engage in mutual petting or oral sex for a while to give the woman's body more time to recover. Couples often need to experiment with different positions and use of lubricants to make intercourse more enjoyable. Almost all women—and some men—report lower sexual desire for a time after the birth of a child. The combination of the effects of pregnancy and the birth on the woman's body can make her feel less sexy and attractive. Hormonal changes and tiredness impact on sexual desire. If the woman is breastfeeding, that can change her own and her partner's feelings about her breasts.

"Most couples successfully recommence having intercourse and their sex lives gradually get back to being mutually enjoyable over a period of 6 months or so. However, about one-quarter of couples report some ongoing difficulty with intercourse a year after the birth of their first child. So the effects of childbirth are quite variable.

"Does anyone have any questions or comments about that statement? Are there other statements that you want to discuss?"

The statements that couples wish to discuss vary considerably across groups. However, a statement that often provokes a lot of discussion is statement 8, that men desire sex more often than women. There are two important points to make about this statement. First, the level of sexual desire varies greatly from man to man, and from woman to woman. Second, the level of sexual desire experienced by an individual varies greatly across the lifespan. It is true that in available studies it is found that, on average, men desire sex somewhat more often than women. However, the relative frequency of desired sex by the man and the woman is likely to vary from couple to couple, and each couple is likely to vary over time.

TALKING ABOUT SEX

The exercises that focus on talking about sex encourage the partners to discuss the frequency with which they have sex and the way in which they have sex. There are two goals in this process. The first goal is to help the partners to understand each other's sexual preferences. The second goal is to identify the strengths and possible challenges in their current sex life.

Discussing the Frequency of Sex and Who Initiates

Figure 9.5 is a series of questions about the frequency with which a couple has sex, and who typically initiates making love. Individuals write down their answers to the first five questions individually, and then discuss their answers together, identifying the strengths of their current pattern of making love and any areas they feel they need to work on. It is often helpful to make a general comment about how often people usually have sex.

> "Some couples wonder about what is normal in terms of the frequency of having sex. So what is a lot of sex? Is there too much? Most couples have sex most frequently early in their relationship. In national surveys couples in their 20s tend to have sex anything from once per week to daily; the average is two or three times per week. As we age that rate declines. But at age 60 the vast majority of couples are still sexually active, and having sex maybe once per week. There is no 'right' level of sexual frequency. If at 60 years of age you can have sex three times a night every night and both of you still manage to get up and go to work, good luck to you. If you save up, and only savor sex on birthdays and anniversaries, and that works for you—fantastic."

A common issue that arises for couples is differences between the partners in sexual desire. It is impossible for two people to always synchronize when they wish to have sex, and for some couples negotiating about when to have sex can be difficult. Differences in sexual desire fall into three broad categories: a situation, a pattern, and a problem. The following is an example of explaining the difference between these categories.

> "Differences in sexual desire fall into three broad categories: a situation, a pattern, and a problem. All couples experience from time to time the situation in which one partner feels like having sex and the other does not. Usually both partners accept this as no big deal. Sometimes the responding partner manages an unwanted sexual invitation by saying 'no' nicely; sometimes by saying 'maybe' and seeing if desire develops. Sometimes he or she might just go along and maybe even then desire develops.
> "In some couples a pattern develops where one of the partners initiates sex most of the time. Often, though not always, it is the man initiating and the woman responding. This pattern of one partner initiating need not be a problem if both partners enjoy their sex life together. However, there is a risk that if the man is always, or almost always, the initiator, then sex occurs only when he is interested. The woman finds herself responding to sex at times not of her choosing, which might

On your own, answer the following questions:

1. Over the last few months we have had sex:

☐ 6–7 days per week
☐ 3–5 days per week
☐ Once or twice per week
☐ Every 2–3 weeks
☐ Once per month or less

2. How often we have had sex over the last few months is:

☐ Much more often than I like
☐ A little bit more often than I like
☐ About right
☐ A bit less often than I like
☐ Much less often than I would like

3. Who initiates sex in your relationship?

☐ Me, most of the time we have sex
☐ Both of us, but me more often
☐ Both of us, about equally
☐ Both of us, but my partner more often
☐ My partner, most of the time we have sex

4. When you do initiate sex with your partner, what do you most often say or do?

_____

_____

5. When your partner initiates sex with you, what does he or she most often say or do?

_____

_____

As a couple, discuss your answers. Write down your thoughts about your current strengths and areas to work on with respect to how you work out how often you have sex.

Strengths about how we decide how often to have sex: _____

_____

_____

Areas to work on: _____

_____

_____

FIGURE 9.5. How often we have sex and how we feel about it.

reduce her enjoyment. If you have the pattern in your relationship that one of you initiates sex most of the time, then you might want to change. But change is not required if both partners are enjoying sex when it occurs.

"A third possibility is that one partner is never, or hardly ever, interested in sex. Many factors can contribute to a lack of interest in sex, such as fatigue, prior learning experiences, alcohol or drug abuse, or a variety of medical conditions. In addition, other sexual problems, such as impotence in the man or painful intercourse in the woman, can result in a lack of interest in sex. Some couples come to accept a lack of sex in their lives. If both partners are OK with this, it need not be a problem. However, if persistent lack of interest in sex is a problem, it is advisable to see a medical practitioner for assessment of whether a medical condition might be contributing to the problem. There are quite effective treatments available for many causes of lack of sexual interest."

Couples should be given the opportunity to discuss ideas about situations, patterns, and problems of differences in sexual desire with their partners. The educator can circulate, answering questions as required.

There is a final point worth making about differences in sexual desire. There are some gender differences in what men and women find promotes sexual desire. On average, men are more likely than women to respond with desire to visual cues. For example, the sight of a naked attractive woman seems to arouse men more than the sight of a naked attractive man arouses women. On average, women are more likely than men to respond with desire to romance cues. For example, a passage in a novel describing a romantic experience seems to arouse women more than men. One way to draw out this point is to ask couples to discuss the following gender difference.

"More than 90% of purchasers of pornography are men. More than 90% of purchasers of romantic fiction are women. Please take a minute to discuss what you think might explain this difference in what men and women choose to buy."

The educator can ask people to report to the group their thoughts on this gender difference. A key point to draw out is that for women, their sexual desire and enjoyment is often closely associated with the overall sense of emotional intimacy in the couple relationship. Women's "pornography" is often focused on the experience of emotional intimacy. For women, great sex typically comes after emotional closeness sets the mood. This is not to say that women are not aroused by the sight of an attractive man, just that romance is important. In contrast, men's sexual desire is more often related to immediate stimulation of sights and sounds. This is not to say that men do not enjoy romance. However, for men in a committed relationship, sex can often be spontaneous and felt as a deep sense of emotional closeness. On average men and women tend to respond sexually to somewhat different things. Both romance and spontaneity have their advantages. A weekend away in a beautiful place, lots of romance, and leisurely lovemaking can be wonderful. A "quickie" to say "I love you" if you have not got much time, or to make up after a minor disagreement, has its place as well.

Talking about How the Couple Has Sex

The aim of this exercise is for participants to review with their partner the range of sensual and sexual behaviors in which they currently engage, and to discuss what changes (if any) they might like to make in their sex life together. Figure 9.6 lists a wide variety of sexual behaviors. Partners are each asked to indicate how they feel about each behavior. This forms the basis for the couple to discuss together their sexual likes and dislikes. A challenge some couples face is different preferences in how they have sex. For example, one partner might greatly enjoy oral sex but the other partner does not. One goal of this exercise is for partners to understand each other's sexual preferences.

A second goal of the exercise is to explore how the couple communicates about sex. While many couples prefer not to divulge the details of their sexual behavior and preferences to the educator, most couples seem comfortable discussing how they communicate about sex. Before couples begin this exercise the educator can make this distinction and talk about how the couple might choose to use the educator as a resource for the exercise.

> "The handout I am about to give you lists a wide variety of sensual and sexual behaviors. The idea is for you to individually rate how you feel about these behaviors, and then discuss this with your partner. One aim is to help you review your sex life and decide together whether you would like to make any changes. A second aim is to have you talk about your sex life and reflect on how you typically communicate about your sex life.
>
> "I am available to help you with your discussions, but I do not want to intrude on your privacy. Some couples prefer to keep the details of what they do in their sex lives private, others find it helpful to talk with me so we can develop ideas they might want to try. If you want to talk to me about sexual positions or your like or dislike of oral sex, that is fine. If you prefer to keep those preferences to yourself, that also is fine.
>
> "If you choose not to talk with me about the details of your sex life, you might still want to talk with me about how you typically communi-

On your own, place a check mark in the appropriate box.

Activity	Love the way we do it now	It's pretty good as it is	It's OK but we could make it better	Haven't done this, I would like to try it	I don't want to do this
Having a long hug with my partner					
My partner and I looking into each other's eyes					
Giving my partner a back rub					
Having my partner give me a back rub					
Giving my partner a foot massage					
Having my partner give me a foot massage					
Initiating sex with my partner					
Having my partner initiate sex					
Kissing each other for more than 1 minute					
Telling my partner my fantasies					
Having my partner tell me his or her fantasies					
Giving my partner a nongenital massage					
Receiving a nongenital massage					
Caressing my partner's nipples/other nongenital area he or she finds stimulating with my hands or lips Area: _____					

(cont.)

FIGURE 9.6. Sexual preferences form.

Activity	Love the way we do it now	It's pretty good as it is	It's OK but we could make it better	Haven't done this, I would like to try it	I don't want to do this
Having my partner caress my nipples/other nongenital area with her or his hands or lips Area: _____					
Caressing my partner's genitals with my hands					
Having my partner caress my genitals with his or her hands					
Giving my partner oral sex					
Receiving oral sex from my partner					
Giving and receiving oral sex simultaneously with my partner					
Watching my partner masturbate					
Having my partner watch me masturbate					
Mutual masturbation					
Having intercourse in the following positions (fill in) 1. _____ 2. _____ 3. _____ 4. _____					
Having sex away from home					
Having dress-up/role-play sex					
Other: _____					
Other: _____					

FIGURE 9.6. *(cont.)*

cate about sex. That is, we might discuss how you express preferences to each other without actually talking about what those preferences might be. I will move around and check with you as a couple what you prefer to talk and not talk with me about."

As the couples discuss their sexual preferences, the educator can move among the couples. The educator should make a comment as he or she approaches a couple like the following:

"[Couple names], I want to ask you to pause for a moment. *Talking about sex can be difficult for some couples. May I ask you how each of you are finding talking about your sexual preferences?*"

It is my experience that beginning with a more abstract general question like this can assist couples to feel more comfortable in talking with the educator. The educator can then ask something like "Is there anything arising from your discussion together that you would like to discuss with me?"

Once a couple has discussed their sexual preferences, each partner is asked to write down two strengths of their sex life with their partner, and one area to work on. Once that is done, the couple discusses the strengths and areas to work on that each has identified. The educator circulates among the couples asking them if there is anything they wish to discuss about their responses. It is important to point out to couples that they might choose to develop a self-change plan about how they communicate about sex, or about the way in which they have sex.

The final step in the unit on sexuality is to ask each partner to develop a self-change plan. I ask the group to comment on what was a key idea that they got from the current session. Then each person individually reflects on the focus of their self-change plan. The handouts on who initiates sex and sexual likes and dislikes are good starting points for partners to develop a self-change plan.

It also is useful to make the point that it is not essential for people to develop a self-change plan on any of the areas covered in Couple CARE. If everything seems satisfactory to the partners about their current sex life, then they might choose not to make a sexual self-change plan. It also is worth pointing out that the next session is the last group session, and hence will be the last chance to review a self-change plan with the educator. So, if participants have a self-change they would like to make about any areas covered in previous sessions (communication, intimacy and caring, or managing differences), this is a good chance to write such a self-change plan. I make a point of saying that I am available to help with development of self-change plans if the participants require assistance.

CHALLENGES IN ENHANCING COUPLE SEXUALITY

One key challenge in working with groups of couples on sexuality is striking the right balance between respecting privacy and encouraging the couples to be open and to use the educator as a resource. It is important to allow couples to control the level of self-disclosure they make about their sex lives to the educator and to other group members. At the same time the educator needs to model comfort with discussing sexuality. The educator does this by using appropriate sexually explicit words. For example, in the introduction to couples talking about sexual likes and dislikes, I make a point of referring to sexually explicit terms like sexual positions and oral sex. It is also important to emphasize the word *some* in saying *some* couples feel a little uncomfortable in talking about sexuality. This prevents the potential trap of the educator implicitly communicating that people should not feel comfortable talking about sexuality. The educator also needs to carefully monitor each partner's responses to the educator's invitation to discuss topics. Look for body language or evasive words that reflect discomfort. The educator can then reflect that the person appears a little uncomfortable and check out that perception with the person.

A second challenge with enhancing couples' sexuality is that there is much specialized knowledge about human sexual functioning that is potentially relevant to couples. For example, many medications (e.g., some antidepressant medications, antihypertensive medications) and medical conditions (e.g., vaginal infections, diabetes) can impact sexual arousal and response. For the majority of couples that present for CRE, the structured exercises contained in Couple CARE can help enrich a satisfactory sexual relationship. However, many relationship educators might lack the specialized knowledge to assist couples experiencing sexual difficulties. Participating in Couple CARE can help couples to identify sexual difficulty. The educator can then assist couples to seek further specialized assistance.

A third challenge is that many adults have experienced some form of sexual abuse, and sometimes disclosure of such abuse can occur during this session. In surveys in Australia, America, New Zealand, and Britain, approximately half of all women and about 15% of men report having experienced sexual abuse as a child (Finkelhor, 1994; Goldman & Padayachi, 1997; Messman-Moore & Long, 2000; Watson & Halford, 2010). For most of these people the abuse was a single episode of unwanted sexual fondling, but others experienced repeated intrusive sexual assault including rape (Watson & Halford, 2010). Occasionally the direct discussion of sexuality included in Unit 5 of Couple CARE leads to disclosure of prior sexual trauma.

If a person's sexual trauma was less severe and the person does not appear to be suffering major adjustment difficulties attributable to the trauma, then the recommended Couple CARE exercises can help. For example, one woman reported to the educator that she rarely enjoyed sex in the position when her male partner was on top of her. She recounted having been sexually molested by a friend of her brother when he lay on her and masturbated. He was a large boy and she felt crushed, and very short of breath at the time. She associated being underneath her partner with that discomfort. Immediately after a group session the educator discussed this with the woman and her partner. Both partners described their sexual relationship as good, and the man and woman both seemed comfortable with adjusting to the woman's preferences in sexual position. The man had been unaware of the prior abuse of his partner, he responded sensitively, and she was emotionally moved by his concern for her.

In other instances, the revelation of prior sexual abuse can indicate a need for further assistance. For example, in a group one man reported that he had been repeatedly raped by his grandfather, who raised him after his parents had separated. The man often suffered from panic attacks, and these sometimes started during sex. After discussing these issues with the man and his partner, it was agreed to refer him to a clinical psychologist for individual and possibly couple therapy.

The issue of revelation of sexual abuse highlights that, while Couple CARE is intended as relationship education and not therapy, there will be some individuals and couples in groups that require therapeutic assistance. One important role of CRE is to identify as yet undiscovered needs for therapeutic assistance. CRE often serves as an important point of access for therapy. Unit 6 explores further the issue of when and how Couple CARE participants might seek additional relationship or individual assistance.

CHAPTER 10

Unit 6

Looking Ahead

Unit 6 of Couple CARE is focused on maintaining relationship satisfaction by looking ahead at what the future is likely to hold, and helping couples to manage that change in relationship-enhancing ways. The content of Unit 6 is summarized in Table 10.1. As with previous units, Unit 6 begins with a review of the content and self-change plan of the previous unit. The unit itself addresses three areas. First, couples identify changes likely to occur in their lives over the next year or two, discuss the possible positive and negative relationship effects of those life changes, and develop a plan to enhance the posi-

TABLE 10.1. Overview of Unit 6: Looking Ahead

Topic and aim	Exercise(s)
Review of sexuality self-change plan	Review implementation and troubleshoot as required.
Managing change	Identifying likely life changes, exploring the relationship effects of life changes, couple management of life change.
Preventing relationship problems	The prevalence of relationship problems, early warning signs of emerging relationship problems, preventing emergence of severe relationship problems.
Maintaining a relationship focus	Reviewing the couple relationship vision, relationship rituals, maintenance of relationship skills.
Self-change plan	Review of key ideas in unit and development of sexuality self-change plan.

tive effects of life changes. Second, the couple is encouraged to consider what might be the early warning signs of future relationship problems, and what they could do to prevent the development of serious relationship problems. Third, the couple is encouraged to maintain a focus on their relationship. This involves reviewing their shared relationship vision based on their learning through Couple CARE, developing rituals to celebrate their relationship, and developing strategies for continuing to practice their most important relationship-enhancing habits.

REVIEWING THE SEXUAL SELF-CHANGE PLAN

Even couples with good sex lives find that the active discussion that Unit 5 encourages can be helpful. The following review illustrates how a husband learned more about the sexual interests of his wife, to whom he had been married for 32 years.

> EDUCATOR: What stands out in your mind, Bob, as the most important part of last week's unit?
>
> BOB: Well, to be honest, I was not feeling like we needed to do too much to change things about sex. Daina and I have generally had a good sex life, except maybe just around when the kids were very young. It was interesting when we did talk, Daina said she wanted more sex. Now, I generally have initiated sex in our relationship. My only real worry was that maybe sometimes she went along to please me but really wasn't into it. It surprised me that she said having sex a bit more would be good.
>
> EDUCATOR: Daina, what is your take on this?
>
> DAINA: I do usually enjoy sex, but Bob is right, he usually does the starting. As we spoke I just thought, sometimes I would like to be in charge—to start things because sometimes I am in the mood.
>
> EDUCATOR: Right, so talking made you both realize that Daina was keen to initiate sex, at least some of the time. And what effect do you think knowing that might have?
>
> BOB: I know what effect it had on Thursday morning. (*Laughs.*)
>
> EDUCATOR: Right. (*Smiles.*) Daina, what, if anything, would you like to say to Bob about the effects of having the discussion together about sex?
>
> DAINA: Just this, that I want to have a good sex life together. I think me approaching Bob sometimes will be good for both of us.

EDUCATOR: Wonderful, thank you for telling me about this. Anything you want to do in the next week to follow up, Daina?

DAINA: I just might look for a chance to initiate, if Bob behaves himself. I quite liked surprising Bob.

Of course not every sexual self-change plan goes exactly as intended. Angelo's self-change plan outcome illustrates how there is usually some useful learning to be had even when plans go slightly awry.

EDUCATOR: Ang, how did the self-change plan go?

ANGELO: Not quite as planned. I had this idea of like a really romantic weekend, out in the woods, you know, all on our lonesome. I cooked up some great pasta, put in some wine, packed the car, the whole deal. Tablecloth, candles, nice linen for the inflatable bed, massage oil. I had thought it all out.

EDUCATOR: Sounding good so far, Anna?

ANNA: *Almost* all of the planning was really good. Though if you're going camping you might want to check the weather forecast. Particularly if you keep your partner in the dark about what you're doing.

EDUCATOR: So how did it go?

ANGELO: Remember the big storm that hit the ranges over the weekend? Knocked our tent down, didn't it? About half an hour after we got there, it suddenly went really dark, and then wham. Long story short, didn't need the massage oil. We slept in the car, no food, drove our soggy selves home early Sunday.

EDUCATOR: So Ang you went to a lot of trouble, by the sound of it. What was good about what you did?

ANGELO: Not much really. Anna has a cold from sleeping in wet clothes, I felt stuffed because I couldn't sleep at all.

EDUCATOR: (*gentle laughter*) He really tried so hard, didn't he, Anna?

ANNA: (*laughing*) Yeah, he did. My smooth Italian lover had it all beautifully planned, and now I am coughing and sneezing so bad he's on the couch trying to get some sleep.

EDUCATOR: So, Anna, what did you like about Ang's effort?

ANNA: It was the effort, that was the good thing. When we first met he was so romantic, but we've got busy and somehow . . . (*dabbing her eye with a tissue*) I miss being . . . like . . . romanced.

ANGELO: Babe, you know I love you. Maybe I'll try again, but no camping.

EDUCATOR: So, Ang, it seems that even though the weekend was wet, and hungry, and cramped in a car, it meant something to Anna that you tried.

This passage illustrates a very important theme that occurs in many couples' experience of doing Couple CARE. When people experience their spouse genuinely making an effort to be loving, to be romantic, to be considerate, to listen more effectively, it makes them feel loved, and draws the two partners closer together. Journalist Dorothy Foltz-Gray had been married for 28 years to Dan and she described doing Couple CARE as "like dating—this person whom I had already loved for so long became new to me . . . we found ourselves talking, sometimes for hours, like two people falling in love" (Foltz-Gray, 2006, p. 145).

MANAGING LIFE CHANGES

All couples will experience a range of changes during a lifetime together. Many of these changes require the couple to adapt their relationship to changed life circumstances. For example, as described in the previous chapter, many couples have children together and this produces a variety of changes. Helping couples to manage the relationship effects of life change involves three steps. First, couples reflect on the common changes in couples' lives, and the possible relationship effects of those changes. Second, each couple identifies life changes that are likely to occur for them in the next year or two, and the relationship effects of those changes. Finally, the couple is asked to develop a plan to maximize the positive gains, and reduce the negative effects, of those anticipated life changes.

The aim of the first task is to introduce couples to the idea of how life changes impact on couple relationships, both positively and negatively, and to explore how couples can manage the relationship effects of life changes. The educator asks the group to identify one or two major life changes many of them might experience in the next year or two. The most appropriate examples depend on the composition of the group. Good examples of common life changes include a job change for one partner that involves more pay and more hours of work; relocation to another town or city; moving house; having a child; or a serious illness in a parent. Selecting one life change, I have the couples brainstorm as many possible positive consequences of that change as they can, and write up these ideas on a whiteboard. We then brainstorm as many possible negative consequences of that change as we can, and write up these ideas on the whiteboard. Figure 10.1 shows the result of such a group discussion, illustrating how life events have the potential for positive and negative relationship effects. It also reinforces the point that standing together in adversity is an extraordinarily powerful developer of intimacy.

I then ask the group to brainstorm things the couple might do to enhance the positive effects and manage the negative effects of the change. Figure 10.2 sets out an example of a change plan a couple prepared for—a life change of the woman going to a new job—and provides space for the couple to develop a change plan of their own. After distributing this table as a handout, the educator needs to explain that the couple first identifies the direct effects of the change. For example, a new job might mean more money and more hours committed to work, or having to work different times of day. Then the couple is asked about the possible impact of these effects of change on the couple relationship, such as reduced time together, or a rebalancing of work and family commitments. Finally, the couple is asked to identify a plan to deal with the relationship effects of the change. A key goal of the planning-for-change exercise is to help couples to think in relationship terms when confronted with change. Such thinking includes being able to consider the potential positive and negative effects of possible changes.

Likely positive relationship effects	Likely negative relationship effects
New, higher paying job with longer hours	
More money for weekends away, vacations Less worry about the mortgage Feel successful Can buy the new fridge Clear the credit card debt	More stressed, tired at the end of the day Less time together during the week Sharing the chores evenly will be harder Will feel pressure to do a good job
Seriously ill parent	
Supporting each other in a tough experience brings us closer Each feeling we are doing the right thing. Showing our kids the importance of family in a real way Focusing us on what is really important, not just the day-to-day stuff Feel giving back for all parents did for us	Stress, worry No time for ourselves Commitments for caring reduce couple time Might be unclear how long the illness might be a problem Should parent live with us? For how long? How would we cope with that?

FIGURE 10.1. Likely relationship effects of common life changes.

Planning for Change: Example		
Change: Naomi is starting a new full-time job next month.		
1. Direct effects of change	2. Possible effects on our relationship	3. Our plan to deal with relationship effects
1. Naomi will have less time to attend to cleaning and cooking. 2. We'll have more money. 3. Naomi will probably be more tired than now; she may need time to adjust to the demands of her new job. 4. We will both be busier.	1. Naomi cannot easily keep doing all her current chores. If she did she might feel resentful. John will find it hard doing more of the chores. 2. We'll be able to save or spend money differently. 3. Naomi might feel the need for support from John. 4. Having less time to talk may stress us.	1. We need to develop new routines for getting chores done. We need to agree on who does what. We need to talk this one through. 2. We could spend our money in lots of ways (e.g., save for a mortgage, get a cleaner to help with chores). We need to agree on priorities and on a budget. We may need to organize for cleaners to come in each week. 3. John will take care to have regular couple time to talk to Naomi. 4. Both of us need to remember that this is a time of change and may be stressful at first. We need to have a regular date to have fun.

Planning for Change		
Change: _____		
1. Direct effects of change	2. Possible effects on our relationship	3. Our plan to deal with relationship effects

FIGURE 10.2. Planning for life changes.

Figure 10.3 sets out possible life changes couples might experience. The educator can read these out, or give it as handout to couples. If it is given as handout, then the couple is asked to check off those changes that they think are likely to occur in the next 2 years, and in the next 10 years. The couple then selects a change likely to occur in the next 2 years, and completes the plan for change as set out in Figure 10.2.

Some couples need assistance in managing change together effectively. One example is Murray and Cherie.

EDUCATOR: What change have you two been discussing?

MURRAY: I am coming up to retirement, and Cherie stopped work a few years back, so we are planning for next year.

EDUCATOR: Retirement—that does sound exciting. Murray, what are you most looking forward to about retirement?

MURRAY: Travel, getting out to see the whole country—like we have always wanted to.

EDUCATOR: Wonderful, wonderful. And do you see any challenges in this change?

MURRAY: None at all. No stress, wondering where we want to go, when we want to go.

EDUCATOR: So it feels like it's all upside, with no possible challenges?

MURRAY: None that I can think of.

EDUCATOR: Cherie?

CHERIE: Well I do want to see the country, but, Murray, I am not sure about leaving my mother for long periods. She manages on her own, but she really is slowing down. I worry that if I am not around for a long time, you know like 6 months or more, that maybe she would not be managing. Remember how fast your dad went downhill in the year before he died?

MURRAY: Yeah, but this is our time now. I mean, I know your mother depends on you a lot but if we don't go next year . . . who knows how long we'll have our health and can do this?

CHERIE: I know, love, I want to do travel with you, it's been our dream for ages.

EDUCATOR: So the challenge for you two seems to be, how do we realize our longtime dream of traveling around the country, but still provide the contact and support for Cherie's mother? Is that the issue? (*Murray and Cherie nod.*) OK, well how about you two write down on the form some of the effects of going on the road, and then talk through some options for managing that. All right?

Change	Within 2 years?	Within 10 years?
One partner changing to a different job		
More responsibility at work		
Changing home within same city/area		
Changing home to a new city/area		
A partner finishing a course or other training		
A partner starting a course or other training		
Birth of a child		
A relative needing special care		
Major purchase (e.g., home or business)		
A partner staying home from paid work		
A major change in social activities		
A major change in sporting activities		
A major change in artistic activities		
Retirement		
Other:		
Other:		

FIGURE 10.3. Identifying and managing likely changes in our life together.

The above discussion illustrates how a brief coaching intervention, in this case prompting Murray to consider challenges in his forthcoming retirement by asking Cherie her views, can lead to further exploration of options. In reviewing this process with Murray and Cherie, Murray commented that he had avoided talking about care for Cherie's mother because he was concerned that considering this issue might prevent the couple from traveling. After the couples discussed this issue further the educator returned and the couple had decided to do some shorter trips, and to ask Cherie's sister to visit her mother more often when Cherie and Murray were away.

In reviewing management of change it is important to recognize that flexibility is often needed. Cherie's mother might have an unexpected deterioration in her health, which might necessitate changing planned activities. Couples anticipating the birth of a child often find their plans have to be modified. For example, Margaret and Blake had a 6-month-old son, Sam. Margaret also had a 19-year-old daughter, Robyn, from a prior relationship. The couple was discussing adjusting to parenting a baby together.

EDUCATOR: What's the issue you two are discussing?

MARGARET: How hard it is to be parents in your late 30s. I was just 18 when I had Robyn. And I pretty much popped her out. Two-hour labor, no drugs, all was sweet. I was studying at the time. I gave birth the day after finishing one examination, and three days after the birth I did another exam. When I was expecting Sam I figured it would be much the same, I planned to take a week or two maternity leave and then back to work. I love my work. But I had a 30-hour labor, and in the end finished needing a caesarian.

BLAKE: Poor Marg was wiped out, she got a postoperative infection, and finished in hospital. Her scar was not healing well and she had a visit to hospital to get that fixed. Sam still doesn't sleep through the night.

EDUCATOR: It sounds like a much tougher journey than you anticipated.

BLAKE: Oh yeah. So we're wondering how to get back in control.

EDUCATOR: What options have you come up with so far?

MARGARET: Well, Blake reckons we should ask the hospital if they ever take babies back. (*Laughs.*) Look we would never give little Sammy back, but some days it feels like we're drowning.

EDUCATOR: Having a young baby can be truly exhausting. I remember when my kids were really young, and our son had been sick. My wife and I had got no sleep for a couple of nights. I stumbled into

the bathroom in the middle of the night and my wife was shower-
ing with a tracksuit on. The poor woman was so tired she had no
idea what she was doing. About that time we asked her mom to
help us out for a few weeks. I am wondering what you guys have
thought about?

Margaret and Blake were initially somewhat stuck with generating other
options. But they recognized that they were not coping, and something
needed to change. Margaret was working half-time, and was reluctant to cut
back work any further. Eventually they resolved that Blake would ask his
employer to let him take some half-time leave, so he could give Margaret
more time off from parenting. The best option for any couple varies according to their circumstances, but those that plan ahead tend to manage stressful life changes more effectively than those couples that do not plan. At the
same time it is important for the educator to draw out the need for couples to
modify their plans when the unexpected comes along.

PREVENTING COUPLE RELATIONSHIP PROBLEMS

Sometimes couple relationships go wrong. The focus in Couple CARE is
working with currently satisfied couples to help them sustain high relationship satisfaction. However, problems might develop in the future. It is important to assist the partners to think about early warning signs that a relationship is developing problems, and to do things early to prevent problems.

There are a couple of issues related to discussing potential future problems. First, many couples have unrealistically optimistic views of their future
relationship satisfaction, particularly in the early stages of a relationship. Fowers and colleagues (1996) found that over 90% of recently married couples
report that there is zero or close to zero probability that they will ever separate
from their spouse. Yet we know that upward of half of all marrying couples
do divorce. The rates of breakup are even higher in cohabiting couples.

Clearly many couples have unrealistic illusions that there are guaranteed
positive relationship outcomes. Often this romantic unreality is conveyed by
comments like "She is my soulmate, we will always love each other" and
"From the moment we met, I knew he was the one." Couples with such positive illusions are sometimes resistant to considering the possibility that their
relationship might encounter difficulties in the future. Due to this potential
resistance to considering future relationship problems, the topic of how to
manage emerging problems is not explicitly dealt with in Couple CARE until
toward the end of the program. This is intended to allow the major focus

of the program to be on relationship enrichment, and leave addressing the potentially sensitive issue of preventing couple problems to when hopefully the relationship between the educator and each couple is strong.

There are a few points worth making about the nature of couple relationship problems and the risk of separation. The educator can summarize these briefly saying something like the following:

"About 40% of married couples and about 60% of cohabiting couples separate. Being here, attending this course, is a really important step you have taken to strengthen your relationship, which reduces your risk of developing relationship problems. Another thing you can do is understand what leads to separations, how you can detect early warning signs of a deteriorating relationship, and what to do about it.

"About half of all divorces result from serious relationship problems. Violence, severe chronic arguments that get nasty, mental health problems like depression or alcohol abuse, affairs. In Couple CARE we emphasize the idea of self-change, of each person taking responsibility for strengthening the relationship. But there are some behaviors that a partner might do that are unacceptable to you, but which you have little influence over. For example, when men are severely violent toward their female partner it seems to have little or nothing to do with her behavior [Babcock, Costa, Eckhardt, & Green, 2004]. Rather, those men often have persistent long-established patterns of violence toward others [Holtzworth-Munroe et al., 2003]. A woman who finds herself the victim of such violence might have little she can do within the relationship to alter the man's behavior. Similarly, if your partner has a drinking or gambling problem, that could wreck things for both of you. What if you have tried to get someone to change a real problem like that, and they refuse? Well, in my view, that is what divorce is for. Getting out of a bad relationship is a good idea.

"However, half of divorces happen in couples that do not have high conflict, or obvious severe problems. It seems more like the relationship has lost its spark. When asked about why they divorced, these people say things like "We just sort of grew apart. We stopped communicating. The magic had faded." Now wanting a good relationship seems pretty reasonable. But divorcing someone because the relationship is a little jaded is a bit like finding your car is low on gasoline and abandoning it at the side of the road. The car needs fuel, not to be abandoned.

"I would like you to think about a relationship that is running low on fuel. It has no major problems, but just lacks spark. What do you think might be some early warning signs of a relationship losing its energy?"

The educator can ask couples to discuss this issue with their partners. You could suggest they try to think about their friends and relatives, and identify a couple whom they think might be struggling a little. Ask them to write down some behaviors they notice in that couple that might be warning signs of impending problems. Asking the couples to report to the group on their thoughts on early warning signs can help to clarify and sharpen the idea of early warning signs. Some commonly identified early warning signs that are worth mentioning if the group does not identify them are (1) not going out on a date as a couple for a long time; (2) noticing that you have not had a long talk to each other for a while; (3) finding you are irritable with each other when talking about a difficult issue on more than one occasion; (4) finding you tend to do the same things over and over, and that the fun is not really there; (5) the frequency of expressing love or caring has dropped away; (6) you have an argument and bad feelings persist; or (7) your interest in or enjoyment of sex has declined. (This list of warning signs might look familiar to the couples, as it summarizes failing to do some of the key things promoted in Couple CARE.)

There are three issues that are useful to highlight after discussing early warning signs of a deteriorating relationship. First, problems often develop over a period of time. Second, addressing problems is most effective when it is done early in the development of the problem. Paying attention to the relationship and working to keep it strong is a vital investment in having a good life together. Third, talk with your partner about any issues that worry you and try to find things you personally can change to make things better. If the relationship does not improve from your own efforts, go for help and go early. Couple therapy is very effective when couples go with smaller problems that have recently developed. A couple tune-up is a very good investment. Couple therapy when there are long-standing and severe problems is worth a try, but it is less effective than going early.

It is important to conclude the review of prevention of relationship problems on a positive note. I often make the transition to a final review of the Couple CARE experience along the following lines:

"We have focused on potential problems because we know problems can occur. If problems develop and you cannot resolve them yourself, then seeking help early gives you a good shot to turn things around. By being attentive to your relationship, using the skills you have learned through Couple CARE, you can reduce the chance that such problems will occur. So let's turn to maintaining a relationship focus and continuing to apply what we have covered in Couple CARE."

MAINTAINING A RELATIONSHIP FOCUS

Couples who sustain relationship satisfaction across a lifetime maintain a focus on their relationship that is central to their lives. Attention to the relationship can decline at times of stress or just with the busyness of life. In this section we try to help couples sustain their relationship focus with three exercises.

Reviewing the Relationship Vision

The first exercise involves reviewing the relationship vision the couple developed in Unit 1. By completing the other units in Couple CARE most couples have developed some new ideas about what can strengthen their relationship. For example, in the case of Bob and Daina described earlier in the chapter, a couple married for 32 years learned more about each other's sexual preferences and ideas. It is helpful to have each partner read what he or she wrote about the vision in the first session, and to identify any changes or additions he or she might want to make to the vision. Then the couple discusses together a revised joint relationship vision. Have each couple report back to the group the changes they identified for their relationship vision. I then ask each couple to discuss an idea they heard from another couple that they liked, and to describe to their partner what appeals to them about that idea.

It is useful to have the couples review their revised relationship vision. Useful questions include, "How would you summarize the most important aspects of your revised relationship vision?" and "What will you do to help you realize this vision?"

Celebrating the Couple Relationship

Most couples develop rituals in which they celebrate their relationship together. Some couples have regular rituals such as a cup of tea together on a morning on the weekend, or a drink together early in the evening. There also might be less frequent rituals like a romantic dinner for their wedding anniversary or a celebration of each other's birthdays.

The idea of relationship rituals can be introduced by describing the idea in similar terms to those in the preceding paragraph.[1] A useful exercise is to have each couple discuss together when, where, and how they currently celebrate their relationship. In a group context couples can report to the larger

---

[1] Alternatively, the different rituals that couples develop, and how those rituals strengthen relationships, are illustrated in a section of Unit 6 of the Couple CARE DVD.

group on important relationship celebration rituals they have developed. Couples are then asked to identify two possible new rituals they would like to introduce to celebrate their relationship together. Figure 10.4 lists some ideas for relationship celebrations that can assist couples who are looking for inspiration.

Maintaining Use of Relationship Skills

After each unit of Couple CARE partners are asked to reflect on what ideas they most liked from that unit, and to identify how they might apply the ideas they liked. The current exercise is an attempt to draw together the learning from across the program, and to help partners to identify what relationship skills they believe are most important for them to sustain. I ask each partner to reflect on the skills that have been covered across the six units in the program. Figure 10.5 lists the key relationship skills covered in the Couple CARE program. I ask each person to rate the extent to which he or she feels

---

- Assembling and looking through together photographs of important relationship events, such as holidays, birthdays, anniversaries, and family gatherings.
- A weekend away for just the two of you.
- A weekend at home together when you don't see anyone else, and you do fun things together that you would not usually do.
- A date during which you tell each other about the importance of your relationship together.
- Cooking a special meal for your partner and telling him or her how special he or she is.
- Having a glass of wine or cup of coffee together and catching up on the day's happenings.
- Planning fun time together, such as a holiday or special outing.
- Working on a fun project together.
- Planning a special meal to celebrate a birthday or anniversary.
- Getting out the diary and booking a special couple activity.
- Getting together with extended family to celebrate your relationship.
- Sending a card to your partner telling him or her how you feel about him or her.
- Doing a community service activity together.

FIGURE 10.4. Couple relationship celebration rituals.

Skills	Do I know?	Important?	My pick(s)
Self-change			
Develop and discuss relationship vision			
Use five-step self-change plan			
Communication			
Describe specifics			
Express positives			
Assert negatives			
Self-disclose feelings			
Attend			
Encourage			
Summarize content			
Paraphrase feelings			
Ask questions			
Hear your partner out			
Caring and intimacy			
Emotion-focused support			
Help partner express feelings			
Encourage, reassure, give affection			
Problem-focused support			
Help define the problem			
Suggest specific plan of action			
Offer partner specific assistance			
Ask what sort of support is needed			

(cont.)

FIGURE 10.5. Key couple care relationship skills.

Skills	Do I know?	Important?	My pick(s)
Caring and fun activities			
Show day-to-day acts of caring			
Keep novelty and variety in caring behaviors			
Maintaining good balance of individual and couple activities			
Managing differences			
Don't try to solve the problem too quickly			
Use the floor technique			
Hear your partner out			
When listening, give feedback			
When speaking, ask for feedback			
Attend and encourage			
Describe problems specifically			
Make specific positive requests for change			
Use conflict management guidelines			
Hold relationship meetings			
Sex			
Express preferences			
Balance responsibility for initiating			
Looking ahead			
Plan for change			
Celebrate the relationship			
Monitor for early warning signs, discuss any issues			
Respond to early warning signs of problems			

FIGURE 10.5. *(cont.)*

he or she understands and could demonstrate that skill if asked. The leader can review any skill with individuals that they feel they do not understand.

The educator should then ask each participant to identify three skills from Couple CARE that he or she wants to keep doing. Some couples find it useful to specify a date and plan to review with their partner how they are maintaining key skills. Most couples seem to prefer less structure, but still find the checklist useful to prompt their memory of what to include in their maintenance planning.

I ask each person to report to the group on the most important thing he or she has learned from attending the sessions, and at least one thing he or she wants to continue to do to enhance his or her relationship with his or her partner. A core message for people is that the Couple CARE learning is just one more step in their relationship together. What matters is that the partners each take responsibility for nurturing and sustaining their relationship. For example, if the couple has a disagreement, this can cue one or both partners to review how they manage differences, and to develop a self-change plan to help them manage conflict more effectively. Similarly, if either partner is feeling the need to express more caring, or be more supportive of their partner, then they can develop a self-change plan to address that identified relationship need.

I usually conclude the final session with couples by asking two questions. First, I ask, "Are there any other questions or comments either of you have about what we have covered across the whole program?" Then I ask each partner what he or she will do in the next week to enhance the relationship. Finally, I suggest that the handouts provided are a useful resource for the couple, particularly the checklist summarizing the skills covered in the program. I encourage the partners to refer back to this list from time to time to generate ideas on how they can continue to enhance their relationship.

SOME FINAL COMMENTS

The couple completes their final session. Hopefully at this point each partner has a broad understanding of the diverse influences on their relationship, and a shared vision of the sort of relationship they want together. This knowledge, combined with the capacity to work effectively on their relationship with self-change, empowers each partner to nurture his or her relationship. When a couple completes relationship education I do not know the long-term fate of their relationship. I know that relationship education is only one influence on their relationship future. The couple may face severe future stresses that undermine their relationship. If that is the case, then I hope our program better prepares them to recognize early the warning signs of problems, and that they take steps to improve the relationship. Couples often find that the effort each extends to succor their relationship, and their collective ability to support each other, enriches their individual and shared fates.

I have savored and been enriched by a loving partnership with my wife Barbara for over 30 years. I have seen the support and joy partners feel when their relationship goes well. I also have seen and felt the suffering of clients and friends when relationships come to painful ends. When my time with a couple comes to an end, I always hope that this couple will experience the joy of truly loving, and being loved by, their spouse. The work you do as a couple relationship educator is an important contribution toward helping more couples achieve lasting, loving relationships. I hope the ideas in this book will assist you in this important work.

References

Afifi, J. D., & Schrodt, P. (2003). Uncertainty and the avoidance of the state of one's family in stepfamilies, post-divorce single parent families, and first marriage families. *Human Communication Research, 29*, 516–532.

Ainsworth, M. D. S., Blehar, M. C., Waters, E., & Wall, S. (1978). *Patterns of attachment: A psychological study of the Strange Situation.* Hillsdale, NJ: Erlbaum.

Amato, P. R. (2000). Consequences of divorce for adults and children. *Journal of Marriage and Family, 58*, 356–365.

Amato, P. R. (2001). Children of divorce in the 1990s: An update of the Amato and Keith (1991) meta-analysis. *Journal of Family Psychology, 15*, 355–370.

Amato, P. R., & Booth, A. (2001). The legacy of parents' marital discord: Consequences for children's marital quality. *Journal of Personality and Social Psychology, 81*, 627–638.

Amato, P. R., & Cheadle, J. (2005). The long reach of divorce: Divorce and child well-being across three generations. *Journal of Marriage and Family, 67*, 191–206.

Amato, P. R., & Rogers, S. J. (1997). A longitudinal study of marital problems and subsequent divorce. *Journal of Marriage and Family, 59*, 612–624.

Arellano, C., & Markman, H. (1995). The Managing Affect and Differences Scale (MADS): A self-report measure assessing conflict management in couples. *Journal of Family Psychology, 9*, 319–334.

Aseltine, R. H., & Kessler, R. C. (1993). Marital disruption and depression in a community sample. *Journal of Health and Social Behavior, 34*, 237–251.

Australian Bureau of Statistics. (2008). *Australian social trends 2007.* Canberra: Australian Government.

Australian House of Representatives Standing Committee on Legal and Constitutional Affairs. (1998). *To have and to hold: Strategies to strengthen marriage and relationships.* Canberra: Attorney General's Department of Australia.

Australian Institute of Family Studies. (1997, April 3). *The Courier Mail,* p. 4.

Australian National Marriage Coalition. (2004). *Why marriage matters.* Wollongong: Author.

Avery, A. W., Ridley, C. A., Leslie, L. A., & Milholland, T. (1980). Relationship enhancement with premarital dyads: A six-month follow-up. *American Journal of Family Therapy, 8*, 23–30.

Babcock, J. C., Costa, D. M., Green, C. E., & Eckhardt, C. I. (2004). What situations induce intimate partner violence?: A reliability and validity study of the Proximal Antecedents to Violent Episodes (PAVE) scale. *Journal of Family Psychology, 18*, 433–442.

Bagarozzi, D. A., Bagarozzi, J. I., Anderson, S. A., & Pollane, L. (1984). Premarital education and training sequence (PETS): A 3-year follow-up of an experimental study. *Journal of Counseling and Development, 63*, 91–100.

Bagarozzi, D. A., & Rauen, P. I. (1981). Premarital counseling: Appraisal and status. *American Journal of Family Therapy, 9*, 13–27.

Bandura, A. (2001). Social cognitive theory: An agentic perspective. *Annual Review of Psychology, 52*, 1–26.

Baucom, D. H., Epstein, N., Rankin, L. A., & Burnett, C. K. (1996). Assessing relationship standards: The inventory of specific relationship standards. *Journal of Family Psychology, 10*, 72–88.

Baucom, D. H., Hahlweg, K., Atkins, D. C., Engl, J., & Thurmaier, F. (2006). Long-term prediction of marital quality following a relationship education program: Being positive in a constructive way. *Journal of Family Psychology, 20*, 448–455.

Baumeister, R. F., & Bratslavsky, E. (1999). Passion, intimacy, and time: Passionate love as a function of change in intimacy. *Personality and Social Psychology Review, 3*, 46–67.

Belsky, J., & Rovine, M. (1990). Patterns of marital change across the transition to parenthood: Pregnancy to three years postpartum. *Journal of Marriage and Family, 52*, 5–19.

Benson, M. J., Larson, J., Wilson, S. M., & Demo, D. H. (1993). Family of origin influences on late adolescent romantic relationships. *Journal of Marriage and Family, 55*, 663–672.

Birch, P., Weed, S., & Olsen, J. (2004). Assessing the impact of community marriage policies on county divorce rates. *Family Relations, 53*, 495–503.

Birchwood, M. (1998). New directions in the psychosocial approach to the psychoses. *Journal of Mental Health, 7*, 111–114.

Birtchnell, J., & Kennard, J. (1984). Early and current factors associated with poor-quality marriage. *Social Psychiatry, 19*, 31–40.

Black, L. E., & Sprenkle, D. H. (1991). Gender differences in college students' attitudes toward divorce and their willingness to marry. *Journal of Divorce and Remarriage, 14*, 47–60.

Block, J., Block, J. H., & Keyes, S. (1988). Longitudinally foretelling drug usage in adolescence: Early childhood personality and environmental precursors. *Child Development, 59*, 336–355.

Bloom, B. L., & Caldwell, R. A. (1981). Sex differences in adjustment during the process of marital separation. *Journal of Marriage and Family, 43*, 693–701.

Bodenmann, G. (2005). Dyadic coping and its significance for marital functioning. In T. A. Revenson, K. Kayser, & G. Bodenmann (Eds.), *Couples coping with stress:*

Emerging perspectives on dyadic coping (pp. 33–49). Washington, DC: American Psychological Association.

Bodenmann, G., & Cina, A. (2006). Stress and coping among stable-satisfied, stable-distressed, and separated/divorced Swiss couples: A 5-year prospective longitudinal study. *Journal of Divorce and Remarriage, 44,* 71–89.

Bodenmann, G., Pihet, S., Shantinath, S. D., Cina, A., & Widmer, K. (2006). Improving dyadic coping in couples with a stress-oriented approach: A 2-year longitudinal study. *Behavior Modification, 30,* 571–597.

Bodenmann, G., & Shantinath, S. D. (2004). The Couples Coping Enhancement Training (CCET): A new approach to prevention of marital distress based upon stress and coping. *Family Relations, 53,* 477–484.

Booth, A., & Johnson, D. (1988). Premarital cohabitation and marital success. *Journal of Family Issues, 9,* 255–272.

Bouma, R., Halford, W. K., & Young, R. (2004). Evaluation of the Controlling Alcohol and Relationship Enhancement (CARE) program with hazardous drinkers. *Behaviour Change, 21,* 229–250.

Bowlby, J. (1973). *Attachment and loss: Vol. 2. Separation: Anxiety and anger.* New York: Basic Books.

Bradbury, T. N. (Ed.). (1998). *The developmental course of marital dysfunction.* New York Cambridge University Press.

Bradbury, T. N., Cohan, C. L., & Karney, B. R. (1998). Optimizing longitudinal research for understanding and preventing marital dysfunction. In T. N. Bradbury (Ed.), *The developmental course of marital dysfunction* (pp. 279–311). New York: Cambridge University Press.

Bradbury, T. N., & Karney, B. R. (2004). Understanding and altering the longitudinal course of marriage. *Journal of Marriage and Family, 66,* 862–879.

Bradford, W. W., Doherty, W. J., Fisher, H., Galston, W. A., Glenn, N. D., Gottman, J., et al. (2005). *Why marriage matters: Twenty-six conclusions from the social sciences* (2nd ed.). New York: Institute for American Values.

Braukhaus, C., Hahlweg, K., Kroeger, C., Groth, T., & Fehm-Wolfsdorf, G. (2003). The effects of adding booster sessions to a prevention training program for committed couples. *Behavioural and Cognitive Psychotherapy, 31,* 325–336.

Burgess, A. W., Hartman, C. R., & McCormack, A. (1987). Abused to abuser: Antecedents of socially deviant behaviors. *American Journal of Psychiatry, 144,* 1431–1436.

Busby, D. M., Holman, T. B., & Taniguchi, N. (2001). RELATE: Relationship evaluation of the individual, family, cultural and couple contexts. *Family Relations, 50,* 308–317.

Busby, D. M., Ivey, D. C., Harris, S. M., & Ates, C. (2007). Self-directed, therapist-directed, and assessment-based interventions for premarital couples. *Family Relations, 56,* 279–290.

Buss, D. (2003). *The evolution of desire: Strategies of human mating* (2nd ed.). New York: Basic Books.

Call, V. R. A., & Heaton, T. B. (1997). Religious influence on marital stability. *Journal for the Scientific Study on Religion, 36,* 382–392.

Carmichael, E. (2001). *Report on the student mentoring program at University of Western Sydney, 2000 (internal report)*. Sydney, Australia: University of Western Sydney, Hawkesbury Campus.

Carrere, S., Buehlman, K. T., Gottman, J. M., Coan, J. A., & Ruckstuhl, L. (2000). Predicting marital stability and divorce in newlywed couples. *Journal of Family Psychology, 14*, 42–58.

Carroll, J. S., & Doherty, W. J. (2003). Evaluating the effectiveness of premarital prevention programs: A meta-analytic review of outcome research. *Family Relations, 52*, 105–118.

Caughlin, J. P., & Huston, T. L. (2002). A contextual analysis of the association between demand/withdraw and marital satisfaction. *Personal Relationships, 9*, 95–119.

Chinese National Bureau of Statistics. (2003). *National registry of marriages and divorces, 96–97*. Beijing: Chinese Government.

Christensen, A., Doss, B. D., & Atkins, D. C. (2005). A science of couple therapy: For what should we seek empirical support? In W. M. Pinsoff & J. L. Lebow (Eds.), *Family psychology: The art of the science* (pp. 43–63). Oxford, UK: Oxford University Press.

Christensen, A., & Heavey, C. L. (1990). Gender and social structure in the demand/withdraw pattern of marital conflict. *Journal of Personality and Social Psychology, 59*, 73–81.

Christensen, A., & Heavey, C. L. (1993). Gender differences in marital conflict. The demand/withdraw interaction pattern. In S. Oskamp & M. Constanzo (Eds.), *Gender issues in contemporary society* (pp. 113–141). Newbury Park, CA: Sage.

Christensen, A., & Jacobson, N. S. (1994). Who (or what) can do psychotherapy: The status and challenge of nonprofessional therapies. *Psychological Science, 5*, 8–14.

Christensen, A., & Shenk, J. L. (1991). Communication, conflict and psychological distance in nondistressed, clinic, and divorcing couples. *Journal of Consulting and Clinical Psychology, 59*, 458–463.

Clarksberg, M., Stolzenberg, R. M., & Wake, L. J. (1995). Attitudes, values and entrance into cohabitation versus marital unions. *Social Forces, 74*, 609–634.

Clements, M. L., Cordova, A. D., Markman, H. J., & Laurenceau, J. (1997). The erosion of marital satisfaction over time and how to prevent it. In R. J. Sternberg & M. Hojjat (Eds.), *Satisfaction in close relationships* (pp. 318–332). New York: Guilford Press.

Clements, M. L., Stanley, S. M., & Markman, H. J. (2004). Before they said "I do": Discriminating among marital outcomes over 13 years based on premarital data. *Journal of Marriage and Family, 66*, 613–626.

Cohen, J. (1992). A power primer. *Psychological Bulletin, 112*, 155–159.

Coie, J. D., Watt, N. F., West, S. G., Hawkins, J. D., Asarnow, J. R., Markman, H. J., et al. (1993). The science of prevention: A conceptual framework and some directions for a national research program. *American Psychologist, 48*, 1013–1022.

Collins, N. L., & Read, S. J. (1990). Adult attachment, working models, and relationship quality in dating couples. *Journal of Personality and Social Psychology, 58*, 644–663.

Collins, N. L., & Read, S. J. (1994). Cognitive representations of attachment: The structure and function of working models. In K. Bartholomew & D. Perlman (Eds.), *Advances in personal relationships: Vol. 5. Attachment processes in adulthood* (pp. 53–90). London: Jessica Kingsley.

Conger, R., Cui, M., Bryant, C. M., & Elder, G. H. (2000). Competence in early adult romantic relationships: A developmental perspective on family influences. *Journal of Personality and Social Psychology, 79*, 224–237.

Coontz, S. (2005). *Marriage, a history: From obedience to intimacy, or how love conquered marriage.* New York: Viking.

Cordova, J. V., Scott, R. L., Dorian, M., Mirgain, S., Yaeger, D., & Groot, A. (2005). The marriage checkup: An indicated preventive intervention for treatment-avoidant couples at risk for marital deterioration. *Behavior Therapy, 36*, 301–309.

Cordova, J. V., Warren, L. Z., & Gee, C. B. (2001). Motivational interviewing as an intervention for at-risk couples. *Journal of Marital and Family Therapy, 27*, 315–326.

Costa, P. T., & McCrae, R. R. (1980). Influence of extraversion and neuroticism on subjective well-being: Happy and unhappy people. *Journal of Personality and Social Psychology, 38*, 668–678.

Cowan, C. P., & Cowan, P. A. (1992). *When partners become parents: The big life change for couples.* New York: Basic Books.

Cowan, C. P., & Cowan, P. A. (1995). Interventions to ease the transition to parenthood: Why they are needed and what they can do. *Family Relations, 44*, 412–423.

Cowan, C. P., & Cowan, P. A. (1999). *When partners become parents: The big life change for couples.* Mahwah, NJ: Erlbaum.

Coyne, J. C., & Smith, D. A. (1991). Couple coping with myocardial infarction: A contextual perspective on wives' distress. *Journal of Personality and Social Psychology, 61*, 404–412.

Coyne, J. C., & Smith, D. A. (1994). Couples coping with a myocardial infarction: Contextual perspective on patient self-efficacy. *Journal of Family Psychology, 8*, 43–54.

Daniel, K. (1995). The marriage premium. In M. Tomassi & K. Ierulli (Eds.), *The new economics of human behavior* (pp. 113–124). Cambridge, UK: Cambridge University Press.

Davila, J., & Bradbury, T. N. (2001). Attachment insecurity and the distinction between unhappy spouses who do and do not divorce. *Journal of Family Psychology, 15*, 371–393.

Davila, J., Burge, D., & Hammen, C. (1997). Why does attachment style change? *Journal of Personality and Social Psychology, 73*, 826–838.

Davila, J., Karney, B., & Bradbury, T. N. (1999). Attachment change processes in the early years of marriage. *Journal of Personality and Social Psychology, 76*, 783–802.

Davila, J., Karney, B., Hall, T. W., & Bradbury, T. N. (2003). Depressive symptoms and marital satisfaction: Within-subject associations and the moderating effects of gender and neuroticism. *Journal of Family Psychology, 17*, 557–570.

de Graaf, A. (1991). De invloed van echtscheiding van de ouders op demografisch gedrag van de vrouw [The impact of divorced parents on women's demographic behavior]. *Maandststistiek van de Bevolking, 39*, 30–38.

de Graaf, P. M., & Kalmijn, M. (2006). Divorce motives in a period of rising divorce: Evidence from a Dutch life-history survey. *Journal of Family Issues, 27*, 483–505.

De Maria, R. M. (2005). Distressed couples and marriage education. *Family Relations, 54*, 242–253.

DeMaris, A., & Rao, V. (1992). Premarital cohabitation and subsequent marital stability in the United States: A reassessment. *Journal of Marriage and Family, 54*, 178–190.

de Vaus, D., Qu, L., & Weston, R. (2003a). Changing patterns of partnering. *Family Matters, 64*, 10–15.

de Vaus, D., Qu, L., & Weston, R. (2003b). Premarital cohabitation and subsequent marital stability. *Family Matters, 65*, 34–39.

Diedrick, P. (1991). Gender differences in divorce adjustment. *Journal of Divorce and Remarriage, 14*, 33–46.

Diener, E., Suh, E. M., Lucas, R. E., & Smith, H. L. (1999). Subjective well-being: Three decades of progress. *Psychological Bulletin, 125*, 276–302.

Doss, B. D., Rhoades, G. K., Stanley, S. M., & Markman, H. J. (2009). The effect of the transition to parenthood on relationship quality: An 8-year prospective study. *Journal of Personality and Social Psychology, 96*, 601–619.

Dutton, D. G., Saunders, K., Starzomski, A., & Bartholomew, K. (1994). Intimacy-anger and insecure attachment as precursors of abuse in intimate relationships. *Journal of Applied Social Psychology, 24*, 1367–1386.

Dyer, C., & Halford, W. K. (1998). Prevention of relationship problems: Retrospect and prospect. *Behaviour Change, 15*, 107–125.

Edin, K., & Kefalas, M. J. (2005). *Promises I can keep: Why poor women put motherhood before marriage*. Berkeley and Los Angeles: University of California Press.

Eidelson, R. J., & Epstein, N. (1982). Cognition and relationship maladjustment: Development of a measure of dysfunctional relationship beliefs. *Journal of Consulting and Clinical Psychology, 50*, 715–720.

Emmelkamp, P. M. G. (2005). Technological innovations in clinical assessment and psychotherapy. *Psychotherapy and Psychosomatics, 74*, 336–343.

Emmelkamp, P. M. G., De Haan, E., & Hoogduin, C. A. I. (1990). Marital adjustment and obsessive–compulsive disorder. *British Journal of Psychiatry, 156*, 55–60.

Epstein, N., & Baucom, D. H. (2002). *Enhanced cognitive-behavioural therapy for couples: A contextual approach*. Washington, DC: American Psychological Association.

Feeney, J. A. (1994). Attachment style, communication patterns and satisfaction across the life cycle of marriage. *Personal Relationships, 1*, 333–348.

Feeney, J. A., Hohaus, L., Noller, P., & Alexander, R. P. (2001). *Becoming parents: Exploring the bonds between mothers, fathers, and their infants*. New York: Cambridge University Press.

Fincham, F. D., Bradbury, T. N., Arias, I., Byrne, C. A., & Karney, B. R. (1997).

Marital violence, marital distress, and attributions. *Journal of Family Psychology, 11*, 367–372.

Fincham, F. D., Harold, G. T., & Gano-Phillips, S. (2000). The longitudinal association between attributions and marital satisfaction: Direction of effects and role of efficacy expectations. *Journal of Family Psychology, 14*, 267–285.

Finkelhor, D. (1994). The international epidemiology of child sexual abuse. *Child Abuse and Neglect, 18*, 409–417.

Floyd, F. J., & Zmich, D. E. (1991). Marriage and the parenting partnership: Perceptions and interactions of parents with mentally retarded and typically developing children. *Child Development, 62*, 1438–1448.

Foltz-Gray, D. (2006, January). Be a better couple. *Health*, pp. 142–145.

Forthofer, M. S., Markman, H. J., Cox, M., Stanley, S., & Kessler, R. C. (1996). Associations between marital distress and work loss in a national sample. *Journal of Marriage and Family, 58*, 597–605.

Fowers, B. J., Lyons, E. M., & Montel, K. H. (1996). Positive marital illusions: Self-enhancement or relationship enhancement? *Journal of Family Psychology, 10*, 192–208.

Fowers, B. J., & Olson, D. H. (1986). Predicting marital success with PREPARE: A predictive validity study. *Journal of Marital and Family Therapy, 12*, 403–413.

Funder, K., Harrison, M., & Weston, R. (1993). *Settling down: Pathways of parents after divorce*. Melbourne: Australian Institute of Family Studies.

Gagnon, A. J., & Sandall, J. (2007). Individual or group antenatal education for childbirth or parenthood, or both. *Cochrane Database of Systematic Reviews*, Issue 3 (Article No. CD002869), DOI: 10.1002/14651858.CD002869.pub2.

Gagnon, M. D., Hersen, M., Kabacoff, R. I., & van Hasselt, V. B. (1999). Interpersonal and psychological correlates of marital dissatisfaction in late life: A review. *Clinical Psychology Review, 19*, 359–378.

Gibardi, L., & Rosen, L. A. (1991). Differences between college students from divorced and intact families. *Journal of Divorce and Remarriage, 15*, 175–191.

Giblin, P., Sprenkle, D. H., & Sheehan, R. (1985). Enrichment outcome research: A meta-analysis of premarital, marital, and family interventions. *Journal of Marital and Family Therapy, 11*, 257–271.

Glenn, N. D. (1998). The course of marital success and failure in five American 10-year marriage cohorts. *Journal of Marriage and Family, 60*, 569–576.

Glenn, N. D., & Kramer, K. B. (1987). The marriages and divorces of the children of divorce. *Journal of Marriage and Family, 49*, 811–825.

Glenn, N. D., & Shelton, B. A. (1983). Pre-adult background variables and divorce: A note of caution about over-reliance on explained variance. *Journal of Marriage and Family, 45*, 405–410.

Goldman, D. G., & Padayachi, U. K. (1997). The prevalence and nature of child sexual abuse in Queensland, Australia. *Child Abuse and Neglect, 21*, 489–498.

Gonzalez, L., & Viitanen, T. K. (2006). *The effect of divorce laws on divorce rates in Europe*. Bonn, Germany: Institute for the Study of Labour.

Gore, S. (1978). The effect of social support in moderating the health consequences of unemployment. *Journal of Health and Social Behavior, 19*, 157–165.

Gottman, J. M. (1993). A theory of marital dissolution and stability. *Journal of Family Psychology, 7,* 57–75.

Gottman, J. M. (1994). *What predicts divorce?: The relationship between marital processes and marital outcomes.* Hillsdale, NJ: Erlbaum.

Gottman, J. M., Coan, J. A., Carrere, S., & Swanson, C. (1998). Predicting marital happiness and stability from newlywed interactions. *Journal of Marriage and Family, 60,* 5–22.

Gottman, J. M., & Krokoff, L. J. (1989). Marital interaction and marital satisfaction: A longitudinal view. *Journal of Consulting and Clinical Psychology, 57,* 47–52.

Gottman, J. M., & Notarius, C. I. (2000). Decade review: Observing marital interaction. *Journal of Marriage and Family, 62,* 927–947.

Greenberg, L. S., & Goldman, R. N. (2008). *Emotion-focused couples therapy: The dynamics of emotion, love, and power.* Washington, DC: American Psychological Association.

Grover, K. J., Russell, C. S., Schumm, W. R., & Paff-Bergen, L. A. (1985). Mate selection processes and marital satisfaction. *Family Relations, 34,* 383–386.

Guerney, B. G. (1977). *Relationship enhancement.* San Francisco: Jossey-Bass.

Guerney, B. G. (1987). *Relationship enhancement manual.* Bethesda, MD: Ideal.

Guerney, B. G., & Maxson, P. (1990). Marital and family enrichment research: A decade review and look ahead. *Journal of Marriage and Family, 52,* 1127–1135.

Hahlweg, K., Baucom, D., Bastine, R., & Markman, H. J. (1998). *Prevention and early intervention: An international perspective on the prediction and prevention of marital and family problems.* Stuttgart, Germany: Kohlhammer.

Hahlweg, K., & Klan, N. (1997). The effectiveness of marital counseling in Germany: A contribution to health services research. *Journal of Family Psychology, 11,* 410–421.

Hahlweg, K., & Markman, H. J. (1988). Effectiveness of behavioral marital therapy: Empirical status of behavioral techniques in preventing and alleviating marital distress. *Journal of Consulting and Clinical Psychology, 56,* 440–447.

Hahlweg, K., Markman, H. J., Thurmaier, F., Engl, J., & Eckert, V. (1998). Prevention of marital distress: Results of a German prospective longitudinal study. *Journal of Family Psychology, 12,* 543–556.

Halford, W. K. (1995). Marriage and the prevention of psychiatric disorder. In B. Raphael & G. D. Burrows (Eds.), *Handbook of preventive psychiatry* (pp. 121–138). Amsterdam: Elsevier.

Halford, W. K. (2001). *Brief couple therapy: Helping partners to help themselves.* New York: Guilford Press.

Halford, W. K. (2004). The future of couple relationship education: Suggestions on how it can make a difference. *Family Relations, 53,* 559–566.

Halford, W. K., Bouma, R., Kelly, A., & Young, R. M. (1999). The interaction of individual psychopathology and marital problems: Current findings and clinical implications. *Behavior Modification, 23,* 179–216.

Halford, W. K., & Casey, L. (2010). Taking it to the people: Using technology to enhance the impact of couple relationship education. In K. Hahlweg, M. Grawe, & D. Baucom (Eds.), *Enhancing couples: the shape of couple therapy to come* (pp. 111–127). Gottingen, Germany: Hogrefe.

Halford, W. K., Gravestock, F. M., Lowe, R., & Scheldt, S. (1992). Toward a behavioral ecology of stressful marital interactions. *Behavioral Assessment, 14,* 199–217.

Halford, W. K., Hahlweg, K., & Dunne, M. (1990). The cross-cultural consistency of marital communication associated with marital distress. *Journal of Marriage and Family, 52,* 487–500.

Halford, W. K., Lizzio, A., Wilson, K. L., & Occhipinti, S. (2007). Does working at your relationship help?: Couple relationship self-regulation and satisfaction in the first 4 years of marriage. *Journal of Family Psychology, 21,* 185–194.

Halford, W. K., Markman, H. J., Kline, G. H., & Stanley, S. (2003). Best practice in relationship education. *Journal of Marital and Family Therapy, 29,* 385–406.

Halford, W. K., Markman, H. J., & Stanley, S. M. (2008). Strengthening couple relationships with education: Social policy and public health perspectives. *Journal of Family Psychology, 22,* 497–505.

Halford, W. K., & Moore, E. (2002). Relationship education and the prevention of couple relationship problems. In A. S. Gurman & N. Jacobson (Eds.), *Clinical handbook of couple therapy* (3rd ed., pp. 400–419). New York: Guilford Press.

Halford, W. K., Moore, E. M., Wilson, K. L., Dyer, C., & Farrugia, C. (2004). Benefits of a flexible delivery relationship education: An evaluation of the Couple CARE program. *Family Relations, 53,* 469–476.

Halford, W. K., Moore, E. M., Wilson, K. L., Dyer, C., & Farrugia, C. (2006a). *Couple commitment and relationship enhancement: A guidebook for life partners.* Brisbane: Australian Academic Press.

Halford, W. K., Moore, E. M., Wilson, K. L., Dyer, C., & Farrugia, C. (2006b). *Couple commitment and relationship enhancement: Professional leaders manual.* Brisbane: Australian Academic Press.

Halford, W. K., Moore, E. M., Wilson, K. L., Dyer, C., Farrugia, C., & Judge, K. (2006c). *Couple commitment and relationship enhancement* [DVD]. Brisbane: Australian Academic Press.

Halford, W. K., Nicholson, J. M., & Sanders, M. R. (2007). Couple communication in stepfamilies. *Family Process, 46,* 471–483.

Halford, W. K., O'Donnell, C., Lizzio, A., & Wilson, K. L. (2006). Brief report: Do couples at high-risk of relationship problems attend pre-marriage education? *Journal of Family Psychology, 20,* 160–163.

Halford, W. K., & Osgarty, S. M. (1993). Alcohol abuse in clients presenting with marital problems. *Journal of Family Psychology, 6,* 245–254.

Halford, W. K., Petch, J., & Creedy, J. (2010). Promoting a positive transition to parenthood: A randomized controlled trial of the couple care for parents program. *Prevention Science, 11,* 89–100.

Halford, W. K., Petch, J., Creedy, D. K., Gamble, J., Heyman, R. E., & Slep, A. (2008, November). *Dissemination of couple care for parents.* Paper presented at the Annual Convention Association for Behavioral and Cognitive Therapies, Orlando, FL.

Halford, W. K., Sanders, M. R., & Behrens, B. C. (1994). Self-regulation in behavioral couples' therapy. *Behavior Therapy, 25,* 431–452.

Halford, W. K., Sanders, M. R., & Behrens, B. C. (2000). Repeating the errors of our parents?: Family-of-origin spouse violence and observed conflict management in engaged couples. *Family Process, 39*, 219–236.

Halford, W. K., Sanders, M. R., & Behrens, B. C. (2001). Can skills training prevent relationship problems in at-risk couples?: Four-year effects of a behavioral relationship education program. *Journal of Family Psychology, 15*, 750–768.

Halford, W. K., Scott, J., & Smythe, J. (2000). Couples and coping with cancer: Helping each other through the night. In K. Schmaling & T. G. Sher (Eds.), *The psychology of couples and illness: Theory, research, and practice* (pp. 135–170). Washington, DC: American Psychological Association.

Halford, W. K., & Simons, M. (2005). Couple relationship education in Australia. *Family Process, 44*, 147–259.

Halford, W. K., & Wilson, K. L. (2009). Predictors of relationship satisfaction four years after completing flexible delivery couple relationship education. *Journal of Couple and Relationship Therapy, 8*, 143–161.

Halford, W. K., Wilson, K. L., Watson, B., Verner, T., Busby, D., Larson, J., et al. (2010). Effective couple relationship education at home: Does skill training enhance relationship assessment and feedback? *Journal of Family Psychology, 24*, 188–196.

Hall, D. R., & Zhao, J. Z. (1995). Cohabitation and divorce in Canada: Testing the selectivity hypothesis. *Journal of Marriage and Family, 57*, 421–427.

Harris, R., Simons, M., Willis, P., & Barrie, A. (1992). *Love, sex and water skiing: The experience of pre-marriage education in Australia*. Adelaide: Center for Human Resource Studies, University of South Australia.

Haskins, R., & Sawhill, I. (2003). *Work and marriage: The way to end poverty and welfare* (Policy Brief #28). Washington, DC: Brookings Institute.

Hawkins, A. J., Blanchard, V. L., Baldwin, S. A., & Fawcett, E. B. (2008). Does marriage and relationship education work?: A meta-analytic study. *Journal of Consulting and Clinical Psychology, 76*, 723–734.

Hawkins, A. J., Fawcett, E. B., Carroll, J. S., & Gilliland, T. T. (2006). The Marriage Moments Program for couples transitioning to parenthood: Divergent conclusions from formative and outcome evaluation data. *Journal of Family Psychology, 20*, 561–570.

Hazan, C., & Shaver, P. (1987). Romantic love conceptualized as an attachment process. *Journal of Personality and Social Psychology, 52*, 511–524.

Heaton, T. B., & Pratt, E. L. (1990). The effects of religious homogamy on marital satisfaction and stability. *Journal of Family Issues, 11*, 191–207.

Heavey, C. L., Christensen, A., & Malamuth, N. M. (1995).The longitudinal impact of demand and withdrawal during marital conflict. *Journal of Consulting and Clinical Psychology, 63*, 797–801.

Heavey, C. L., Layne, C., & Christensen, A. (1993). Gender and conflict structure in marital interaction: A replication and extension. *Journal of Consulting and Clinical Psychology, 61*, 16–27.

Hetherington, E. M., & Clingempeel, W. G. (1992). Coping with marital transitions: A family systems perspective. *Monographs of the Society for Research in Child Development*, 57(2–3, Serial No. 227).

Hetherington, E. M., & Stanley-Hagen, M. (2000). Diversity among stepfamilies. In D. H. Demo, K. R. Allen, & M. A. Fine (Eds.), *Handbook of family diversity* (pp. 173–196). New York: Oxford University Press.

Hewitt, B., & de Vaus, D. (2009). Change in the association between premarital cohabitation and separation, Australia 1945–2000. *Journal of Marriage and Family, 71*, 353–361.

Heyman, R. E. (2001). Observation of couple conflicts: Clinical assessment applications, stubborn truths, and shaky foundations. *Psychological Assessment, 13*, 5–35.

Heyman, R. E., & Schlee, K. (2003). Stopping wife abuse via physical aggression couples treatment. *Journal of Aggression, Maltreatment and Trauma, 7*, 135–157.

Higginbottom, S. F., Barling, J., & Kelloway, E. K. (1993). Linking retirement experiences and marital satisfaction: Testing a mediational model. *Psychology and Aging, 8*, 508–516.

Holman, T. B. (2001). *Premarital prediction of marital quality or break up: Research, theory and practice*. New York: Kluwer.

Holman, T. B., Busby, D. M., Doxey, C., Klein, D. M., & Loyer-Carlson, V. (1997). The relationship evaluation (RELATE). Provo, UT: RELATE Institute.

Holtzworth-Munroe, A., & Meehan, J. C. (2004). Typologies of men who are maritally violent: Scientific and clinical implications. *Journal of Interpersonal Violence, 19*, 1369–1389.

Holtzworth-Munroe, A., Meehan, J. C., Herron, K., Rehman, U., & Stuart, G. L. (2000). Testing the Holtzworth–Munroe and Stuart (1994) batterer typology. *Journal of Consulting and Clinical Psychology, 68*, 1000–1019.

Holtzworth-Munroe, A., Meehan, J. C., Herron, K., Rehman, U., & Stuart, G. L. (2003). Do subtypes of maritally violent men continue to differ over time? *Journal of Consulting and Clinical Psychology, 71*, 728–740.

Hu, Y., & Goldman, R. (1990). Mortality differentials by marital status: An international comparison. *Demography, 27*, 233–250.

Huang, W. J. (2005). An Asian perspective on relationship and marriage education. *Family Process, 44*, 161–173.

Hunt, R., Hof, L., & DeMaria, R. (1998). *Marriage enrichment: Preparation, mentoring, and outreach*. Philadelphia: Brunner/Mazel.

Huston, T. L., Caughlin, J. P., Houts, R. M., Smith, S. E., & George, L. J. (2001). The connubial crucible: Newlywed years as predictors of marital delight, distress and divorce. *Journal of Personality and Social Psychology, 80*, 237–252.

Huston, T. L., McHale, S., & Crouter, A. C. (1986). When the honeymoon's over: Changes in the marriage relationship over the first year. In R. L. Gilmour & S. W. Duck (Eds.), *The emerging field of personal relationships* (pp. 109–132). Hillsdale, NJ: Erlbaum.

Johnson, C. A., Stanley, S. M., Glenn, N. D., Amato, P. A., Nock, S. L., Markman, H. J., et al. (2002). *Marriage in Oklahoma: 2001 baseline statewide survey on marriage and divorce*. Stillwater: Bureau for Social Research, Oklahoma State University.

Johnson, D. R., & Booth, A. (1998). Marital quality: A product of the dyadic environment or individual factors? *Social Forces, 76*, 883–904.

Johnson, M. D., Cohan, C. L., Davila, J., Lawrence, E., Rogge, R., Karney, B., et al. (2005). Problem-solving skills and affective expression as predictors of change in marital satisfaction. *Journal of Consulting and Clinical Psychology, 73,* 15–27.

Johnson, M. P. (1995). Patriarchal terrorism and common couple violence: Two forms of violence against women. *Journal of Marriage and Family, 57,* 283–294.

Johnson, S. M., & Talitman, E. (1997). Predictors of success in emotionally focused marital therapy. *Journal of Marital and Family Therapy, 23,* 135–152.

Jones, A. C., & Chao, C. M. (1997). Racial, ethnic and cultural issues in couple therapy. In W. K. Halford & H. J. Markman (Eds.), *Clinical handbook of marriage and couple intervention* (pp. 157–178). Chichester, UK: Wiley.

Kaiser, A., Hahlweg, K., Fehm-Wolfsdorf, G., & Groth, T. (1998). The efficacy of a compact psychoeducational group training program for married couples. *Journal of Consulting and Clinical Psychology, 66,* 753–760.

Kalmijn, M., & Poortman, A. (2006). His or her divorce?: The gendered nature of divorce and its determinants. *European Sociological Review, 22,* 201–214.

Kaltenthaler, E., Parry, G., & Beverley, C. (2004). Computerized cognitive behaviour therapy: A systematic review. *Behavioural and Cognitive Psychotherapy, 32,* 31–55.

Karney, B. R., & Bradbury, T. N. (1995). The longitudinal course of marital quality and stability: A review of theory, methods, and research. *Psychological Bulletin, 118,* 3–34.

Karney, B. R., & Bradbury, T. N. (1997). Neuroticism, marital interaction, and the trajectory of marital satisfaction. *Journal of Personality and Social Psychology, 72,* 1075–1092.

Karney, B. R., Story, L. B., & Bradbury, T. N. (2005). Marriages in context: Interactions between chronic and acute stress among newlyweds. In T.A. Revenson, K. Kayser, & G. Bodenmann (Eds.), *Couples coping with stress: Emerging perspectives on dyadic coping* (pp. 13–32). Washington, DC: American Psychological Association.

Karoly, P. (1993). Mechanisms of self-regulation: A systems view. *Annual Review of Psychology, 44,* 23–53.

Kember, G., Jenkins, W., & Ng, K. C. (2003). Adult students' perceptions of good teaching as a function of their conceptions of learning—part 1: Influencing the development of self-determination. *Studies in Continuing Education, 25,* 239–251.

Kesner, J. E., & McKenry, P. C. (1998). The role of childhood attachment factors in predicting male violence toward female intimates. *Journal of Family Violence, 13,* 417–432.

Kiecolt-Glaser, J. K., Bane, C., Glaser, R., & Malarkey, W. B. (2003). Love, marriage, and divorce: Newlyweds' stress hormones foreshadow relationship changes. *Journal of Consulting and Clinical Psychology, 71,* 176–188.

Kieran, K. (2002). Cohabitation in Western Europe: Trends, issues, and implications. In A. Booth & A. Crouter (Eds.), *Just living together: Implications of cohabitation on families, children, and social policy* (pp. 308–326). Mahwah, NJ: Erlbaum.

Kincaid, S. B., & Caldwell, R. A. (1995). Marital separation: Causes, coping, and consequences. *Journal of Divorce and Remarriage, 22,* 109–128.

Knutson, L., & Olson, D. H. (2003). Effectiveness of PREPARE Program with premarital couples in a community setting. *Marriage and Family*, 6(4), 529–546.

Kobak, R. R., & Hazan, C. (1991). Attachment in marriage: Effects of security and accuracy of working models. *Journal of Personality and Social Psychology*, 60, 861–869.

Kolb, D. A. (1984). *Experiential learning: Experience as the source of learning and development*. Englewood Cliffs, NJ: Prentice-Hall.

Krokoff, L. J., Gottman, J. M., & Roy, A. K. (1988). Blue-collar and white-collar marital interaction and communication orientation. *Journal of Social and Personal Relationships*, 5, 201–221.

Kurdek, L. A. (1991a). Marital stability and changes in marital quality in newlywed couples: A test of the contextual model. *Journal of Social and Personal Relationships*, 8, 27–48.

Kurdek, L. A. (1991b). Predictors of increases in marital distress in newlywed couples: A 3-year prospective longitudinal study. *Developmental Psychology*, 27, 627–636.

Kurdek, L. A. (1993). Predicting marital dissolution: A 5-year prospective longitudinal study of newlywed couples. *Journal of Personality and Social Psychology*, 64, 221–242.

Kurdek, L. A. (1995). Assessing multiple determinants of relationship commitment in cohabiting gay, cohabiting lesbian, dating heterosexual, and married heterosexual couples. *Family Relations*, 44, 261–266.

Larsen, A. S., & Olson, D. H. (1989). Predicting marital satisfaction using PREPARE: A replication study. *Journal of Marital and Family Therapy*, 15, 311–322.

Larson, J. H., & Brimhall, A. S. (2005). Marital tune-ups. In S. M. Harris, D. C. Ivey, & R. A. Bean (Eds.), *A practice that works: Strategies to complement your stand alone therapy practice* (pp. 155–165). New York: Routledge.

Larson, J. H., & Halford, W. K (in press). Couple relationship education for the future: A customized stepped approach. *Journal of Couple and Relationship Therapy*.

Larson, J. H., & Holman, T. B. (1994). Premarital predictors of marital quality and stability. *Family Relations*, 43, 228–237.

Larson, J. H., Newell, K., Topham, G., & Nichols, S. (2002). A review of three comprehensive premarital assessment questionnaires. *Journal of Marital and Family Therapy*, 28, 233–239.

Larson, J. H., Vatter, R. S., Galbraith, R. C., Holman, T. B., & Stahmann, R. F. (2007). The RELATionship Evaluation (RELATE) with therapist-assisted interpretation: Short-term effects on premarital relationships. *Journal of Marital and Family Therapy*, 33, 364–374.

Laurenceau, J. P., Stanley, S. M., Olmos-Gallo, A., Baucom, B., & Markman, H. J. (2004). Community-based prevention of marital dysfunction: Multi-level modeling of a randomized effectiveness study. *Journal of Consulting and Clinical Psychology*, 72, 933–943.

Laurillard, D. (1992). Learning through collaborative computer simulations. *British Journal of Education Technology*, 23, 164–171.

Laurillard, D. (2002). *Rethinking university teaching: A conversational framework for the effective use of learning technologies*. London: Routledge.

Lawrence, E., & Bradbury, T. N. (2001). Physical aggression and marital dysfunction: A longitudinal analysis. *Journal of Family Psychology, 15*, 135–154.

Leonard, K. E., & Roberts, L. J. (1998). Marital aggression, quality, and stability in the first year of marriage. In T. N. Bradbury (Ed.), *The developmental course of marital dysfunction* (pp. 44–73). New York: Cambridge University Press.

Leonard, K. E., & Senchak, M. (1996). Prospective prediction of husband marital aggression within newlywed couples. *Journal of Abnormal Psychology, 105,* 369–380.

Lichtman, R. R., Taylor, S. E., & Wood, J. V. (1988). Social support and marital adjustment after breast cancer. *Journal of Psychosocial Oncology, 5,* 47–74.

Liefbroer, A. C., & Dourleijn, E. (2006). Unmarried cohabitation and union stability: Testing the role of diffusion using data from 16 European countries. *Demography, 43,* 203–221.

Lindahl, K. M., & Markman, H. J. (1990). Communication and negative affect regulation in the family. In E. Blechman (Ed.), *Emotions and the family: For better or for worse* (pp. 99–115). New York: Plenum Press.

Lizzio, A., & Wilson, K. (2004). First-year students' perceptions of capability. *Studies in Higher Education, 29,* 109–128.

Mahoney, A., Pargament, K. I., Tarakeshwar, N., & Swank, A. B. (2001). Religion in the home in the 1980s and 1990s: A meta-analytic review and conceptual analysis of links between religion, marriage, and parenting. *Journal of Family Psychology, 15,* 559–596.

Markey, B., & Micheletto, M. (1997). *Instructor manual for FOCCUS.* Omaha, NE: Archdiocese of Omaha.

Markman, H. J. (1981). The prediction of marital distress: A 5-year follow-up. *Journal of Consulting and Clinical Psychology, 49,* 760–762.

Markman, H. J., Floyd, F. J., Stanley, S. M., & Storaasli, R. D. (1988). Prevention of marital distress: A longitudinal investigation. *Journal of Consulting and Clinical Psychology, 56,* 210–217.

Markman, H. J., & Hahlweg, K. (1993). The prediction and prevention of marital distress: An international perspective. *Clinical Psychology Review, 13,* 29–43.

Markman, H. J., & Halford, W. K. (2005). International perspectives on couple relationship education. *Family Process, 44,* 139–146.

Markman, H. J., Halford, W. K., & Cordova, A. D. (1997). Future directions in the study of marriage. In W. K. Halford & H. J. Markman (Eds.), *Clinical handbook of marriage and couples intervention* (pp. 695–716). Chichester, UK: Wiley.

Markman, H. J., Renick, M. J., Floyd, F. J., Stanley, S. M., & Clements, M. (1993). Preventing marital distress through communication and conflict management training: A 4- and 5-year follow-up. *Journal of Consulting and Clinical Psychology, 61,* 70–77.

Markman, H. J., Stanley, S. M., & Blumberg, S. L. (2001). *Fighting for your marriage* (2nd ed.). San Francisco: Jossey-Bass.

Markman, H., Williams, T., Einhorn, L., & Stanley, S. (2007). The new frontier in relationship education: Innovations and challenges in dissemination. *The Behavior Therapist, 31,* 14–17.

Matthey, S., Kavanagh, D. J., Howie, P., Barnett, B., & Charles, M. (2004). Prevention of postnatal distress or depression: An evaluation of an intervention at preparation for parenthood classes. *Journal of Affective Disorders, 79,* 113–126.

McDonald, P. (1995). *Families in Australia: A sociodemographic perspective.* Melbourne: Australian Institute of Family Studies.

McLanahan, S., & Sandefur, G. (1996). *Growing up with a single parent: What hurts, what helps.* Cambridge, MA: Harvard University Press.

McLaughlin, D. K., & Lichter, D. T. (1997). Poverty and the marital behaviour of young women. *Journal of Marriage and Family, 59,* 582–594.

Messman-Moore, T. L., & Long, P. J. (2000). Child sexual abuse and revictimization in the form of adult sexual abuse, adult physical abuse, and adult psychological maltreatment. *Journal of Interpersonal Violence, 15,* 489–502.

Midmer, D., Wilson, L., & Cummings, S. (1995). A randomized, controlled trial of the influence of prenatal parenting education on postpartum anxiety and marital adjustment. *Family Medicine, 27,* 200–205.

Mihalic, S. W., & Elliot, D. (1997). A social learning theory model of marital violence. *Journal of Family Violence, 12,* 21–47.

Miklowitz, D. J., George, E. L., Richards, J. A., Simoneau, T. L., & Suddath, R. L. (2003). A randomized study of family-focused psychoeducation and pharmacotherapy in the outpatient management of bipolar disorder. *Archives of General Psychiatry, 60,* 904–912.

Miller, S., Miller, P., Nunnally, E. W., & Wackman, D. B. (1992). *Couple communication instructor manual.* Evergreen, CO: International Communication Programs.

Miller, W. R., & Rollnick, S. (2002). *Motivational interviewing: Preparing people for change.* New York: Guilford Press.

Mouzos, J., & Makkai, T. (2004). *Women's experience of male violence: Findings from the Australian component of the International Violence against Women Survey* (Research and Public Policy Series No. 56). Canberra: Australian Institute of Criminology.

Murphy, C. M., & O'Leary, K. D. (1989). Psychological aggression predicts physical aggression in early marriage. *Journal of Consulting and Clinical Psychology, 57,* 579–582.

Neff, L. A., & Karney, B. R. (2004). How does context affect intimate relationships?: Linking external stress and cognitive processes within marriage. *Personality and Social Psychology Bulletin, 30,* 134–148.

Nezu, A. M., D'Zurilla, T. J., Zwick, M. L., & Nezu, C. M. (2004). Social problem-solving therapy for adults. In E. C. Chang, T. J. D'Zurilla, & L. J. Sanna (Eds.), *Social problem solving: Theory, research and training* (pp. 171–191). Washington, DC: American Psychological Association.

Nicholson, J. M., Phillips, M., Whitton, S., Halford, W. K., & Sanders, M. R. (2007). Promoting healthy stepfamilies: Couples' reasons for seeking help and perceived benefits from intervention. *Family Matters, 77,* 48–57.

Nicholson, J. M., Sanders, M. R., Halford, W. K., Phillips, M., & Whitton, S. W. (2008). The prevention and treatment of children's adjustment problems in stepfamilies. In J. Pryor (Ed.), *The international handbook of stepfamilies: Policy and practice in legal, research, and clinical environments* (pp. 485–522). New York: Wiley.

Nolan, M. L. (1997). Antenatal education—where next? *Journal of Advanced Nursing, 25*, 1198–1204.

Notarius, C., & Markman, H. J. (1993). *We can work it out: Making sense of marital conflict.* New York: Putnam.

O'Brien, M., & Peyton, V. (2002). Parenting attitudes and marital intimacy: A longitudinal analysis. *Journal of Family Psychology, 16*, 118–127.

O'Driscoll, M., Brough, P., & Kalliath, T. (2006). Work–family conflict and facilitation. In F. Jones, R. J. Burke, & M. Westman (Eds.), *Work–life balance: A psychological perspective* (pp. 117–142). New York: Psychology Press.

O'Leary, K. D., Barling, J., Arias, I., Rosenbaum, A., Malone, J., & Tyree, A. (1989). Prevalence and stability of physical aggression between spouses: A longitudinal analysis. *Journal of Consulting and Clinical Psychology, 57*, 263–268.

Olson, D. H., Dyer, P., & Dyer, G. (1997). *Growing together: Leaders manual. A group program for couples.* Minneapolis, MN: Life Innovations.

Olson, D. H., Fournier, D. G., & Druckman, J. M. (1996). *PREPARE.* Minneapolis, MN: Life Innovations.

Olson, D. H., & Fowers, B. J. (1986). Predicting marital success with PREPARE: A predictive validity study. *Journal of Marital and Family Therapy, 12*, 403–413.

Ooms, T., & Wilson, P. (2004). The challenges of offering relation and marriage education to low-income populations. *Family Relations, 53*, 440–448.

Orbuch, T. L., Veroff, J., Hassan, H., & Horrocks, J. (2002). Who will divorce: A 14-year longitudinal study of black couples and white couples. *Journal of Social and Personal Relationships, 19*, 179–202.

Pasch, L. A., & Bradbury, T. N. (1998). Social support, conflict, and the development of marital dysfunction. *Journal of Consulting and Clinical Psychology, 66*, 219–230.

Pinsof, W. M. (2002). The death of "till death us do part": The transformation of pair-bonding in the 20th century. *Family Process, 41*, 135–157.

Pistole, M. C., & Tarrant, N. (1993). Attachment style and aggression in male batterers. *Family Therapy, 20*, 165–173.

Pope, H., & Mueller, C. W. (1976). The intergenerational transmission of marital instability: Comparisons by race and sex. *Journal of Social Issues, 32*, 49–66.

Prado, L. M., & Markman, H. J. (1999). Unearthing the seeds of marital distress: What we have learned from married and remarried couples. In M. Cox & J. Brooks-Gunn (Eds.), *Conflict and cohesion in families: Causes and consequences* (pp. 148–178). Mahwah, NJ: Earlbaum.

Purdie, N., Hattie, J., & Douglas, G. (1996). Student conceptions of learning and their use of self-regulated learning strategies: A cross-cultural comparison. *Journal of Educational Psychology, 88*, 87–100.

Qu, L. (2003). Expectations of marriage among cohabiting couples. *Family Matters, 64*, 36–39.

Qu, L., & Weston, R. (2001). Starting out together through cohabitation or marriage. *Family Matters, 60*, 76–79.

Quigley, B. M., & Leonard, K. E. (1996). Desistance of husband aggression in the early years of marriage. *Violence and Victims, 11*, 355–370.

Rea, M. M., Tompson, M. C., Miklowitz, D. J., Goldstein, M. J., Hwang, S., & Mintz, J. (2003). Family-focused treatment versus individual treatment for bipolar disorder: Results of a randomized clinical trial. *Journal of Consulting and Clinical Psychology, 71*, 482–492.

Ridley, C. A., Jorgensen, S. R., Morgan, A. G., & Avery, A. W. (1982). Relationship enhancement with premarital couples: An assessment of effects on relationship quality. *American Journal of Family Therapy, 10*, 41–48.

Riessman, C. K., & Gerstel, N. (1985). Marital dissolution and health: Do males or females have greater risk? *Social Science and Medicine, 20*, 627–635.

Rodriguez, J., & Borgen, W. A. (1998). Needs assessment: Western Canada's program administrators' perspectives on the role of EAPs in the workplace. *Employee Assistance Quarterly, 14*, 11–30.

Rogge, R. D., & Bradbury, T. N. (1999). Till violence does us part: The differing roles of communication and aggression in predicting adverse marital outcomes. *Journal of Consulting and Clinical Psychology, 67*, 340–351.

Rogge, R. D., Cobb, R. J., Story, L. B., Johnson, M. D., Lawrence, E. E., Rothman, A. D., et al. (2006). Recruitment and selection of couples for intervention research: Achieving developmental homogeneity at the cost of demographic diversity. *Journal of Consulting and Clinical Psychology, 74*, 777–784.

Rourke, L., & Anderson, T. (2002). Using peer teams to lead online discussions. *Journal of Interactive Media in Education, 1*, 1–21.

Sabatelli, R. M., & Bartle-Haring, S. (2003). Family-of-origin experiences and adjustment in married couples. *Journal of Marriage and Family, 65*, 159–169.

Sanders, M. R., Halford, W. K., & Behrens, B. C. (1999). Parental divorce and premarital couple communication. *Journal of Family Psychology, 13*, 60–74.

Sanders, M. R., Nicholson, J. M., & Floyd, F. J. (1997). Couples' relationships and children. In W. K. Halford & H. J. Markman (Eds.), *Clinical handbook of marriage and couple intervention* (pp. 225–253). Chichester, UK: Wiley.

Sayers, S. L., Kohn, C. S., & Heavey, C. (1998). Prevention of marital dysfunction: Behavioral approaches and beyond. *Clinical Psychology Review, 18*, 713–744.

Schafer, J., Caetano, R., & Clark, C. L. (1998). Rates of intimate partner violence in the United States. *American Journal of Public Health, 88*, 1702–1704.

Schilling, E. A., Baucom, D. H., Burnett, C. K., Sandin-Allen, E., & Ragland, L. (2003). Altering the course of marriage: The effect of PREP communication skills acquisition on couples' risk of becoming maritally distressed. *Journal of Family Psychology, 17*, 41–53.

Schmaling, K., & Sher, T. G. (2000). *The psychology of couples and illness.* Washington, DC: American Psychological Association.

Schoeni, R. F. (1995). Marital status and earnings in developed countries. *Journal of Population Economics, 8*, 351–359.

Schulz, M. S., Cowan, C. P., & Cowan, P. A. (2006). Promoting healthy beginnings: A randomized controlled trial of a preventive intervention to preserve marital quality during the transition to parenthood. *Journal of Consulting and Clinical Psychology, 74*, 20–31.

Schumacher, J. A., & Leonard, K. E. (2005). Husbands' and wives' marital adjustment, verbal aggression, and physical aggression as longitudinal predictors of physical aggression in early marriage. *Journal of Consulting and Clinical Psychology, 73*, 28–37.

Schumm, W. R., Resnick, G., Silliman, B., & Bell, D. B. (1998). Premarital counseling and marital satisfaction among civilian wives of military service members. *Journal of Sex and Marital Therapy, 24*, 21–28.

Scott, J. L., Halford, W. K., & Ward, B. (2004). United we stand?: The effects of a couple-coping intervention on adjustment to early stage breast or gynaecological cancer. *Journal of Consulting and Clinical Psychology, 72*, 1122–1135.

Seefeldt, K. S., & Smock, P. J. (2004). *Marriage on the public policy agenda: What do policy makers need to know from research?* (PSC Research Report No. 04-554). Ann Arbor, MI: Population Studies Center.

Seligman, M. E. P. (1995). The effectiveness of psychotherapy: The Consumer Reports study. *American Psychologist, 50,* 965–974.

Shapiro, A. F., & Gottman, J. M. (2005). Effects on marriage of a psycho–communicative–educational intervention with couples undergoing the transition to parenthood: Evaluation at 1-year post intervention. *Journal of Family Communication, 5*, 1–24.

Shapiro, A. F., Gottman, J. M., & Carrere, S. (2000). The baby and the marriage: Identifying factors that buffer against decline in marital satisfaction after the first baby arrives. *Journal of Family Psychology, 14*, 59–70.

Shelton, J. L., & Levy, R. L. (1981). *Behavioral assignments and treatment compliance: A handbook of clinical strategies.* Champaign, IL: Research Press.

Silliman, B., & Schumm, W. R. (2000). Marriage preparation programs: A literature review. *Family Journal, 8*, 133–142.

Silliman, B., Stanley, S. M., Coffin, W., Markman, H. J., & Jordan, P. L. (2002). Preventive interventions for couples. In H. A. Liddle, D. A. Santisteban, R. F. Levant, & J. H. Bray (Eds.), *Family psychology: Science-based interventions* (pp. 123–146). Washington, DC: American Psychological Association.

Simons, M., Harris, R., & Willis, P. (1994). *Pathways to marriage: Learning for married life in Australia.* Adelaide: Centre for Research in Education and Work, University of South Australia.

Simons, M., & Parker, R. (2002). *A study of Australian relationship education service activities.* Canberra, Australia: Department of Family and Community Services.

Skuja, K., & Halford, W. K. (2004). Repeating the errors of our parents?: Parental violence in men's family of origin and conflict management in dating couples. *Journal of Interpersonal Violence, 19*, 623–638.

Smock, P. J., Manning, W. D., & Gupta, S. (1999). The effects of marriage and divorce on women's economic well-being. *American Sociological Review, 64*, 794–812.

Snyder, D. K., Castellani, A. M., & Whisman, M. A. (2006). Current status and future directions in couple therapy. *Annual Review of Psychology, 57*, 317–344.

Snyder, D. K., Mangrum, L. F., & Wills, R. M. (1993). Predicting couples' response to marital therapy: A comparison of short- and long-term predictors. *Journal of Consulting and Clinical Psychology, 61*, 61–69.

Snyder, D., & Whisman, M. (Eds.). (2003). *Treating difficult couples: Helping clients with coexisting mental and relationship disorders.* New York: Guilford Press.

South, S. J. (1985). Economic conditions and the divorce rate: A time–series analysis of the post-war United States. *Journal of Marriage and Family, 47*, 31–41.

Stanley, S. M. (2001). Making the case for premarital education. *Family Relations, 50*, 272–280.

Stanley, S. M., Allen, E. S., Markman, H. J., Saiz, C., Bloomstrom, G., Thomas, R., et al. (2005). Dissemination and evaluation of marriage education in the army. *Family Process, 44*, 187–201.

Stanley, S. M., Amato, P., Johnson, C. A., & Markman, H. J. (2006). Premarital education, marital quality, and marital stability: Findings from a large, random household survey. *Journal of Family Psychology, 20*, 117–126.

Stanley, S. M., Bradbury, T. N., & Markman, H. J. (2000). Structural flaws in the bridge from basic research on marriage to interventions for couples: Illustrations from Gottman, Coan, Carrere, and Swanson (1998). *Journal of Marriage and Family, 62*, 256–264.

Stanley, S. M., Markman, H. J., Prado, L. M., Olmos-Gallo, P. A., Tonelli, L., St. Peters, M., et al. (2001). Community-based premarital prevention: Clergy and lay leaders on the front lines. *Family Relations, 50*, 67–76.

Stanley, S. M., Markman, H. J., St. Peters, M., & Leber, B. D. (1995). Strengthening marriages and preventing divorce: New directions in prevention research. *Family Relations, 44*, 392–401.

Stanley, S. M., Rhoades, G. K., Olmos-Gallo, P. A., & Markman, H. J. (2007). Mechanisms of change in a cognitive behavioural couples prevention programs: Does being naughty or nice matter? *Prevention Science, 8*, 227–239.

Stanley, S. M., Whitton, S. W., & Markman, H. J. (2004). Maybe I do: Interpersonal commitment and premarital or non-marital cohabitation. *Journal of Family Issues, 25*, 496–519.

Statistics Canada. (2003). *Canadian social trends.* Ottawa: Ministry of Industry.

Story, L. B., & Bradbury, T. N. (2004). Understanding marriage and stress: Essential questions and challenges. *Clinical Psychology Review, 23*, 1139–1162.

Story, L. B., Karney, B. R., Lawrence, E., & Bradbury, T. N. (2004). Interpersonal mediators in the intergenerational transmission of marital dysfunction. *Journal of Family Psychology, 18*, 519–529.

Straus, M. A., & Gelles, R. J. (1990). How violent are American families?: Estimates from the National Family Violence Resurvey and other studies. In M. A. Straus & R. J. Gelles (Eds.), *Physical violence in American families: Risk factors and adaptations to violence in 8,145 families* (pp. 95–112). New Brunswick, NJ: Transaction.

Sullivan, K. T., & Bradbury, T. N. (1997). Are premarital prevention programs reaching couples at risk for marital dysfunction? *Journal of Consulting and Clinical Psychology, 65*, 24–30.

Sweeper, S., & Halford, W. K. (2006). Assessing adult adjustment to relationship separation: The Psychological Adjustment to Separation Test (PAST). *Journal of Family Psychology, 20,* 632–640.

Teachman, J. (2003). Premarital sex, premarital cohabitation and the risk of subsequent marital dissolution among women. *Journal of Marriage and Family, 65,* 444–455.

Thomas, A., & Sawhill, I. (2005). For love "and" money?: The impact of family structure on family income. *Future of Children, 15,* 57–74.

Thompson, B. M. (1997). Couples and the work–family interface. In W. K. Halford & H. J. Markman (Eds.), *Clinical handbook of marriage and couples intervention* (pp. 273–290). Chichester, UK: Wiley.

Thornton, A., & Young-DeMarco, L. (2001). Four decades of trends in attitudes toward family issues in the United States: The 1960s through the 1990s. *Journal of Marriage and Family, 63,* 1009–1037.

Thuen, F., & LÊrum, K. (2005). A public/private partnership in offering relationship education to the Norwegian population. *Family Process, 44,* 175–185.

Ting-Toomey, S., & Takai, J. (2006). Explaining intercultural conflict: Promising approaches and directions. In J. G. Oetzel & S. Ting-Toomey (Eds.), *The SAGE handbook of conflict communication: Integrating theory, research, and practice* (pp. 691–723). Thousand Oaks, CA: Sage.

United Nations Economic and Social Affairs Population Division. (2003). *World fertility report.* New York: United Nations.

U.S. Census Bureau. (2003). *Census 2000 special report: Married couples and unmarried partner households 2000.* Washington, DC: U.S. Government Printing Offices.

van Poppel, F., & de Beer, J. (1993). Measuring the effect of changing legislation on the frequency of divorce: The Netherlands, 1830–1990. *Demography, 30,* 425–441.

van Widenfelt, B., Hosman, C., Schaap, C., & van der Staak, C. (1996). The prevention of relationship distress for couples at risk: A controlled evaluation with nine-month and two-year follow-ups. *Family Relations, 45,* 156–165.

van Widenfelt, B., Markman, H. J., Guerney, B., Behrens, B. C., & Hosman, C. (1997). Prevention of relationship problems. In W. K. Halford & H. J. Markman (Eds.), *Clinical handbook of marriage and couples intervention* (pp. 651–677). Chichester, UK: Wiley.

Veroff, J., Douvan, E., & Hatchett, S. J. (1995). *Marital instability: A social and behavioral study of the early years.* Westport, CT: Praeger.

Vinokur, A. D., Price, R. H., & Caplan, R. D. (1996). Hard times and hurtful partners: How financial strain affects depression and relationship satisfaction of unemployed persons and their spouses. *Journal of Personality and Social Psychology, 71,* 166–179.

Waite, L. J., & Gallagher, M. (2000). *The case for marriage: Why married people are happier, healthier, and better off financially.* New York: Doubleday.

Watson, B., & Halford, W. K. (2010). Classes of childhood sexual abuse and women's adult couple relationships. *Violence and Victims, 25,* 518–535.

Wampler, K. S., & Sprenkle, D. H. (1980). The Minnesota Couple Communication Program: A follow-up study. *Journal of Marriage and Family, 42,* 577–585.

Wekerle, C., & Wolfe, D. A. (1998). The role of child maltreatment and attachment style in adolescent relationship violence. *Development and Psychopathology, 10*, 571–586.

Whisman, M. A., & Jacobson, N. S. (1990). Power, marital satisfaction, and response to marital therapy. *Journal of Family Psychology, 4*, 202–212.

Whisman, M. A., & Uebelacker, L. A. (2003). Comorbidity of relationship distress and mental and physical health problems. In D. K. Snyder & M. A. Whisman (Eds.), *Treating difficult couples: Helping clients with coexisting mental and relationship problems* (pp. 3–26). New York: Guilford Press.

Whisman, M. A., Uebelacker, L. A., & Bruce, M. L. (2006). Longitudinal association between marital dissatisfaction and alcohol use disorders in a community sample. *Journal of Family Psychology, 20*, 164–167.

White, L. K., & Booth, A. (1985). The quality and stability of remarriages: The role of stepchildren. *American Sociological Review, 50*, 689–698.

Widom, C. S. (1989). The cycle of violence. *Science, 244*, 160–166.

Williams, L., & Jurich, J. (1995). Predicting marital success after five years: Assessing the predictive validity of FOCCUS. *Journal of Marital and Family Therapy, 21*, 141–153.

Wilson, J. Q. (2002). *The marriage problem: How our culture has weakened families.* New York: HarperCollins.

Wilson, K. L., Charker, J., Lizzio, A., Kimlin, S., & Halford, W. K. (2005). Assessing how much couples work at their relationship: The Behavioral Self-Regulation for Effective Relationships Scale. *Journal of Family Psychology, 91*, 385–393.

Wilson, K. L., & Halford, W. K. (2008). Processes of change in the flexible delivery of couple relationship education. *Family Relations, 57*, 625–635.

Index